OFF THE

RAILS

by

Rudy Sarzo

Contents

Kudos

I would like to express my own appreciation for the following.

My beautiful wife, Rebecca, thank you for being my best friend, the rock upon which I've built my dreams and my fountain of inspiration throughout all these years. To our Dog-ter Tory, my muse and comfort during the writing of this book. Tooka we miss you.

My loving Mother and Father, Magnolia and Rodolfo, for making countless sacrifices so my brother and I could live in freedom. Dad we miss you.

My mother-in-law, Ruth Garrard, for her support and inspiration during the writing of this book. Granny we miss you.

My nephew Robert Jr., Julian, my sister-in-law Suzie and especially my brother, Robert, for sharing all those rocking childhood Miami nights. Suzie we miss you.

The Fiallos. Gina, Cyrina, Vinny and Abbey for always inspiring me to keep the faith and follow my dreams.

My eternal gratitude to Sharon and Ozzy for giving a break to the kid from Cuba and welcoming him into their family.

The Rhoads family, Kathy, Kelle and especially Delores for bringing into the world such a brilliant musical talent and extraordinary human being. Delores we miss you.

Ozzy, Randy, Tommy Aldridge and Don Airey for kicking my butt on stage every night.

All the members of Quiet Riot, Kevin, Frankie and Carlos, with whom I've had the pleasure of banging our heads.

Ronnie, Wendy, Craig, Simon, Scott and the rest of the DIO family for putting the joy of making music back into my life.

To God and my Lord Jesus Christ for guiding and often carrying me through this amazing journey.

And to the countless fans around the world who've asked me "What was it like to play with Randy?" this is book is for you. I hope you enjoy reading it as much as I did writing it.

Dedication

This book is dedicated to the memory of my father Rodolfo Sarzo, mother-in-law Ruth Garrard, my Sister-in-Law, Suzie Sarzo, my dear friends Rachel Youngblood, Randy Rhoads and Delores Rhoads and my Dog-ter Tory.
Thank you for being a part of my life. God bless you all.

Introduction

March 19, 1982

"Rudes! Rudes! Come on, get up!" I hear a voice yelling to me through the curtains in my bunk.

As I slide the curtains open I see Randy standing in the doorway of the tour bus.

"What's going on?" I ask with a yawn as I wipe the sleep from my eyes.

"We're at the bus depot and Andy's going to take Rachel and me up on a plane to see the country side. Get dressed and come with us! It'll be fun."

"What time is it?" I ask, fighting back a yawn.

"Oh, I don't know," Randy says with a shrug. "About 8 a.m." "Oh that's all right, Rand, you go ahead. I'm just going to wait until we get to Orlando before I get up." I put my head back down on my pillow.

"OK, but you'll be sorry you missed it!" Randy kidded as I watch him step out of the tour bus and into the quiet Florida morning.

I pull back the curtains in my bunk and go back to sleep, never to see my friend Randy Rhoads again.

1
All Aboard!

It was an early morning in March 1981 as I lay down on a bed sheet spread across a spare bedroom floor of my former Quiet Riot band mate Kevin DuBrow's Sherman Oaks apartment. The phone rang. Seconds later Kevin yelled,

"Rudy, phone call for you!" I grabbed the phone.

"Rudy? Hi, this is Sharon. I'm with Ozzy's management.

We're looking for a bass player and Randy has spoken very highly of you. We would like for you to come down and audition."

Without hesitating I replied,

"Well, I really appreciate the call but, you see, I'm already in a band."

Sharon snapped back at me.

"You mean you don't want to come down?"

I apologetically replied,

"Sorry, but I can't."

There was a short pause on Sharon's end, and then,

"OK, I'll tell Ozzy."

I stood frozen for a moment listening to the dial tone wondering if I had done the right thing.

"What's wrong? Who was that?" Kevin asked.

"Oh, that was somebody from Ozzy's management asking me to come down and audition. But I turned it down."

"You what!?" yelled Kevin in disbelief. "You turned down the gig with Ozzy? Are you fucking nuts?"

At that moment I realized that, yeah, I probably was. Not only was this the kind of opportunity you hope and work for your whole life, but it was also a chance to play again with my Quiet Riot band mate, Randy Rhoads. And besides, passing on Ozzy's—or any other paying gig, for

1

that matter—didn't make any sense under my current strapped economic situation.

Yes, I was already committed to another band, Angel. These were guys who dressed up in white outfits and had perfect, big hair, something I thought was real cool at the time. Casablanca Records had just dropped Angel prior to my joining, so we spent most of our time making demos at the Record Plant studios in Los Angeles and showcasing for major labels. But no matter how much I enjoyed playing in Angel or how promising the future looked for the band, the reality was that I was broke and sleeping on the floor in Kevin's apartment. I spent the rest of the day locked in my room, meditating. The following afternoon the phone rang.

"Hello?" I answered.

"Is this Rudy?" asked an unfamiliar male voice.

" Y e s . . I said with trepidation.

"Rudy, hi this is Ozzy. Listen man, we had some guys come down yesterday and they were all a bunch of bloody hacks. Randy tells me you're the guy. So just come down and meet with me."

"When do you wanna get together?" I asked.

"Tonight," Ozzy said quickly. "Randy's here and says he'll pick you up"

"I'll be ready!" I answered before Ozzy could finish. I couldn't believe it, lightning isn't supposed to strike twice! "Kevin, you're not going to believe who just called!" I ran into the kitchen.

"I overheard congratulations!" he said. "Just don't blow it." "Hey Rudes!" I heard Randy say as I got in his Volkswagen Scirocco.

"Hey, thanks for talking me up to Ozzy," I said as we shook hands.

"It's no big deal," Randy shrugged.

It had been a year since I'd seen him. He had just returned from England where he'd been recording and touring with Ozzy and I couldn't help but notice how much more mature and worldly he looked. Even though he was as humble and friendly as ever, he now reflected a dazzling rock star image. The diamond in the rough that I had shared the stage with in Quiet Riot was at last beginning to shine.

"So, Rand, tell me: How do you like playing with Ozzy?" My question was intended to get some insight into my pending situation.

"Oh, it's been great, and crazy at the same time," Randy said with a smile.

"But I've got to warn you. Ozzy and Sharon are very different from anyone you've dealt with before."

I was puzzled.

"What do you mean?"

Randy paused.

"Don't get me wrong. They're the nicest people you'll ever meet. Let's just say that they have different ways of doing things. So if you get the gig and down the line they do things you don't understand, don't take it personally. That's just the way they are."

"I'll keep that in mind," I replied gratefully as we drove up Coldwater Canyon heading towards Beverly Hills.

We arrived at Trader Vic's, a restaurant located in the Beverly Hills Hotel where Ozzy was staying. Ozzy was waiting for us along with Sharon and drummer Tommy Aldridge. Ozzy gave us a very warm welcome and asked me to sit next to him. He ordered a round of drinks and proceeded to tell me how excited he was about touring the U.S. for the first time since he left Black Sabbath.

Meanwhile, unbeknownst to me, Sharon and Tommy were closely eyeing me and looking under the table to see what shoes I was wearing. Randy had told them that I was playing in Angel. Tommy then told Sharon that the bass player in that band had stolen his shoes from a mutual friend's house in Chicago where Tommy was staying.

3

Fortunately, I was quickly cleared when Tommy heard my Cuban accent and realized I wasn't the same guy!

After a few drinks and casual conversation, Ozzy turned to me and said,

"Rudy, you seem like a nice bloke. Just know the songs when you come to the audition tomorrow."

"Don't worry, Ozzy. I'm gonna give it all I've got." I answered with the confidence of someone who'd been preparing for this moment all his life.

"Ozzy, I'm going to go over the songs with Rudy before we get to rehearsal," Randy said.

He didn't have to do that, but that's the kind of friend Randy was. Ozzy guzzled his drink and slammed his empty glass on the table and invited everybody up to his suite. As we were leaving Randy pulled me to his side, whispering,

"He's gonna test you to see what you're made of, so if he offers you anything don't take it." I nodded.

When we got to the suite Ozzy went straight to his bedroom and returned with a small bag of coke.

"Hey man, want some waffle dust?" Ozzy said with a devilish grin, as he waved the bag in my face.

"Oh no, thanks." My eyes shifted to Randy.

"Ozzy," Randy jumped in, "Rudy has a long day ahead of him and I need to get him back to his place so we can go over those songs."

"Yeah, we'd better go," I said in support.

Ozzy opened the bag anyway, stuck in a thick straw, and did a quick, strong snort. When he sat back, he looked like his head was about to explode. His eyes rolled like a slot machine, his head shook, and he yelled, "Rock and Roll!" He grabbed a bottle of booze and stumbled into the bedroom.

The following afternoon, when Randy and I pulled up to Frank Zappa's rehearsal studio in Hollywood there were close to 20 bass players waiting outside for a chance to audition. Tommy was already there tuning his drums.

Randy suggested we go over the songs since Ozzy and Sharon hadn't arrived yet. This was a good idea; Tommy had just joined the band himself and he also needed the opportunity to familiarize himself with the new material.

As soon as Randy started in on the intro to "I Don't Know" from the Blizzard of Ozz record I saw that this sure wasn't the same Randy I had played with in Quiet Riot. Even though he was still using his favorite cream-colored Les Paul, he had switched over to playing Marshall stacks with an English-built custom pedal board. His new rig gave him a heavier and more biting tone than the one he had in Quiet Riot when he was using a hybrid of a solid state Peavey head with an Ampeg cabinet. His new aggressive sound fully complemented the songs he had composed and recorded with Ozzy. The stage was ablaze, fueled by Randy's guitar pyrotechnics and Tommy's rapid fire drumming. I just tried to do my best to keep up with what was going on as the awaiting bass players looked on anxiously.

After a couple of run-throughs, Ozzy and Sharon arrived. Ozzy went straight up on stage:

"So are you ready, Rudy?" He turned to me and grabbed his microphone. I looked at Randy for support.

"Ready as I am ever gonna be, Ozzy."

"All right! Let's rock and roll, man!"

We went into "I Don't Know" followed by "Crazy Train." I played each note like there was no tomorrow, at the same time eyeing Ozzy and Sharon to pick up on clues as to how I was doing. Sharon asked us to play the songs one more time as Ozzy stood next to her watching us perform. I was beginning to get nervous. Randy looked at me and smiled.

"Don't worry, Rudes. You're doin' fine!"

After we finished the two songs, Ozzy and Sharon went outside to talk things over while I stood onstage waiting for the verdict. Suddenly Ozzy re-enters, runs up to my side of the stage, and says, "So, do you want the gig, man?" I couldn't believe my ears. I didn't think for a second.

"Of course!"

Ozzy stretched out his hand.

"Welcome aboard!" Randy and I smiled at each other as I shook Ozzy's hand.

I did it! I was the new bass player in Ozzy's band, and just as exciting was that fact that I was going to play with Randy again. Sharon walked over to the other bass players and announced,

"Sorry boys, but the auditions are over. We've found our bass player."

I had never seen so many pissed off guys in one room. One of them came up to me and said,

"Congratulations dude, but if I had the chance I would have smoked your ass!"

Seeing as I was in a state of total bliss, I brushed it off. Nothing any of those guys could say would have ruined the moment.

"Hey, so where are we going?" I asked Randy as we left the rehearsal studio.

"We're goin' up to Sharon's house," Randy replied as we followed Sharon, Ozzy, and Tommy out of the parking lot.

"Now remember, they're going to test you again. So, if Ozzy offers you any booze or drugs, don't take it."

I couldn't blame Ozzy and Sharon for wanting to be completely sure. Here they were letting a perfect stranger into their inner sanctum based on a couple of songs and Randy's word. Plus, the stakes were high. They were banking on the upcoming tour to establish Ozzy's career as a solo artist, and they couldn't afford to make a single mistake.

"You're sounding better than ever," I told Randy, "especially your rhythm chops. I've never heard you play with so much aggression!"

"Thanks," said Randy with humility. "You know, it's been great working with Ozzy. When we first got together to write I asked him what he wanted me to play and he just told me to be myself. He even encouraged me to take classical guitar lessons from a teacher in London."

"He sounds like he's receptive to your ideas," I said, contemplating the positive musical environment that lay ahead. "Yeah, definitely. I've even composed a classical piece with a vocal choir for the new record. I think we're gonna call it Diary of a Madman."

"Wow, I can't wait to hear it."

We were driving down Sunset Strip past all the local clubs where just a year and a half ago Quiet Riot struggled to get noticed by record labels.

We drove up to the very top of a street off Benedict Canyon in Beverly Hills. As we turned in the driveway we came upon an imposing iron gate. Once Randy identified himself to the security guard over the intercom, we drove through the gate, up a long cobblestone driveway, past a stable with midget ponies and a multitude of dogs. Driving into the courtyard, I was mesmerized by the idyllic setting created by the magnificent Mediterranean-style estate, perfectly surrounded by a cluster of enchanting bungalows.

"Oh my God, this place is amazing," I said to Randy in awe.

"Wait till you see the inside!" said Randy.

I stepped through the doorway and froze. I couldn't believe my
eyes.

"Don't just stand there! For fuck's sake come in!" Ozzy yelled from behind the game room bar.

As I slowly headed toward Ozzy—feeling completely out of place— I bumped into Don Arden. Not only was Mr. Arden Sharon's father, he was also Ozzy's manager, owned JET Records, Ozzy's label. He also happened to be one of the most intimidating characters I'd ever meet.

"Who the fuck are you?" Don asked as he stood there wearing a monogrammed white terrycloth bathrobe, puffing a cigar while giving me a once over. I stood there stammering. Sharon ran to my rescue.

"Daddy, this is Rudy. He's Ozzy's new bass player." He stared me down and walked away.

"Don't be scared," Sharon said to me. "I think Daddy likes you.

"Oh, that's good," I said, still shaking in my boots.

"Here let me show you around. This house was built by
Howard Hughes for one of his girlfriends," Sharon said as she led me through the beautiful grounds and pointed out the magnificent view of Los Angeles and the home's many priceless antiques. There was even a sliding ceiling in the living room.

When I returned from my tour, Randy, Tommy, and Ozzy were shooting pool in the game room.

"Want a drink?" Ozzy asked, grabbing a bottle of vodka.

"Oh, no thanks, maybe later." I said cautiously. "I think I'll just have a Coke for now."

"OK, suit yourself."

I sensed a little disappointment in his voice. I didn't want to be rude, but after hearing Randy's advice I felt I had to be on my best behavior. On the other hand, I thought maybe Ozzy was looking for a kindred spirit. We spent the next couple of hours shooting pool and talking.

"Ozzy, I gotta get Rudy back home before I meet Jody," Randy said, grabbing his car keys and leather jacket.

Sharon interjected.

"Rudy, why don't you stay and spend more time with Ozzy?"

I looked at Randy for his approval and he seemed to be comfortable with the idea.

"Yeah, OK, that would be great."

Sharon had a knack for making you feel welcome. By the time Randy left, Tommy had already gone to his guest room and I was alone with Ozzy and Sharon. After a little casual conversation regarding my family and Latino background, Sharon retired for the night, leaving me alone with Ozzy. This was a good thing.

Even though we had just met the night before, he had this uncanny ability, like Sharon, to honestly open up to you and make you feel at ease. We chatted about his good and bad times with Sabbath, how appreciative he was to have Randy in his life, and how much he loved playing and writing with him.

"You know, Rudy, I've been doing this for over fifteen years, man, and was getting real tired about the whole thing. I was ready to quit until I found Randy. He's the reason I'm still doing this."

Ozzy spoke with fatherly pride as he went on to reminisce about the first time he saw Randy play. It was at his audition for the band, and he could clearly see the magical qualities that would later make him a legend. By now I couldn't help but feel a kinship with Ozzy. Besides our mutual admiration for Randy there was an air of unpretentiousness about him that I found quite disarming even after he had downed a whole bottle of booze.

"Do you want a toot?" Ozzy asked with a devilish smile, holding out a single gram bottle of blow.

"Oh, no thanks," I said; Randy's words echoed in my mind.

"It's late. I'd better get some sleep."

"OK, that means more for me then," Ozzy said, doing the bump intended for me. After the snort he looked at me for a second, then said,

"You look like you could use some rock-star rags, man."

There was no arguing about that. I was broke, sleeping on a floor, and had a shabby wardrobe. Ozzy left the room and came back with an armload of regalia.

9

"Here, try these on," he said as he threw them on the pool table. I must have tried on enough clothes from Ozzy's wardrobe to fill up a whole Hard Rock Cafe. I recognized some of the outfits from Black Sabbath album cover photos.

"Now you look like a fucking Rock Star!" he said as he walked behind the bar. I went over and stood in front of the mirror to check out my new threads. When I looked back at Ozzy, I saw that he was pissing in the bar sink.

Suddenly, Don Arden walked into the room.

"Ozzy, are you pissing in the sink!?" Don shouted in disbelief. Ozzy tried to pull his dripping member back in his trousers, causing a stream of urine to splash all over Don. "You fucking animal! Get out of my house! Now!" Don yelled at Ozzy while trying to control his anger.

I beat it pretty quick, passing Ozzy as he wobbled out, still trying to pull his johnson back in his pants, still spraying pee on the carpet.

"I need to get back home," I said to Ozzy as he finally met me outside of the house.

"Sorry, but I can't drive," he said. "You're gonna have to stay over."

Ozzy pointed to one of bungalows as he headed towards his own. I approached the one at the front of the courtyard and cautiously opened the door. Turning on the lights I found that the picture-perfect English cottage was empty. I flopped down on an inviting California king-size bed with a massive brass headboard and quickly got under the covers. I stayed fully dressed in case someone found me and chased me from the premises.

As I lay in bed, I began to realize how long it had been since I felt the comfort of a warm bed. Slowly, the ticking of the alarm clock faded and I drifted off to sleep. I don't remember what I dreamed about that night but I can assure you that it wasn't as fantastic as the last 24 hours had been.

The next morning Sharon knocked on my door.

"Rudy, get up and have some breakfast. We have a full day ahead of us."

"I'll be right over, Sharon." I yelled through the door as I jumped out of bed. After a quick shower I followed the smell of
country cooking all the way to the breakfast nook adjacent to the kitchen. Sharon was sitting next to Ozzy.

"Come in, Rudy; have a seat next to Daddy."

Oh shit! There goes my appetite. I thought. They were sitting at the table as if nothing had happened the night before. I took a seat next to Don. He was draped in another monogrammed terrycloth robe; he was yelling on the phone at some record executive or other, shouted a stream of expletives while feeding Jet, his Great Dane, bacon from his plate. A dish full of delicious Southern cooking was placed in front of me. Rachel Youngblood, the Arden's housekeeper, smiled as she put the plate in front of me.

"Rachel, this is Rudy," said Sharon. "He's Ozzy's new bass player."

"Well, he's just too skinny! We're gonna have to do something about that." Rachel said as she winked. "Eat all you want dear; there's plenty more."

"Did you get a good night's sleep?" Sharon asked as I began to feel relaxed enough to take my first bite.

"Yeah, the bed was really comfortable." I still couldn't remember the last time I had slept in a real bed.

"I'm glad you like it. You're welcome to stay here as long as you like," Sharon added, smiling.

"That's quite generous. Thank you."

I had never experienced so much kindness from anyone outside my immediate family before. I couldn't believe it. In less than 24 hours I had gone from sleeping on the floor of an apartment in the San Fernando Valley to staying in a mansion in the Hollywood Hills. Of course, one thing that I always kept in mind was that none of this belonged to me. I had to respect it and appreciate it for as long as it was offered to me.

Halfway through my breakfast Jet came over to my plate and started chomping on my breakfast.

"Jet likes you," Don said. "He doesn't eat off just anybody's plate." I guess that made me part of the family.

2
Excuse Me, Mr. Sarzo ...

It seems like there isn't a day that goes by when some wide-eyed young fan doesn't come up to me and say,

"Excuse me, Mr. Sarzo, but can I ask you a question?" I smile and reply,

"You want to know what Randy Rhoads was like, don't

you?

As I see them nervously grinning with anticipation I think to myself, "How can I tell them in just a few words who Randy was?"

It was an unusually cool Saturday night in late August 1977. I had just arrived in Los Angeles from the Midwest and was itching to check out the local scene. The big buzz around town was about a young guitarist named Eddie in a recently signed band called Van Halen. I attempted to finagle my way into the Whisky a Go Go on the Sunset Strip to catch Van Halen perform but the show was sold out. So I opted to go down the street to the Starwood, a club on the corner of Crescent Heights and Santa Monica Boulevard.

As I made my way inside the bowels of the noisy, cavernous venue, I noticed how young most of the patrons were. There were plenty of scantily clad and dangerously willing teenage girls ready to make the new kids in town feel right at home.

"Hey! How are you?" said a flirtatious petite brunette with just enough baby fat pouring out of her sequined tube top to betray her womanly posture.

"Hi, I'm Rudy!" I shouted over the blaring sounds coming from the nearby stage. "I just got into town a few days ago."

"Oh, you look very familiar. I thought you were somebody else," she said with an air of disappointment as she quickly turned to watch the band.

"Who are these guys?" I said, trying to keep our conversation from fizzling.

"They're called Bad Axe!"

As I watched this traditional metal band I focused on their bass player, as it was my custom to check out the local competition.

His name was Dana Strum and would later become an instrumental figure in connecting Ozzy with Randy.

"Make sure you catch the next band," the brunette shouted enthusiastically.

"Oh, yeah? Who are they?"

"They're called Quiet Riot. Check out the guitar player!" She rushed over to claim her spot in front of the stage.

To my surprise, Quiet Riot came on like gangbusters. Immediately after the stage went black, police lights began to flash from both sides of the stage. An intro tape came blaring through the loudspeakers with the sounds of police sirens, choppers flying overhead, the cacophony of an unruly mob and a newscaster's voiceover announcing the breaking news of a "Quiet Riot" breaking out somewhere in the city.

"This is quite ambitious for a club band," I thought to myself as I waited for the music to kick in.

When the intro came to an end, an avalanche of guitar chords came ferociously ripping from the right side of the stage. Suddenly, the spotlight hit the sonic assailant revealing a diminutive young man with long blond hair, matching polka dotted vest and bow tie. The chainsaw riffs from his cream-colored Les Paul along with his glam- rock looks drove the young girls in front of the stage into a frenzy.

"Who is this guy?" I asked the petite brunette up front.

"That's Randy Rhoads!" She yelled into my ear, never taking her eyes off him.

14

Suddenly the stage was bathed in multi-colored lights as the rest of the band joined Randy in their opening song, "There's Gonna Be a Riot." To the left of the stage was Kelly Garni on bass, behind the drums was Drew Forsythe, and on center stage behind a black-and- white striped microphone stand, Kevin DuBrow. Endowed with star qualities, Quiet Riot had an extraordinary image that complemented their heavy sound. That night they gave an arena-style performance the likes of which I had never before experienced in a club. Needless to say, I was impressed.

After Quiet Riot finished their set, I made the rounds around the club looking to see what kind of trouble I could get myself into, when I spotted Kevin. I went up to him and introduced myself.

We decided to grab a table in the corner of a small crowded room that separated the live Rock Room from the Disco Room.

"Kevin, I'm really impressed with your band's performance. I believe you guys will be signed to a major label and playing in arenas before too long," I said with unbridled honesty.

"Thanks, man," Kevin quickly replied, as his eyes shifted across the room like laser beams honing in on the young girls passing by. "You know, I get what you guys are doing. The whole image thing and putting on an arena show in a club. I think you guys could be huge."

"Thanks, man. What's your name again?" Kevin said as his eyes kept wandering.

"It's Rudy, Rudy Sarzo," I said, humored by Kevin's distractions. "Listen, Rudy, thanks for the words of encouragement. It's been nice talking with you." Kevin said as he spotted a familiar female face. "Maybe we'll run into each other some time." Kevin got up and disappeared into the crowded room.

As I left the Starwood and prowled endlessly into the cool Hollywood night, little did I know what our brief encounter would lead to in the next few months.

I spent most of the summer of 1977 surviving the Hollywood scene off the kindness of female strangers while playing in a string of unsuccessful local outfits. In the fall I received a phone call from my brother, Robert, asking me if I wanted to travel to New Jersey and join him and his wife Suzie in their Top 40 act. I immediately accepted his offer and flew out to New Jersey the next day. My brother and I grew up playing together in rock clubs around South Florida and it was a great opportunity to play with him again, even though the repertoire of his act, called "A New Taste," consisted mostly of Top 40 and disco.

With the intention of returning to Los Angeles and continuing my pursuit of the rock-and-roll dream, I saved most of my wages after expenses and was able to stash a sizable nest egg. In the summer of 1978, one week before I was scheduled to return to Los Angeles, I got a phone call.

"Hello, I'm looking for Rudy," a cheerful young voice said. "Ahhh, this is Rudy. Who's calling?" I said befuddled.

"Oh great, I've been trying to track you down for days. This is Kevin DuBrow, the singer of Quiet Riot. We met a few months ago at the Starwood." His voice reflected unexpected enthusiasm, something that was absent when we first met.

"Oh yeah, I remember you!" I said, wondering what the phone call was about.

"Quiet Riot's looking for a bass player and everyone around town is telling me that you're the guy. I hear you'll be in L.A. soon."

"Yes! As a matter of fact, I've already made my flight reservation for next week."

"Great!" Kevin sounded excited and so was I. "So let me send you a tape of our songs so you can learn them and audition for us as soon as you get here."

"Fantastic! I can't wait to play for you guys."

"Have a safe trip and we'll see you in L.A."

As I hung up the phone, I couldn't believe my good fortune. I had intended to go back to L.A. without any prospects, and now I had the opportunity to play with one of the most promising unsigned bands I had ever seen. Upon my arrival in Los Angeles I contacted Kevin and let him know I was ready for the audition. The following evening I arrived at Quiet Riot's rehearsal space near downtown Burbank. The spacious wall-to-wall mirrored room housed one of Queen's previously owned multi-leveled drum risers. This set up gave the band the opportunity to rehearse the show in a pseudo arena stage environment. Now I could see how Quiet Riot was able to polish their live show.

After Kevin introduced me to Randy and Drew we immediately began to jam. This is when I was first able to bask in the light of Randy's magic. I noticed how effortlessly he managed to alternate from playing rhythm to soloing without loosing the fullness of his sound. Even though we were jamming on a blues-based riff, Randy was capable of improvising in modes not often associated with the blues. I could tell that he had a rich musical vocabulary reaching well beyond the average rock guitarist.

After the jam, the guys decided to try "Killer Girls," one of Quiet Riot's original songs from the audition tape. Back in New Jersey I assumed that there were discrepancies between the playback speed of Kevin's and my tape machine. It didn't make sense to me that a song with a typical open E guitar riff would be played half a step up in F, thus eliminating the possibility of playing the open E string. So I went ahead and took the liberty of transposing the song to the key of E.

"Wow, stop! What's going on?" Kevin yelled as

soon as we started the song.

"Aren't you guys playing the song in E?" I asked, puzzled.

"Yeah, don't worry about the mistake. I know that it sounds like a typical E riff but it's actually played in F," Randy explained with his typical unassuming music-teacher demeanor. "We like to do things a bit different in this band." He smiled and lit up a Winston.

That's when I first realized that Quiet Riot was intent on breaking the mold.

The rest of the audition went smoothly and I was able to land the spot as the new bass player. It was all very casual, no big celebratory atmosphere. They were just relieved to know that they had finally found a player that they could carry on with. I, on the other hand, couldn't have been more excited about the opportunity to play with Quiet Riot. We arranged to meet the next evening to begin full rehearsals and prepare for the upcoming shows.

A few days after my arrival in Los Angeles I moved into a small apartment off the Sunset Strip with a cute, raven-haired young lady that I met at the Rainbow Bar & Grill. As my nest egg slowly shriveled up, I managed to get a job across the street from my apartment at "McNaturals'", a fast health food restaurant. Besides the health conscious Hollywood celebrities that used to frequent the place, McNaturals also became a favorite spot for Quiet Riot fans to hang out and have a smoothie before catching one of our shows at the Whisky a Go Go a couple of blocks up the Sunset Strip.

Before I joined Quiet Riot, the guys had performed close to a couple of dozen shows around the Los Angeles area. In this relatively short period they had managed to release an album in Japan for Sony Records entitled Quiet Riot I. They were already in the mixing stages of their second Japanese release, Quiet Riot II, by the time I joined the group. Both albums received rave reviews in the Japanese press, claiming Quiet Riot to be the "next big thing." Unfortunately, these recordings didn't garner the band a U.S. label deal. While there was a substantial demand from Japanese fans for Quiet Riot to tour Japan, their managers, David Joseph and Warren Entner of Toby Management, turned down the offers. The decision left the band no other choice but to stay in town and slug it out with the rest of the local bands.

The first order of business was to give me a stage makeover that would complement the visual concept of the band. As their trademark, Kevin had gone for striped shirts and microphone stand. Randy had the polka dotted vest and bow tie. Drew was behind the drum kit so his outfit was a pair of wrestling tights. Kevin suggested that I should go over to see Randy's girlfriend, Jody Raskin, who happened to be the band's clothes designer and hairdresser.

Short and slender with a thick curly red mane, Jody was one of the sweetest girls I've ever met and a perfect match for Randy in every way. She took one look at me and came up with a simple solution: the fringe accented western outfit. When it came time to do the album cover photo session for Quiet Riot II, I had already replaced Kelly Garni, their former bass player. I didn't feel comfortable having my photo on the cover of an album that I had not performed on, so I asked if I could overdub Kelly's performance. I was told by the band's management that the record was in the final mixing stages and that it would be cost prohibitive to do so.

Finally on October 5th, 1978, a little over a year after first seeing Quiet Riot, I stepped onto the same Starwood stage in my six-inch platform boots ready to take on the world alongside my new bandmates. The fans were anxious to see the new version of Quiet Riot and their reaction was overwhelming. On the other hand, the local music industry had grown ambivalent towards the band due to the fast growing popularity of the homegrown New Wave scene. From that first weekend of October 1978 until October 27th, 1979, Quiet Riot performed approximately three dozen shows at various Los Angeles nightspots. During this period we watched a number of New Wave bands get signed to major record labels as apathetic record executives passed on Quiet Riot, dismissing us as local rock dinosaurs.

Though it was clear to see that our chances of getting picked up by a major record company were getting slimmer, we just weren't ready to give up yet. So in the spring of 1979 we gathered at the Rhoads' residence for an emergency afternoon meeting.

"What are we gonna do, guys?" asked a concerned Kevin as we sat around the kitchen table.

"I have a couple of new song ideas that I can show you guys at our next rehearsal," Randy said as he poured spoonfuls of sugar in his tall glass of iced tea.

"Oh, please no!" Kevin snapped as he threw his arms up in the air. "I'm tired of making demos and getting rejected by all these record company assholes," he said in disgust.

"The problem is that they never come to our shows," Randy said, as he puffed his Winston.

"Yeah, its pretty discouraging to look up at the Starwood VIP section and see all those empty reserved tables," Drew added.

"If they only saw the reaction of our fans I know they'd take us seriously," Randy said, as he took a sip from his frosty glass of iced tea.

"Hey, guys, I have an idea. How about if we get our fan club to go to every record company in town and demand that they sign Quiet Riot?" I said jokingly, trying to lighten up the mood. "Wait a minute!" Kevin shouted as he jumped off his chair. "That's a great idea!"

"I was only joking," I said, trying to reject any accountability for my inane suggestion.

"No wait, I think that we can make it work." I could

see the wheels turning inside Kevin's brain. We always believed that one of our biggest assets lay in the devotion of our fans, so that afternoon a master plan was forged.

A couple of weeks after our emergency meeting we gathered about 100 members of our fan club on a Sunday afternoon at a park across the street from the NBC studios in Burbank for a pep rally. The fans showed up with homemade banners and picket signs with slogans expressing their allegiance to the band.

"We want to thank every one of you for taking the time to show your appreciation for Quiet Riot!" Kevin said as he addressed the fans seated on the grass.

"The plan is for all of you to meet here tomorrow at 9 a.m. You'll be transported in these flatbed trucks to each major record company and then picket in front of their buildings." Two flatbed trucks were draped with huge Quiet Riot banners. "We truly appreciate what every one of you is doing for Quiet Riot," Randy said as he smiled at the smitten teenage girls surrounding him.

It was quite a touching site to watch such honest dedication coming from the fans as we all mingled on that sunny afternoon in the park.

The following morning the trucks made their first scheduled stop at the Warner Bros. Records building in Burbank. Shortly after the fans began picketing on the sidewalk the police arrived demanding to see a permit. Unbeknownst to us, anyone holding a public demonstration within the municipality of Burbank was required to obtain a permit. So the local authorities quickly herded everyone back into the flatbed trucks and ordered them to leave the city limits within 10 minutes or else they would all be arrested. This unforeseen blunder made our schedule run an hour early, which meant that all the arrangements our publicist had made with the local news media were now out of sync. This put a major wrinkle on our planned media coverage. It wasn't until our last scheduled stop at the CBS building in Century

City that the news media was able to catch up with the picketing fans.

Finally that evening, as we gathered in front of our TV sets, we were pleased to see the local newscasts run the story of our devoted fans and their efforts to let the local music industry know that Quiet Riot was a band worth adding to their roster. Pleased with all the media attention that the demonstrations received, we decided to increase our performing scheduled while we waited for a reaction from the record companies.

A few days later at rehearsal, Randy asked me if I would be interested in teaching bass guitar at Musonia, a North Hollywood music school. I quickly accepted his offer and joined Randy and the rest of the teaching staff the following day. Randy's mom, Delores Rhoads, a soft-spoken, nurturing music teacher with a classy smile and sparkling eyes, owned the school, housed in a quaint Cape Cod structure surrounded by a white picket fence. Next to raising Randy and his siblings, Doug and Kathy, teaching at Musonia was the most fulfilling role in Delores's life.

Teaching at Musonia gave me plenty of opportunities to witness Randy patiently dedicate his time to young guitar hero wannabes.

One day, after a frustrating afternoon of tutoring, I approached Randy for some advice.

"Rand, I need help," I said as I stuck my head through the door of his small, dark wood-paneled classroom.

"Come on in, Rudes. I got a few minutes before my next lesson. What's up?"

"I don't know. I've been teaching for over a week now and I get the feeling that my students aren't interested in learning the basics of music theory. All they're interested in is how to play the songs they want to learn."

"Well, the way I look at it is like this," Randy said as he laid his guitar in its case. "These kids aren't any different than you and me when we were their age. They just can't wait get up onstage and tear it up. But it's my responsibility to prepare them for that moment the best I can. So when they ask me to teach

them how to play 'Eruption' or 'Stairway to Heaven,' I just ask them to practice their homework. Once they come back and show me that they've learned their assignment, be it a new scale or arpeggio, then I teach them whatever song they want."

"I see. You really enjoy teaching, don't you?" I asked, marveling at his dedication.

"You know, one of the things that I enjoy the most about it is that I often learn something new from my students. Their way of looking at things with a fresh approach gives me new insight into my own playing."

Randy's next student arrived and I made my way back to my classroom with a new positive attitude towards my teaching methods.

In the weeks following the fans' demonstrations we managed to garner interest from only one label, Capitol Records. One of their A&R staff members felt that our fans' devotion merited giving a listen to some of our new material.

"You know what you guys need?" said the A&R man seated behind his cluttered desk as we crammed into his office. "You guys need to write a hit song. If you guys can make me a demo with a batch of songs that sound like any of the Top 40 hits on this chart, you guys got a deal." He held up the latest issue of Billboard magazine, the industry bible.

So we reluctantly went back in the studio to record a new batch of songs. In a desperate attempt to please the record company, we took our music into uncharted commercial territory, thus producing results that were inferior to any of our previous efforts.

After Capitol Records rejected our latest demos, a dark cloud fell upon the band, casting shadows of disillusion, anger and dissent. One night in October after another redundant rehearsal, I approached Randy with my concerns.

"Rand, I'm tired of banging my head against the wall. I don't know how much longer I can keep doing this."

"Yeah, I'm getting pretty frustrated myself. Some guy named Dana keeps calling me to audition for Ozzy, the ex-singer in Black Sabbath," Randy said, as he packed away his guitar.

"I can't believe this!" I cut in, overwhelmed by the surprise.

"I've been trying all week long to contact Ozzy's manager and he's been trying to get a hold of you."

"I don't really wanna go," Randy said, "but I figure that once I audition for Ozzy, then Dana will leave me alone." He put on his leather jacket.

"I think that's great, Rand. So when are you meeting Ozzy?" "Tonight. I've got to be at some studio in half an hour," Randy said as he locked away his guitar in the trunk of his car.

"That's wonderful, Rand. Best of luck and I hope everything goes well for you."

He got in his Volkswagen Scirocco.

"Thanks Rudes, see ya tomorrow at Musonia." Randy smiled as he drove away to meet with Ozzy.

The next day, upon my arrival at Musonia, I rushed over to see Randy.

"So tell me Rand, how did it go?"

"Well, it was kind of strange. I walked in the studio and set up my equipment while Ozzy stayed in the control room. So I started to tune my guitar and just play a few riffs from my guitar solo and then Dana came in the room and told me I had the job!" Randy said, still unsure of the situation.

"My God, that's great! Congratulations!" I said as I shook his hand. "So what's Ozzy like?" I asked, filled with curiosity.

"I don't know, but I'm supposed to go and meet him

tonight at this hotel."

"So what does your mom think of all of this?"

"She's 100 percent behind any decision I make. I just hate to leave her to run the school all by herself," Randy said with concern.

"Yeah, it's a tough decision, but I know you'll make the right one," I said, confident in his judgment.

With the reality of Randy's departure from Quiet Riot looming in the horizon, I was left with no other choice than to pursue other musical opportunities. On October 2, 1979, Randy, Kevin, Drew, and I performed our last show as Quiet Riot at the Starwood. It was a bittersweet occasion, celebrating Kevin's birthday, and in my heart and soul my farewell performance with Quiet Riot.

The following day I called up Kevin and told him I was leaving the band. Kevin tried to keep Quiet Riot together and he even auditioned a few bass players before Randy left for England around Thanksgiving.

Musonia felt empty without Randy's guitar playing echoing through the hallways, so shortly after his departure Delores hired George Lynch to fill in, on Randy's recommendation. Randy had a very high regard for George's talent and considered him one of the great local guitar players.

A few days after Randy left for England I approached Delores. "Mrs. Rhoads, have you heard from Randy since he left?"

"You mean he hasn't called you?" Delores wondered.

"Well, I don't expect him to. I know how costly the phone calls are from England."

"Oh, no. He's here at home!" Delores exclaimed.

"What happened?" I said, confused.

"I think you better ask him yourself," Delores said as she walked away to greet her next student.

I couldn't wait to get home and call Randy.

"Hello?" Randy said, apprehensively answering the phone.

"Hey Rand, its Rudy. I didn't know you were back!"

"Oh, I'm too embarrassed to call anyone."

"What the hell happened?" I anxiously inquired.

"It's a long story. After my first flight ever, a 10-hour trip to London, I go through customs at Heathrow Airport and the agent asks me if my visit was business or pleasure. I told him that I was there to record an album. So he asked me for my work permit and of course I didn't have one. Some other agents come over and take me to a room and tell me I have one phone call to clear things up. So I called Jet Records' office in London and explained to the person in charge my situation. He tells me that he'd be right over to take care of it. But instead, he decides to go to the horse races on his way here and forgets about me. I had to spend the night in a cell with a bunch of illegal Pakistani immigrants. The next day they handcuff me and put me on a plane back to Los Angeles!"

"Wow, unbelievable!" I exclaimed. "So have you heard from Ozzy?"

"Yeah, he called me apologizing and has already made arrangements for me to fly back to England in a couple of days." One November morning in 1979 as I faced my 29th birthday, I looked in the mirror and grabbed my waist-length locks and chopped them back to shoulder length. I needed to put behind everything that represented hard rock, as I was determined to join the New Wave scene. I then joined forces with other Hard Rock refugees in a band called Private Army that included my old rhythm section partner and future Quiet Riot drummer, Frankie Banali.

I met Frankie back in 1973 after witnessing his impressive drumming behind a massive kit in a band called Ginger during a set opening for David Bowie's Ziggy Stardust and the Spiders from Mars at a South Florida rock venue called Pirate's World. Private Army managed to assemble an impressive collection of tunes that were rejected by the record labels, all of whom considered us a hard rock band disguised as New Wavers.

Taking advantage of one of Randy's trips back home in 1980, Quiet Riot reunited at Kevin's urging for a string of dates at the Starwood from May 29th through the 31st. Even though it was wonderful to play with Randy once again and all the shows were sold out, the emotional strain of reliving Quiet Riot's failures was hard to endure. Soon after, Randy returned to England to finish writing and recording with Ozzy.

That fall I moved out of the apartment I was sharing with my girlfriend. Deep inside we both knew that our unstable pairing was nothing more than a union of convenience and that our relationship was doomed to fail from the beginning.

Fortunately, Kevin came to my rescue and offered to let me stay at his place as long as I could pay my share of the rent. Kevin also asked me to play in his band, DuBrow, which helped keep my chops up and subsidized my income.

After spending years in a seductive, callous town, enduring rejection and surviving economic hardships my faith was in need of improvement. I've always looked at my life as a spiritual journey, having practiced catechism during my childhood in my native Cuba and experiencing all sorts of alternative religions along the way. But I had never before felt a direct connection with God. I believe that spiritual enlightenment is a personal journey and no one can lead you to the straight and narrow path but yourself. I started to read the Bible, which brought me the spiritual comfort I desperately needed. It was during this time that I experienced my epiphany.

Here I was, at the lowest material point in my life, yet my faith couldn't have been stronger. It was at this moment that I made a commitment to God expressing that if I was ever able to make a living as a musician, I would be eternally grateful—and if not, then I would accept it peacefully. From that moment on, my relationship with God would always be the single most important concern in my life.

A couple of weeks later I received the phone call from Ozzy. A coincidence you might ask? I think not.

3
Let Me Put the Little Bastard Out of Its Misery

Immediately after my first morning at the Arden's mansion, Randy, Tommy, and I kicked off a full rehearsal schedule. With the first date of the Blizzard of Ozz Tour just a few weeks away, the anticipation and tension were running high. While Ozzy was busy doing all of the record release and pre-tour interviews, we carried on at Frank Zappa's rehearsal studio, going over the set list and getting acquainted musically with each other. The bulk of the live show was made up of tunes from the Blizzard of Oz record: "I Don't Know," "Crazy Train," "Mr. Crowley," "Revelation (Mother Earth)," "Steal Away" and "Suicide Solution." "Believer" and "Flying High Again," from the soon-to-be-released Diary of a Madman record, were added to the list. To finish, the set featured three Black Sabbath tunes: "Iron Man," "Children of the Grave," and the heavy metal anthem "Paranoid."

As we rehearsed the set list I was impressed by Randy's craftsmanship at tailoring each of his compositions to showcase his innovative styles. He incorporated into his songs an aggressive double picking rhythm technique that soon after became a staple of heavy metal rhythm guitar. He also took the art of guitar soloing into new realms by writing individual musical passages within the songs to perform his soaring solos over. Randy's blend of classical music and pop sensibilities, along with Ozzy's eerie vocals, gave each song a distinctive sound, laying the foundation for a new generation of heavy metal.

I was also impacted by Tommy's freedom of musical expression in more ways than one. Being one of rock's most respected drummers and Ozzy's first choice, he was free to take liberties interpreting the drum parts on the records by adding his own percussive thumbprint. I, on the other hand, as a newcomer, was asked to adhere as close as possible to the recorded bass lines. But Tommy's assertive drumming and Randy's charging rhythm guitar inspired me to reshape the bass parts from the records; I tried to match their musical intensity. By the time we hit the stage on opening night of the Blizzard of Ozz tour, the three of us had become an airtight rhythm section.

One afternoon after rehearsal I went over to the Jet Records office located in a converted guesthouse on the grounds of the Arden's estate. I was there to discuss business with Sharon. As I followed the fragrant blossoming pathway, I ran into Ozzy dressed in a plaid jacket and looking rather spiffy.

"Hey Oz! What's that all over your clothes?" I asked, wondering about the messy crimson stains on his white dress shirt.

"Oh, it's just blood, man." Ozzy sounded unconcerned.

"Cut yourself shaving?" I pried.

"Oh no," Ozzy said, brushing off any such possibility. "You wanna hear what happened?" he said, flashing a wicked grin. "Sharon insisted that I go over to the CBS Records offices and introduce myself to everyone. Then she got this fuckin' great idea that I bring with me some fuckin' doves and release them as a goodwill gesture. When we get there, we find out that some bloody wanker named Adam Ant is having a fuckin' big record release party and no one wants fuck all to do with us. So they drag us into this bloody tiny piece of shit office and we wait for fuckin' ever until some bird shows up," Ozzy rambled in his thick Midlands accent.

"You mean, a bird flew into the room?" I asked, trying to make some sense of the story.

"No, no! You know a skirt, a chick, a girl. So Sharon brings in a photographer and tells me to sit next to this bird. We started waffling a bit and then I pulled a dove out of my coat pocket and without thinking about it I bit its fuckin' head off! You should've seen it! Blood was dripping out of my mouth, feathers were flying all over the fuckin' place." Ozzy said as he laughed. "What did the girl do?" I inquired.

"She ran out of the fuckin' room screaming for security, and then these guards came in and kicked us out of the building." Ozzy was obviously amused by his deeds. Then his coat pocket started shaking.

"Oh, here's the other one!" He pulls a semiconscious dove out of his pocket.

"Let me put the little bastard out its misery." Ozzy chomped its head off with one quick bite, splattering still more blood over his clothes. "Tastes like chicken!" he says, flashing a devilish grin.

As I watched Ozzy walk down the pathway towards the house, I realized that my life was about to become very interesting indeed.

As I finally made my way inside the Jet office, I heard Sharon's girlish voice.

"Rudy, come in and have a seat," she said from behind her desk where she was on the phone. I couldn't help but notice the wall lined with gold and platinum records from ELO, Air Supply, and other Jet acts.

"How are rehearsals coming along?" Sharon asked as she hung up the phone.

"Oh fine, we'll have the songs down by the time we get to San Bernardino."

"Ozzy and I are concerned that you boys might not be ready by the 22nd with such little time to rehearse the full production." Sharon looked deeply into my eyes, trying to detect apprehension.

"Don't worry. I think you'll both be pleased when you hear how tight we sound."

"Fine, well, let's talk about your salary. I'm not sure if you know this, but money's a bit tight on this tour." I could read her sincerity. "We're not getting enough support from CBS to cover all of the touring expenses, so Daddy has put up most of the money himself. I really can't offer you much right now but I promise you a raise when the financial situation improves, hopefully in a couple of months."

"That's fine, I understand," I said without hesitation.

I had already heard some rumors regarding the financial status of the tour and I was ready to lend my support in any way I could. "Good," she said with a smile. "Here, let me give you some money for stage clothes." She reached in a drawer and pulled out some cash from an envelope. "Just make sure you do all your shopping before we leave. We'll have a dress rehearsal for the CBS executives on the last day of pre- production. We've got to get them excited about the tour, so you boys need to look and sound your best."

It sounded like a half time locker room pep talk.

"Sharon, don't worry. Consider it done," I said as I got up to leave.

"And don't forget to bring me the receipts for the clothes!" Sharon yelled as I walked out the door.

The night before we left Los Angeles for full rehearsals, Tommy and I hit the town. This was the first night I was out since joining the band. It was amusing running into local musicians. They joked about how rich I was and offered half-hearted congratulations. I thought it was strange that no one mentioned how great it must be to play with Randy again or with such accomplished musicians, or even that I had finally been given the opportunity of a lifetime. Not seeing the need to go into the details of my private arrangement with Sharon, I would just smile and say,"Yeah, life is good." And indeed it was.

On April 7th we began pre-production rehearsals at the Swing Auditorium, situated in the Orange Pavilion Fair Grounds in San Bernardino, 70 miles east of Los Angeles. Having spent all my years playing clubs, the barn-like, 8,000-capacity venue felt ominous and cold at first sight. By the time we arrived, the back line, sound, and lights were already rigged up. I climbed onto the stage and stood alone, taking in the moment. I surveyed the hovering, massive lighting rig, the rows of floor monitors, the side-fill monitors, the miles of cables connected to the massive stacks of the PA. A feeling like no other swept over me. I felt like a kid who had run away from home to join the circus, except that I wasn't running away from home. I was finally home.

"So whaddaya think?" I heard Tommy's Southern drawl as we stood side by side looking out into the empty venue.

"I've got to tell you, it's really exciting and a little scary at the
same time."

"Don't worry," Tommy said as he walked towards his drum kit.

"You'll get used to it."

And he was right. Soon, real soon, there would be no safer place than on a concert stage.

I made the rounds, introducing myself to the sound and light crew. Most of the guys were from England and had already worked with Ozzy in Sabbath. Through the years I'd come to deeply respect and appreciate our crews. They get to the venue early in the morning to rig the whole production up and tear it back down only to do it again the next day and the day after that. Most of the time they're gone for months, and the only link to their loved ones are the photos you see hanging from their backstage passes and road cases.

By now our keyboard player, Lindsay Bridgewater, had joined us for pre-production. Lindsay had already toured with Ozzy and Randy on the British leg of the Blizzard Tour and was familiar with the set list, with the exception of the two new songs from Diary of a Madman. His familiarity with the material immediately added a cohesive element to our sound. This was Lindsay's first trip to America, however, and his innocent demeanor would soon fall victim to Ozzy's pranks.

After a few days of rehearsal we were pleased enough with our progress to go out and blow off some steam. The band and crew decided to meet that Saturday night at a nearby Black Angus restaurant for dinner and drinks. Randy and I were the first to arrive. After a few dirty looks from the local rednecks we made our way to the bar to await our table.

"Hey Rand," I said, "After listening to Blizzard non-stop for the past couple of weeks, I've got some questions."

"What do you wanna know?" Randy answered, calmly looking through the menu, oblivious to the tension in the room.

"The intro to 'Mr. Crowley,' who came up with that?"

Our rowdy road crew was just arriving.

"That was a keyboard player named Bill, a friend of a friend of Ozzy's, who had come down to audition. Bob and I started jamming on this chord pattern that Bill had. When Ozzy came in and heard what we were playing he thought it sounded a bit like 'Mr. Crowley.' So when it came time to record the song, Don Airey came in and added his own touches and arranged it as the intro."

"That's one of my favorite moments on the record," I said. "Don's a real talented musician," Randy added. "He would be on this tour if it weren't for a previous commitment he had with Rainbow."

By this time, the road crew was bellying up to the bar.

"Is that him on 'Revelation (Mother Earth)'?"

"Yeah, that's him. Isn't that a beautiful piano?" Randy said, as we greeted the crew.

"Yeah, I love the arpeggios."

"Don's also playing the piccolo trumpet line on

'Goodbye to Romance' on the synthesizer," said Randy.

"It sounds like something off a Beatles record," I said, giving the waitress my drink order.

"Believe it or not, Ozzy's a huge Beatles fan. He's always coming up with these real melodic vocal ideas."

I was surprised, completely unaware of Ozzy's musical roots. "Well, I think it's a real well-balanced record. I love 'Dee,' your acoustic piece," I told him.

"That's dedicated to my mom," Randy said. "I'd been practicing it for quite some time, and then late one night after we finished our recording sessions I felt I was ready. We were recording and living at Ridge Farm so I woke up Max our engineer in the middle of the night and had him come down and record it."

"It has a real peaceful feel to it," I said.

The bartender was eyeing our crew with suspicion. "Mom likes it," Randy said, still oblivious of the escalating tension. "For the second record I also wrote an acoustic piece for the intro of 'Diary of a Madman,'" Randy added.

"Isn't that the one with the choir?"

"That's the one. It's a bit of a rip-off of "Carmina Burana" but I guess it works," Randy smiled.

"Your classical technique has improved so much in such a short time," I said as the waitress arrived with drinks.

"I found this teacher in London who's really amazing. Plus Ozzy's been very supportive."

"I picked up on your double tracking solos on the new record,"

I said, winking.

"Old habits are hard to break I guess," he answered. "I just like the way the solos sound when they're doubled. You don't hear too many guitar players doing it."

"Maybe it's because not many guitar players can do it like you." The waitress was now flirting with the crew.

"By the way," I asked, "how did Max Norman get to be involved in the recording?"

Out of the corner of my eye, I saw the bartender motion to a couple of the locals.

"It was really tough getting the whole thing off the ground," said Randy. "We spent months looking for a drummer until Lee Kerslake finally came on board. Bob Daisley came from one of Don Arden's bands, Widowmaker. A nice guy and a real good player and songwriter. After being rejected by just about every producer in town we finally got one to come in, but Ozzy didn't like him so we got rid of him. So out of desperation Ozzy goes up to Max, points at the recording console and says, 'Hey, mate! Do you know how to turn this thing on?' Max was caught off guard, and said, 'Well yeah, I'm the house engineer.' 'Great,' said Ozzy. 'Then you're the producer!'"

I burst out laughing, only to see what I had been half-expecting: one of the local rednecks punched a crew member. All hell broke loose. It was like a scene out of an old western. One of our burly crew grabbed Randy and me.

"I gotta get you guys outta here! If either of you gets hurt then we ain't got a tour" He dragged us through the melee and out the door, then ran gleefully back inside to mix it up a little.

"We'd better leave before the cops get here," Randy said wisely, as we headed back to the hotel.

"What's the deal with 'No Bone Movies'?" I asked. "It's so different from everything else on the record."

"You mean, you don't know? Bone movies, porn flicks!" Randy giggled.

"Oh, I get it."

"When Jody came over to visit in England," Randy

36

explained, "we all went out to the movies. There was all this sex and stuff in it, so after the show Bob came up with the idea of writing a
song about porn. I suggested the title. It's just a silly fun song, originally a B-side. But somehow it wound up on the record."

"I wasn't familiar with all the Sabbath tunes, but I'm having a blast playing them," I admitted.

"To be honest Rudes, I wish we didn't have to include them. After doing two albums with Ozzy there's enough material to play a full set without the Sabbath stuff. But I realize that Ozzy's fans expect him to do a few every night. Maybe later we can drop them."

"Well, I think we've got a really strong set list," I said. "It's all the great heavy stuff—'I Don't Know,' 'Crazy Train,' 'Suicide Solution.' Plus there's 'Believer' and 'Flying High Again' and the Sabbath tunes."

"We're gonna need all the heavy stuff we can play," Randy said. "Motorhead's gonna be opening the first leg of the tour!" "Motorhead? Never heard of 'em." "Oh, you will, and so will everybody else within a 20-mile radius of the stage!"

Randy grabbed a candy bar out of the vending machine and headed down the hallway to his room.

April 16th. The final day of pre-production rehearsals had finally arrived. The tension in the air was thick. Ozzy sat in a corner of the dressing room staring into space, rocking back and forth, as we were getting ready to perform for the CBS record executives. Meanwhile, Sharon was helping us out with wardrobe.

"Let me see what you bought!" she said, sifting through my clothes bag. "What's this?" She shrieked as she held up a pair of red vinyl trousers.

"I couldn't find any metal clothes in L.A. Everyplace is selling all that New Wave crap," I explained.

37

"You should have gotten two pairs," Tommy said. "One to shit on and another to cover it with!"

"I did. I got these in black too!"

"Go with the black," Sharon ordered. "OK, let me see your shirts." She dug through my bag, irritated. "Put this one on ... What about shoes?"

"I thought I'd wear my cowboy boots."

"No way! You'll look like one of the Village People. Just go with your street shoes."

As I was checking myself out in front of a full-length mirror, I saw Ozzy's reflection.

"You look like a poofter," Ozzy said as we looked at each other's reflection in the mirror.

"Sharon!" I heard Ozzy yell as he ran out of the dressing room. My fashion attack was cut short by the arrival of the CBS suits. As I stood behind my bass rig I saw their black stretch limousine enter the venue and pull up in front of the stage. A small group of well-dressed men got out of the car and took their pre-arranged seats up front. A giant knot swelled in the pit of my stomach; my Quiet Riot nightmare of playing for the suits was beginning to come back to me. Ozzy quickly gathered everyone backstage for a last-minute pep talk.

"OK guys, let's play like there's no tomorrow. 'Cause if we fuck up there will be no tomorrow. Rock and roll!"

When the lights came up, we ripped into our first song. At that moment, all my fears and anxieties disappeared and the comforts of performing with world-class musicians kicked in. Ozzy, Randy, and Tommy gave it their all. It made no difference if we were playing for 50,000 or five. I just needed to find my groove and keep up with everyone else. Immediately after the first song ended a deafening silence reverberated in the venue. The suits sat there frozen, silhouetted by Ozzy's spotlight throwing a long, dark, motionless shadow across the stage. Puzzled, Ozzy turned and yelled out the next song.

We didn't stop until the set was over. As the last, fading chords of "Paranoid" echoed through the building, the suits clapped quietly, got back in their limousine, and drove away. Just like that. Ozzy stood on the stage looking down at the floor.

"Ozzy," I heard Sharon softly call as she stepped out of the shadows.

"Yeah?" Ozzy answered, slowly looking up.

"They loved it!" Sharon's face was glowing with pride. Ozzy collapsed in her arms as they hugged. Randy smiled and lit up a cigarette.

4
Welcome to the Club

After our last day of pre-production in San Bernardino, we all returned to Los Angeles as our equipment trucks made their way across country bound, for the first city of the tour.

On the morning of April 21st, Sharon, Ozzy, Randy, Tommy, Rachel, and I departed from Los Angeles International Airport for our first date of the Blizzard of Ozz tour: Towson, Maryland. Mr. Pook, Sharon's Yorkshire terrier, rounded out our Heavy Metal circus.

Our tour bus picked us up at the airport and drove us to the hotel. As I was relishing my first ride ever on a tour bus, everyone else was claiming his bunk of choice. By the time I realized what was going on, I was left with the worst possible choice: upper bunk adjacent to the bathroom. Rule Number One: On any tour bus toilet, you're allowed to urinate only. Never #2! Why? In the summer it would stink up the bus and in the winter it would freeze, clog up the pipes, and then stink up the bus with the stench of #1 and #2.

Now fully aware that Ozzy was not one to follow rules, I took the precaution of purchasing industrial strength deodorizers at the first truck stop we fueled at and lined my bunk with them. Despite the peril, my dubious cocoon soon became my sanctuary amid the mayhem. Plus, it sure beat the hell out of sleeping on a floor.

On the afternoon of April 22nd, Randy, Tommy, Lindsay, and I headed for sound check. Often Ozzy would stay behind, resting in his hotel room or in the back lounge of the bus and skip sound check. As soon as the tour bus arrived at the venue, we rushed to the stage. The equipment trucks had taken longer to arrive than planned and the production was running a couple of hours behind.

The Towson Center's doors would be opening in a few hours and both bands still had to do sound checks. After a quick survey—an equipment once-over that merely amounted to a line check—we yielded the stage to make room for Motorhead's back line. After a couple of weeks of pre-production it wasn't all that imperative to do a full sound check. We just needed to make sure that our backline was in one piece after a bumpy cross-country ride. On the other hand, Motorhead had just arrived from England where the voltage difference could cause a major problem with the sound quality of their amplifiers. Not that you would ever notice the difference, since they played at 120 decibels, the noise level of a jet taking off.

"Hey Lemmy!" Randy shouted as we headed towards catering.

"Randall!" Lemmy's gravelly voice echoed through the backstage

area.

Lemmy was dressed in a faded blue denim shirt and jeans, a bullet belt, and white Beatle boots, the only outfit I ever saw him wear on and off stage. He was nursing a half empty bottle of Smirnoff with a faint hint of orange juice and carrying a small bag stuffed with paperback books. His pupils were as big as silver dollars.

"Welcome to the tour!" Randy said, as they shook hands.

"This is Rudy, our new bass player." Since I had joined the band I had already experienced a series of British dialects, but I wasn't ready for Lemmy's indecipherable accent. As he finished delivering his message he raised his bottle and offered me a drink.

"No thanks," I said. "I never drink before a show." Lemmy took a long hard swig from the bottle, flashed a buccaneer grin and walked away.

"What did he say?" I asked Randy.

"He just said it was great to be in the Colonies and he was

lookin' forward to the tour."

"Colonies?"

"Some Englishmen still like to think of the U.S. as part of the

British colonies!"

I made a habit of not returning to the hotel after sound check so I spent most of my pre-show time wandering about the venue and getting a feel for the place. About an hour before show time, everybody gathered in the dressing room. The mood backstage was jovial, in contrast to our previous performance. Ozzy was ridiculing Lindsay for putting on makeup, since he spent most of the show on the side of the stage and in total darkness. Tommy was firing wisecracks in rapid succession while twirling his drum sticks. Randy was in a corner smoking and warming up on his guitar. Sharon and Rachel were helping Ozzy get dressed. I sat quietly in the comer hugging my bass and trying to stay calm.

I'll never forget our first performance. The roar of the crowd as the venue went completely dark. The smell of the fog machine as it draped the stage in a misty blanket. The ominous strains of "Carmina Burana" heralding the band's arrival onstage. Randy and I looked at each other, moved by the sight of the crowd flicking their lighters as they turned the place into a surrealistic galaxy. Ozzy incited the crowd as we stepped onstage. Then suddenly Randy ripped into the intro of "I Don't Know" as Tommy banged on the gong behind his drum kit. I felt like I had reached the top of a rollercoaster and was about to go on the most thrilling ride of my life.

But just like an amusement park ride, with the last chords of "Paranoid," it had to come to an end. When it did, I couldn't wait to get back on it again.

A local rock journalist wrote about that night's performance.

"By rights, Osbourne should be a

burnout case by now. What happened? First off, Osbourne got a great band together. Guitarist Randy Rhoads is the focal point here. That which sounded strained or portentous on the album was hard-hitting and believable in concert. My favorite song was from his as- yet-unreleased Diary of a Madman. An irritable ditty called "I Don't Like New Wave" is about just that, crabbily ranting against bands like the Damned or the Dead Kennedys. Opening the show was Motorhead, a band that may well make current conceptions of loud and fast obsolete."

Not a bad review for the first show of the tour. It's amusing how the reviewer obviously couldn't understand the lyrics to "Flying High Again" and mistook its title and message.

Immediately after we took our bow, we were ushered off the stage, just like Elvis, and onto the tour bus. This became a nightly tradition. We all then piled into the back lounge as the tour bus drove out of the parking lot. It was always nice to see Rachel's smiling face and hear her comments about the show as we peeled off our wet stage clothes and put them in plastic bags. As I lay in my bunk and basked in the afterglow of that first show, I couldn't help but reflect on how blessed I was to be a part of this band and to have all these wonderful people in my life.

The following morning, April 23rd, we woke up in front of the Holiday Inn in downtown Harrisburg, Pennsylvania. While we waited for Sharon to check us in, I experienced my first case of "bus hair." This is a phenomenon that occurs when you spend the night in your bunk. The effect looks pretty much like rats running laps through your hair while you sleep.

The evening's show was at the Forum Theater. This was our first performance in a theater setting. Unlike the cacophonous acoustics of the average hockey/basketball arenas, a theater can offer a warm, rich sound experience for both the audience and the performers. The band played more relaxed than the previous night since we could hear ourselves better on the proscenium stage. This intimate setting gave me an opportunity to take a good look at our audience. I was disappointed to discover that most of them were bikers and old Black Sabbath fans. I couldn't find a single female in the whole crowd. Not that it mattered, since Sharon had a "No Groupies" backstage policy and we always left town after the show. This was obviously one of Sharon's tactics to keep Ozzy out of trouble.

On our way to the next city we pulled into a truck stop to refuel. We all filed out of the bus and went inside for a late night meal. It was amusing to see the stunned truckers as we were whisked to the back of the restaurant. Ozzy sat at the head of the table with Lindsay at the other end. As we finished our meal I heard Lindsay yell, "What the hell?!" He jumped out of his chair, revealing wet trousers. I looked at Ozzy who was laughing uncontrollably. He pissed on Lindsay under the table! We threw our money on the table and scrambled back to the bus.

The next morning, April 24th, we woke up in Passaic, New Jersey. I called my brother Robert after we checked into the local Howard Johnson and arranged to meet him for lunch. It was great to see him again and to finally meet his son, Robert Jr., who was born after I returned to California.

That night's show was at the Capitol Theater. Sharon arranged for our second group photo session with a fledgling rock photographer named Mark Weiss. Before long, the talented rookie lensman would become one of the most respected and sought-after photographers in the music business. It was very emotional for me to perform that night in the same area where just three years before I had been performing on the lounge circuit with my brother and his wife.

The New Jersey Journal printed a pre-show backstage interview with Ozzy. Such boastful quotes as, "Not too many performers can hold the attention of an audience the way I do," were totally out of character with Ozzy's unpretentious personality. Though the interviewer got all of the band member's names right, the paper printed a photo of the previous lineup.

By this time, Randy and I were developing our after-show/back- lounge ritual. We would get out of our wet clothes, put on our robes, open a bottle of wine, eat some yogurt and listen to Lee Ritenour before hitting the sack. In contrast, it was interesting to watch Ozzy and Tommy, veteran road warriors, and how they adjusted to life on the road. Tommy had amassed an impressive little black book from all the years of traveling with Black Oak Arkansas, Pat Travers, and other acts. There was always some pretty young lady waiting for him in each city we played. During our days off, Tommy would disappear, only to turn up the following day at sound check with some beauty in tow. I could have sworn he had his own tour going. For his part, Ozzy became more reclusive and dependent on booze as the tour gained momentum.

The following morning, April 25th, we woke up in Philadelphia. After checking into the Marriott hotel, Randy and I agreed to meet for lunch and see the sights. That evening's show was at the Tower Theater. I always looked forward to playing in those ornate, historical buildings in the decaying downtown areas of so many cities around the country.

After sound check I felt it was time to meet the rest of Motorhead's band members and crew. I had seen them running around backstage and since they all wore head-to-toe blue denim at all times it was hard for me to differentiate the band from the crew.

"Anybody home?" I yelled as I entered Motorhead's

tour bus. Quite the contrast to our bus, to say the least. There were empty bottles of Smirnoff—the only item, along with orange juice, included in their backstage rider—scattered throughout the front lounge. Dirty ashtrays, stacks of empty pizza boxes, dirty plates, and porno magazines were everywhere. This is what a rock-and-roll tour bus was supposed to look like! A young, leather-clad female appeared from the back of the bus as I stood in the middle of the smelly mess. "You must be Rudy," I heard her disheveled companion say.

"My name is Phil," he said, a cigarette dangling from his lip.

"My friends call me 'Philthy,' as in 'Philthy Animal.'" His skull rings embellished his hands.

"You must be the drummer," I confirmed, as we shook hands. "Yeah, I've been accused of that!" he said as he playfully spanked his companion.

"Where's your guitar player?" I asked.

"Eddie's sleeping. Big party last night, mate." He paused for a moment. "Or has it been going on for two nights? ... Anyway, he's out like a light and Lemmy's in the back lounge reading." "Yeah, I noticed the bag of books he carries. Looks like they'll last him the whole tour."

"Are you kidding? Lemmy stays up for days reading. He's already gone through that bag!"

He sucked the last drops from a bottle of vodka. "Better get some more!" he said, holding the bottle upside down. "You know what they say: breakfast's the most important meal of the day!"

Though that night we enjoyed another in a string of strong performances, the weekend entertainment preview column of the local Philadelphia newspaper read:

"For those who take their blasts from the past quite literally, the headbanging, speed freak sounds of Ozzy Osbourne and

Blizzard of Ozz will surely chill the cockles of your hearts at the Tower Theater tomorrow night. Frankly, wild horses couldn't drag me to see Ozzy and Company. Their latest group recording is as bloated and insipid as all the Sabbath LPs."

A local rock critic reported,

"For years, Black Sabbath was one of those bands the critics loved to hate, and for 11 of those years its leader was Ozzy Osbourne, shrill-voiced vocalist and dark-eyed sex symbol. On bass, there's Bob Daisley and on drums Lee Kerslade. Young guitarist Randy Rhoads rounds out Ozzy's Blizzard."

Not only did the writer misspell Lee's last name but also mistakenly printed Ozzy's name under Lee's headshot. I wonder if he was discouraged by the negative preview and decided to skip the show altogether. On the other hand, this other rock journalist appeared to have actually made the show when he wrote this review:

"If the heavy metal rock was any heavier this weekend at the Tower Theater, the ceilings and walls could not have stood it. The opening act, Motorhead, is known for being one of the loudest acts in the realm of rock- and-roll. Fronting his new power trio, the Blizzard of Ozz, Osbourne has found a perfect vehicle for his sardonic vocals. Ozzy Osbourne was living proof that you cannot keep an old rock-and-roller down, especially if they are as talented as Osbourne and his current group, Blizzard of Ozz."

The following morning, April 26th, we woke up in

Bethlehem, Pennsylvania. After we checked into the Holiday Inn, Randy and I grabbed a cab and went to the local shopping mall just to keep from going stir crazy in our rooms. That evening's show was at the Stabler Arena, situated on the Lehigh University campus. Though we were performing in front of the smallest crowd to date, we still put on another high-energy show.

A local journalist wrote of that evening's performance,

"Last Sunday night's bout between two heavy metal monsters at Lehigh University's Stabler Arena in Bethlehem yielded a clear cut winner with opening act Motorhead outperforming headline act Ozzy Osbourne's Blizzard of Ozz. But the estimated crowd of 1,200 apparently saw the outcome otherwise than did this reviewer as it responded enthusiastically to every token gesture given by Osbourne. Osbourne's new band fell prey to a number of heavy metal cliches, the most blatant of which were overly long drum and guitar soloing and a tendency to plod. To his credit, Osbourne has discovered melody. The trick almost worked on 'No Bone Movies'."

Interesting comment since we didn't get to perform "No Bone Movies" until the 1982 Diary of a Madman tour.

After a 300-mile overnight drive we woke up the next morning, April 27th, in Rochester, New York. After five consecutive shows, a couple of days off was a welcomed break, especially for our road crew who had been working nonstop. Sharon made arrangements that afternoon for the band and crew to have dinner together at an Italian restaurant in downtown Rochester.

That evening we took over the banquet room of the family style establishment as Ozzy, Sharon, Rachel, the band and crew shared one large table. I was seated between Brooksie, a burly member of Tasco's crew, our light and sound company and Ox, Tommy's husky drum tech. As the evening progressed, our table gathered an impressive collection of empty wine bottles.

Caught in the spirit of celebration I got completely hammered. I began to playfully toss empty lobster shells at our dinner companions when suddenly Brooksie and Ox get up and poured bowls of Roquefort cheese dressing on my head. I immediately jumped off my chair and staggered to the bathroom stunned and almost sobered by the pungent stench of the dripping sauce, which by now covered most of my upper body. After a futile attempt to wipe the dressing off my head, I fumbled my way out of the restaurant and into the bustling streets of downtown Rochester. Each cab I hailed rejected my fare after they took a close look at my condition and smelled the stench. I was left with no other choice than to walk a couple of miles back to the hotel on that chilly night.

I jumped in the shower as soon as I reached the hotel and washed my hair at least half a dozen times. But each time I blew it dry the pungent smell of the cheesy dressing got worse. The room spun as I lay in my bed drunk and naked.

Suddenly, the door burst open and the party from the restaurant charged in. They dragged me off the bed and threw me onto the ground. They emptied trashcans on me and threw anything else they could find on my naked, immobilized body. When the attackers finally left the room I stood up and saw the crime scene outline of my body drawn on the carpet by all the debris.

I took another shower and went next door where the party continued.

"Hey Rudes! You took it like a real man!" Ozzy said as he smiled and gave me a hug. "You're one of us now. Welcome to the club!"

Everyone else gathered around and congratulated me on passing my strange initiation. The next morning, April 28th, I got a call from Sharon.

"Rudy, Pat Siciliano from Jet has made arrangements

for Ozzy to perform tonight at a local television station. We will only need you boys for four songs. So be dressed and ready to be picked up around 8 tonight."

"What the fuck!" Ozzy blurted out as we entered the small television studio. "For fuck's sake, Sharon! There's no room for us in here. We'll bring down the bloody roof and it's gonna sound like shit!" Ozzy exclaimed.

"It'll be all right, Ozzy. Just trust me." She pleaded.

Sharon had taken preventive measures by arranging for our soundman, Chuck Weisner, to mix the live sound and for the use of our own monitor system. I wasn't sure it was a good move for us to broadcast our live performance with only five shows under our belt.

"What do you think, Rand?" I asked while we were checking our tuning.

"It'll be all right," he answered. "I don't think anybody else besides them is ever gonna see this." Randy smiled as he pointed at the studio audience—about 20 fans.

We ran through "I Don't Know," "Crazy Train," "Mr. Crowley," and "Suicide Solution" with the carefree attitude of a frat house party band. In retrospect, I thank God we had the opportunity to capture the moment. This so-called "After Hours" show is the only professional quality video recording available of Randy in all his glory.

The following night, April 29th, we performed at Rochester's Auditorium Theater. There was a persistent interference emitting from the transmitting aerials surrounding the venue. I was left with no other choice than to use a guitar cord instead of my wireless system during the show. Towards the end of "Paranoid," I tripped over my guitar cord and fell on my ass. Ozzy hovered over me as his spotlight highlighted the embarrassing moment. I looked like an upside down turtle struggling to get up as I continued playing my bass. Needless to say, I couldn't wait to get the hell out of Rochester.

5
Make me a cheeseburger like Wonder Woman!

The morning of April 30th, we woke up in downtown
Syracuse, New York. After we checked into the Holiday
Inn, Randy and I went sightseeing, a hobby on the tour
that had become a daily event. That evening's show was
at the Landmark Theater where we took advantage of the
proscenium stage's intimacy and delivered another strong
performance in front of a near sellout crowd.

On the after-show bus ride Ozzy had that
mischievous look on his face. He had been pressuring
Sharon to relocate Lindsay from our bus to one of the
crew buses. I don't think it had anything to do with
Lindsay's musicianship. He was definitely holding his
own when it came to duplicating all the intricate, multi-
layered keyboard tracks that Don Airey previously
recorded. But there was something about Lindsay's
personality that rubbed Ozzy the wrong way. So on the
way out of town, Ozzy slipped Lindsay a sleeping pill and
within minutes he had passed out in the front lounge.

As soon as Lindsay started snoring, Ozzy picked him
up and dragged him into his bunk, leaving his head
dangling from the edge. Ozzy quickly returned with a
grooming kit and started chopping off the right side of
Lindsay's shoulder length blonde locks. Not quite
satisfied with his prank, Ozzy continued by shaving his
right eyebrow also. A couple of hours later we pulled into
a truck stop to refuel. We went in the dining area and
ordered our late night snacks while Lindsay remained
passed out in his bunk. As I sat at the counter with Randy,
Lindsay stormed in. He grabbed a stool next to me,
slammed his fist on the counter, and demanded the
waitress.

"Make me a cheeseburger like Wonder Woman! Right
now!"
Lindsay slurred as the poor waitress stared at him.

She was horrified at the sight of the English lunatic with half his hair and one eyebrow missing.

"What are you looking at!?" Lindsay spun and slipped off his stool as he yelled with contempt at the appalled patrons.

While I watched Lindsay gobble up his cheeseburger, completely oblivious of his freakish appearance, I didn't have the heart to tell him what had happened, or how he looked.

The next morning, we woke up in front of the Park Plaza Hotel in bustling downtown Boston. As I was getting out of my bunk I heard a bloodcurdling scream coming from the bathroom.

"Aaah! Aaah!" Lindsay yelled as he bumped into Ozzy in the front lounge.

"I tried to stop you from doing this to yourself, man," Ozzy said while grabbing and shaking Lindsay by the shoulders. "But you were so fuckin' high last night we couldn't hold you down."

Ozzy convincingly explained to Lindsay in an effort to ease his anger. "I'm sorry but you can't be seen with us looking like a bloody punk rocker. It's just not good for the image."

Lindsay looked at himself in the mirror, weeping and running his hands through his chopped hair.

"Here, go get a haircut right now in the hotel barbershop and even out the rest of your hair." Ozzy handed Lindsay some cash. After breakfast I ran into Lindsay in the hotel gift shop sporting a fresh crew cut.

"What do you think?" I heard Lindsay ask as he held up two eyebrow pencils.

"I think the one on the left matches your natural color better," I said, feeling sorry for him.

That afternoon, a jubilant Ozzy got his wish when Lindsay was moved to one of the crew buses.

The sound check at the Opheum Theater in Boston marked the beginning of what was to become a trend throughout most of the tour. After a couple of weeks on the road, word was beginning to spread about Ozzy and his band, especially his new hotshot guitar player with the rock star looks. Guitar students from many of the Boston area schools gathered outside the theatre waiting to get a glimpse of Randy and hopefully chat with him. After sound check, he ventured outside to meet the throng of young guitarists and answered questions about his playing and writing techniques. Randy reconnected with the guitar teacher in him, as demonstrated by the articulately outstanding performance he gave that evening. Not only did the audience get a great show for their hard-earned money but also the best guitar lesson of their lives.

After a 200-mile after show drive we arrived in New York City. Sharon had arranged for a pre-dawn check-in at the Park Plaza Hotel. The exasperated night manager finally decided to check me into one of their suites after half a dozen futile attempts to find me a clean, unoccupied room. I couldn't believe my eyes as I walked into a gorgeous suite with picture postcard views of Central Park. I had seen photos of these opulently furnished rooms with the cathedral ceilings when Life magazine chronicled the Beatles' appearances on "The Ed Sullivan Show." I was so excited I couldn't go to sleep, so I called my parents and close friends to share the moment with them. After a couple of hours of sleep, Randy and I hit the town. With only a few hours to see the sights, Randy surprised me with his suggestion to take a glass bottom helicopter ride around Manhattan. Why not?

We took off from a heliport on the Hudson River. The small chopper with the translucent floor gave the impression we were riding on clouds as we flew over and around Yankee Stadium, Central Park, the Empire State Building and other points of interest.

"Look Rand, there's Madison Square Garden!" I pointed out as we approached the prestigious venue.

"Wow! Of all the places in the world, that's the one

I've always dreamed of playing," Randy said as he stared down at the round building like a little boy looking at a new bike in a toy store window. "Someday Rudes, someday."

The revered landmark faded into the horizon. It was an unforgettable—not to mention—scary ride, something we decided not to do again in the near future.

That evening we performed two shows at the historical New York Palladium. The first show had sold out in a flash so the promoter convinced Sharon to add a second one. It's hard to explain but there's something about a New York City crowd that can bring out the best in any performer. Maybe it's their heartfelt dedication to a band or their brutal honesty when they let you know you sucked. But that night, inspired by the crowd, the band performed two of the tour's most memorable gigs. After the second, Sharon arranged for a party back at the hotel. For the band, the label, and many CBS folks, it was one of many nights to remember on the tour.

May 3rd we stopped at Lower Manhattan's Battery Park for a group photo session on our way to Poughkeepsie, New York. That day we skipped the hotel and spent our time at the venue, the Mid Hudson Civic Center.

Before sound check, Sharon asked me to see her in the dressing room.

"Rudy, Ozzy is a bit concerned with your stage antics," she explained quietly. "As you know, he comes from a very traditional heavy metal stage presentation and he feels that you're moving too much around the stage. So here are the rules. You cannot stand in front of Ozzy. If he's in front of you and he moves back, you move back with him. You cannot go over to Randy's side of the stage. You cannot turn your back to the audience or set your foot on the drum riser." She expounded laying down the law. "You see this area?" Sharon asked as she drew with her finger an invisible 2-foot square around me. "This is your spot." She paused to watch my reaction. "I'm sorry but that's the way it is."

What was I going to do? I was in Ozzy's band. That's what he wanted, and that's what he got. Nevertheless, I wasn't about to stand there on stage like a tree stump, especially with all of the incredible energy coming off the stage. I took it as challenge to do the best performance I could within that limited space. So from that night on I just opened my legs as wide as I could, swung my bass and banged my head from the first note to the very last.

Ozzy was quickly becoming a favorite subject among journalists who followed his prankish antics. During an interview Ozzy was asked about life after Black Sabbath.

"I've been in this business 13-14 years," he said. "I'm in my early 30's and I've got my youth back. I'll do it as long as the kids want to hear it. When I left Sabbath, it was a question of whether to retire or continue. I tried something else for a while and it didn't work. I tried to sit behind a desk. It'll be a sad day when I have to stop."

The following morning we woke up in Springfield, Massachusetts. After checking into the Marriot it was time for Randy and me to hit the mall once again. Inspired by the fan's word-of- mouth recognition that the band was beginning to receive, we searched the newsstands for any rock magazines that featured Ozzy related articles. Much to our disappointment we couldn't find any. In the pre-MTV and Internet era, news traveled slowly and it took a few weeks until we saw Ozzy on the cover of a rock publication.

That evening's show was at the Civic Center in front of a near sellout crowd of 4,000. As our audience mushroomed, I was beginning to recognize some of the familiar faces in the crowd from previous shows in the area. I also noticed that most of them were guitar gods in the making gathered in front of Randy, their new hero.

A local rock reviewer wrote of that evening's show:

"Volume reigned supreme Monday night as the biggest heavy metal concert of the year reverberated through Springfield Civic Center. Featured on a triple bill were former Black Sabbath lead vocalist Ozzy Osbourne and his Blizzard of Ozz, the new and improved Joe Perry Project, and English hard rock/heavy metal wonder Motorhead. Although the evening had moments of energy and finesse courtesy of Perry, the overall effect was dull, repetitive and very forgettable. Opening with the up-tempo "I Don't Know," it was clear that the success of Blizzard of Ozz rested on what Osbourne had learned in his nearly 10-year stay with Black Sabbath. Guitarist Randy Rhoads made his presence felt early in the set with his feedback laden screeches and blinding speed on "Crazy Train." Osbourne exhibited great faith in his new band and the bulk of the songs played were either from Blizzard of Ozz or his upcoming Diary of a Madman album. Three hours of so much noise, except for a brief interim by Joe Perry, all of this heavy metal seemed like so much scrap iron."

The following morning, after a 300-mile drive, we arrived in Buffalo, New York. This was our next day off. Upon checking into the Holiday Inn, Sharon let everyone know about the evening's CBS Records dinner plans. The event took place at a picturesque Italian restaurant decorated with mock Mediterranean facades simulating the ambiance of Tuscany. A school bus filled with devoted Canadian fans made the three-hour trip from Toronto to Buffalo to join us for dinner.

Tony Martell, one of the CBS/Epic Records executives attending the dinner and the man responsible for signing Ozzy to the label, sat at the table between Randy and me. I was very impressed with Tony when he casually prompted our conversation and seemed sincerely interested in what Randy and I had to say. By the end of the evening, Tony had removed my deep-rooted distrust for the suits. Throughout the years, Tony has been the most sincere, kindest man I've ever met in the record industry. After dessert, the band posed for photos with the elated Canadian group before they boarded the bus back to Toronto.

The next day, May 6th, Randy and I took a trip to nearby Niagara Falls. While playing tourists for a couple of uneventful hours, Ozzy was up to his old tricks again as chronicled in this amusing anecdote from a Buffalo, NY newspaper:

> **"Word is out that some punk rock fanatics were disappointed when rocker Ozzy Osbourne appeared at Shea's. It seems Ozzy usually highlights his performances by biting off the head of a chicken.**
> **Well, although Shea's stage manager chauffeured Ozzy around to numerous pet stores, Ozzy couldn't find a bird he liked. Thank goodness."**

That evening's show was at Shea's Buffalo Theatre with the sellout crowd of over 3,000 witnessing another solid performance from the band.

In a colorful Ozzy interview published in a Toronto newspaper, the rock columnist wrote,

"In England they're already calling me

the Godfather of Heavy Metal. I'm only 31, not that ancient, but because I've been around, I'm treated this way at times. It's amazing really, the way this thing, this kind of music, keeps on, isn't it?"

On May 7th we woke up in Johnstown, Pennsylvania. After checking into another Holiday Inn, and faced with one more boring day off, Ozzy went on a relentless quest to find where our road crew was staying. Sharon had a policy of not booking the band and crew in the same hotel in an attempt to keep Ozzy from partying with the rowdy bunch. So that morning Ozzy began his mayhem by urinating in the ice machines of every floor of the hotel. Unbeknownst to Sharon, who as usual was taking care of day-to-day business in her hotel room, Ozzy found his way to the road crew's hotel where he drank and snorted until Sharon finally tracked him down that evening.

Upon his arrival back at the hotel, Ozzy continued his rampage by defecating in the ice machines before retiring from another full day of mischief. Due to countless incidents of day off shenanigans, I truly believe that Ozzy is responsible for the modifications that have been made to the design of today's hotel ice machines.

The following night we performed at the War Memorial Auditorium. During the show, Ozzy suffered from a massive hangover and fatigue. I spent most of the show watching Ozzy, who seemed lost, wandering about aimlessly from one side of the stage to the other while mumbling his lyrics. But every time I looked over at the audience, I was amazed to see the delirious fans worshipping their working class hero like some demigod. Ozzy is truly blessed with the ability to whip a crowd into a frenzy no matter what his condition. With time, I became used to this unexplainable phenomenon.

During our after-show bus ride I was inspired by Ozzy's exemplary misbehavior—and a whole bottle of

French white wine— as I tried my hand at some mischief of my own. I took the shotgun seat next to our bus driver and started a casual conversation while I began hurling Oreo cookies over my shoulder at everyone seated in the front lounge. By the time I got to the bottom of the bag Ozzy snuck up from behind and poured a bucket of water over my head. As I wobbled after him down the narrow aisle of the bus I lost my balance and fell flat on my face. As soon as I hit the ground Ozzy ripped my sweat suit off and left me once again buck-naked on the ground. Being too drunk to get up, I passed out on the front lounge floor for the duration of the bus ride. By now I was sure everybody had tired of seeing my naked butt. While I passed out, I dreamt that the front lounge was filled with beautiful young ladies. Randy,
Tommy and I were sitting among them, and oddly, I was naked.

I woke up that morning with a pounding headache as I surveyed the unfamiliar hotel room through bloodshot eyes. Through my haze I didn't know where I was or remember how or when I had checked in. With shaky hands I grabbed the phone and dialed the front desk and discovered that I was in Dayton, Ohio. After a long, cold, sobering shower I made my way to the hotel restaurant where I joined Randy for lunch.

"So how are you doing today?" I heard the young pretty waitress ask as she smiled and handed me a menu.

"Wow, Randy," I said, "the waitresses here are really cute. If I didn't know any better I'd think they were flirting with us." I said with studly pride.

"Rudes, they're not flirting with you, they're laughing at
you!" Randy laughed. "Don't you remember anything from last
night?"

Fragmented images of the night before hit me like a sledgehammer.

"Oh my God!" I gasped, sliding slowly under the table.

"When we got to the hotel last night Tommy and I went to the bar," Randy explained as he sipped his iced tea. "We chatted up these girls and invited them back to the bus while Sharon checked us in. When we got back you were still passed out naked on the floor. The girls thought it was real funny, one of them painted with her lipstick a smiley face on your butt. That's when you came to and sat with us."

"Was I still naked?"

"Yep, you were naked until Rachel put a robe on you, dragged you through the lobby and tucked you in."

"Oh, no," I groaned another waitresses snickered past our table. "Would you like more coffee?" she asked.

"No thanks," I said, avoiding eye contact. "I'll take my lunch to go.

When I picked up the check I noticed the waitress had drawn a smiley face on it. When I got back to the room I pondered my behavior. I came to the conclusion that I just couldn't keep up with Ozzy's rock star lifestyle and if I was going to make something out of myself then I had better get my act together in a hurry.

6
Tonight Could Be a Good One

We woke up in the Holiday Inn parking lot in Toledo, Ohio the next morning. After Sharon checked us in, Randy and I visited the local shops and went out to do some sightseeing. It's funny how a first visit to a city like Toledo can somehow be interesting. We performed that evening at the Sports Arena to a half-full house. On the after-show bus ride Randy seem quieter than usual in the back lounge.

"What's up Rand? You haven't said a word since we got on the bus," I asked him.

"Oh, I don't know Rudes. I've been away from home a lot and I'm beginning to miss my Mom and Jody."

"Why don't you ask Jody to come and visit?" I suggested.

"Well, it's actually more than that." Randy paused. "I thought things were going to be different. In England the record shot up the charts really fast and we were selling out tickets even before we played our first show. But it's taking a lot longer to build a following in the States."

"Maybe after tomorrow's radio broadcast everyone one will have a chance to hear the band and thins will improve," I rationalized. "I hope so," he said. "I'm beginning to have my doubts after spending almost two years away from home, pouring my heart and soul into the records and live shows only to have a handful of fans get into our music." He paused again. "I don't know, maybe New Wave and punk killed our music."

The next morning, May 11th, we woke up in Cleveland, Ohio. After checking into the Holiday Inn, Randy and I decided to skip the usual sightseeing for the day and rest for the big show ahead of us. When we arrived for our 4 p.m. sound check at the Music Hall, our backline was set up and ready to go, but our crew and local stage hands were nowhere to be found.

"Stop! You can't touch anything!" yelled the local stage manager. "This is a union hall and only the union crew's allowed to touch or move the equipment."

"So when can I check my bass rig?" I asked.

"Not now. The stage is dark while we're on a half-hour union break." He abruptly walked off stage.

"Tonight's gonna be as much fun as a roomful of nuns,"

Tommy complained as he threw down his sticks and got off his riser.

As Randy and I stood on the silent proscenium stage, we looked out into the plush hall and observed the red velvet covered seats and ornate curtained walls. The balcony felt so close you could almost reach out and touch it. Randy clapped his hands to check the acoustic and was pleased to hear the rich quick echoes bouncing off the back of the hall and then trapped by the velvet curtains and seats. The theater had all the right acoustical elements for a perfect live recording and the intimacy of the hall was going to provide a great setting for us all.

"What do you think?" I asked Randy.

"Tonight could be a good one, Rudes, a real good one."

Tensions were high backstage before the show; Ozzy paced up and down the confined quarters of our dressing room like a caged tiger waiting to be unleashed into a Roman coliseum. Randy, with a look of complete focus and determination, quietly warmed up in the corner of the dressing room. Meanwhile, I just tried to relax and not think too much about the show. I repeatedly ran my stiff fingers up and down the fretboard of my bass while Tommy twirled his drumsticks and pranced around, amused by all the somber mood of the room.

"Don't worry, boys," Sharon said. "Tonight's gonna be a great show. I can just feel it. Think of all the people around the world that are going to hear the band for the first time. Isn't that exciting?" She rubbed Ozzy's shoulders.

"Sharon, I don't feel well. I think I'm coming down with something." Ozzy complained as he grabbed Sharon's hand and put it on his forehead. "Get me a Doctor. I need a shot of B12." "Ozzy stop it! You're fine," Sharon said, slapping Ozzy on the head. "And besides, the show's about to start in a few minutes and we can't be late. This concert is for a radio broadcast. You all know this, right?" Sharon reiterated as she scanned the room for approval.

"But we can always go back and fix the flubs, right Sharon?" Ozzy asked.

"No can do, sorry," she replied.

"You mean we can't go back and fix anything?" Ozzy complained, as he stood up to face Sharon. "Fuck Sharon, I'm gonna sound like shit!"

"Don't worry, Ozzy, Chuck will be mixing the show from the remote truck. He'll make you boys sound beautiful, just like he does every night." She smiled confidently.

"I'm not doing it. I'm not doing it!" Ozzy uttered over and over as he paced the floor with his head hung low.

We all followed Ozzy and Sharon out of the dressing room as the crowd roared at the opening strains of "Carmina Burana." I could see Ozzy still mouthing the words: "I'm not doing it" while standing in the wings next to Sharon. I waited behind the backline for my cue to go on stage,

Suddenly, right on his musical cue, I saw Ozzy run to the middle of the stage like some crazed fan that had slipped by the security guards. "Are you ready to rock and roll!" There was a thunderous roar. "You're beautiful!"

Ozzy yelled back as the intro reached its climax and the audience roared with anticipation. There was something different about the band that night. Ozzy's edginess at performing live without a net and Randy's determination to prove his worth to the radio audience gave this performance a level of intensity unlike other nights. I, on the other hand, was only concerned with providing the strongest rhythmic foundation possible. So I laid back on my head banging and concentrated on my musical execution.

Randy's opening chords of "I Don't Know" ripped out of his Marshall stack buzz saw as I watched Ozzy crouch and leap up into the air like a demented frog, sprint over to the mike stand and strangle the microphone as his ethereal voice filled the venue. The stage was intentionally brighter than usual that night, a fact that provided us with a visual advantage and minimized mistakes. I could clearly see the urgency on Randy's face as he issued squeals and wails out of his Les Paul, while Ozzy exhorted the capacity crowd to get on their feet. The band's stage volume was quieter than usual in order to keep the instruments from bleeding into each other's microphones, thus aiding Chuck in creating the best mix possible.

During the quiet bridge section I could hear the harmonics from my bass guitar clearly resonating throughout the hall while Randy's guitar and Lindsay's synthesizer weaved a rich melodic tapestry. During Randy's guitar solo, Ozzy unexpectedly darted over to his side clapping his hands and bopping his head like a mad cheerleader. Randy reciprocated by throwing his head back and leaning into Ozzy and as he dug into his Les Paul and pulled out a flurry of notes. As the song reached its coda, the wailing sounds of Randy's wah wah pedal fused with Ozzy's echoing howls of "I Don't Know!" I looked over to the side of the stage and saw Sharon, seated in the wings behind the monitor board, her smiling face beamed in the dark. In total contrast, the local union crewmembers sat on road cases with wads of tissue paper sticking out of their ears as they kept an eye on our road crew.

I had to rush over to the drum riser to make eye contact with Tommy as the roar of the crowd drowned out his count off into the next song. Ozzy punched the air in rhythm to the percussive accents of the "Crazy Train" intro as he ran from one side of the stage to the other. His unpredictable stage moves always reminded me of a raving lunatic trying to hail a cab during a Manhattan rush hour. Unlike other singers of his generation who projected machismo and sexuality, Ozzy's unpretentious onstage persona struck me as that of the working class fan who got his wish to be onstage with his favorite heavy metal band.

Hundreds of pulsating light beams bathed the stage as I pounded on the top horn of my bass guitar, a habit I developed during my South Florida club years while attempting to provide our three-piece bands with a fuller sound.

"I know you're gonna get wild tonight!" Ozzy provoked the crowd. "Come on everybody! Let me see you clap your hands." Ozzy yelled as thousands of arms rose skyward flailing to the rhythm of the music.

Though our backline's volume was quieter, our monitors were cranking. I could hear Randy loud and clear through the towering side-fills on my stage right as he bent the living daylights out of his heavy gauge strings while rocking back and forth on his pedal board.
I always requested an evenly balanced mix in my side-fill. I like the mix to sound like a record, with the drums, guitar, keyboards and vocals evenly mixed while the sound of my bass comes from the backline behind me.

"OK! That's what rock and roll is all about!" Ozzy teased the crowd as "Crazy Train" came to an end.
I rushed over to my bass tech and did the customary

switch from my Black Music Man Stingray to my 1967 Sunburst Fender Jazz. The switch always guaranteed me a varied bass tone and fresh tuning. As I began the intro bass riff to "Believer" I deliberately tried to pull back on my usual performing antics, playing with my fretting hand over the neck, for a more articulate execution. But half way through the intro I began to feel awkward performing the riff in the traditional manner. That's when I realized that my antics had become second nature to my performance. So I just let go and returned to the way it felt natural.

"Stand up!" Ozzy yelled as he thrust peace signs to the beat as Randy's guitar ripped through the plodding thud of the bass riff. "Let me see your hands!" Ozzy commanded the crowd as he leapfrogged up to Randy's shoulders.

Ozzy never failed to amaze me. Just a few minutes ago he was complaining about his health and threatening not to do the show, and now he's got more energy onstage than most of the fans half his age in the audience.

"Get up!" Ozzy yelled, totally out of control as he choked the microphone and continued singing.

The song ended with a furious flurry of Tommy's drum fills as the stage went pitch black. Lindsay, in full stage makeup and crew cut, introduced the ominous strains of "Mr. Crowley" from the shadows of the stage right wing. I have to give Lindsay a lot of credit for trying. Even though he was hidden from the audience, he still got dressed up in his stage clothes and put on a show from the sidelines as he bounced from one keyboard rack to the next in total darkness. A circle of white lights slowly faded in to reveal Ozzy standing motionless at center stage, his arms raised towards the sky like a druid preparing for a sacrifice. I always considered this side of Ozzy's stage persona a carry over from his Sabbath image.

During the time I spent off stage with Ozzy I never

caught a glimpse of any occult practices or leanings. On the contrary, his onstage rants were filled with "God Bless you alls!" aimed at the audience throughout the shows. Also, the lyrics to "Mr. Crowley" are critical of the occult practices and beliefs. Unlike stage and screen actors who portray such occult characters, the public seems to have a hard time separating Ozzy's "Prince of Darkness" onstage persona from the real Ozzy.

Unlike his virtually static performances with Black Sabbath, a band in which he had little or no eye contact onstage with the rest of the band members, Ozzy was adapting and testing the limits of his and Randy's onstage chemistry. So right before the guitar solo, Ozzy ran over to Randy's side and grabbed him by the hair. Maybe it was the pain from Ozzy's playful torture or the pleasure from his majestic sounding instrument that inspired Randy to perform one of the most riveting solos I ever heard him play.

"We want to do another number entitled 'Flying High' so keep
on smoking them joints!" Ozzy yelled as the crowd let out a deafening cheer.

One of the most distinguishing qualities of Randy's prolific songwriting style was his technique of crafting separate musical passages for him to solo over thus creating a unique musical centerpiece within the body of a song, and this tune was no exception. Randy churned out a solo showcasing his fluid musical vocabulary.

"Alright!" yelled Ozzy as he watched Randy perform. The uptempo feel of the song was also a perfect showcase for Tommy's aggressive style, as he played lightning fast drums fills and syncopated accents while twirling his sticks high above his head.

"This is a song called 'Revelation, Mother Earth,'" said Ozzy, introducing the song.

The soft guitar and piano intro filled the room. The harmonizer on Randy's Les Paul made it sound like an acoustic 12-string guitar as he gently picked arpeggiated chords during the quiet verse section. This song was one of my favorite moments in the set. Even though Randy wrote it, the song was truly a showcase for the piano. A composer of a lesser ability would had chosen to make this composition a centerpiece for their instrument, but Randy, being an altruistic musician, chose "Revelation, Mother Earth" as one of the vehicles to compliment the Blizzard of Ozz record with as many shades of sound and mood as possible.

"Steal away the night! Let's go crazy!" Ozzy bellowed at the roaring crowd.

There are three levels of intensity at which rock bands play, behind the beat, on top of the beat and in front of the beat. A band with our level of intensity would play in front of the beat. Every night on this particular song, much like galloping stallions in a chariot race, we leaned forward and accelerated the tempo in anticipation of the drum solo that lay ahead. That night we constantly looked over our shoulder as we made a conscious effort to assure that all the run away horses were pulling Ozzy's chariot at the same pace.

"Mr. Tommy Aldridge on drums, thank you!" Ozzy announced as the elated crowd responded with an earsplitting cheer.

During all my years sharing the stage with Tommy I can honestly say that at his worst he is a great drummer and at his best he is awesome. All spotlights converged on Tommy, bathing him in white as the rest of us disappeared into the wings. The lightning fast double-bass drum locomotive chug laid a solid foundation for the avalanche of cymbal crashes, snare and tom tom fills.

The crowd responded with a thunderous roar as Tommy raised his arms and hurled the drumsticks into the audience. I could see Ozzy and Sharon enjoying the moment from the wings. Tommy had been Ozzy's first choice from the very beginning and Ozzy never concealed his appreciation for having him in the band. Tommy continued playing aggressively with his bare hands like a tribal drummer, as he seemed to embrace his Native American roots. After the last cymbal and bass drum crunch Tommy raised his arms victoriously igniting a long appreciative roar from the crowd.

"Tommy Aldridge on drums! All right!" Ozzy yelled as Tommy took a graceful bow while we rejoined him on stage.

"We're gonna do a song now featuring Randy Rhoads our lead
guitarist," Ozzy announced. "This is a number titled 'Suicide Solution!'"

The mid-tempo feel of the song was the perfect set up for Randy's solo feature. The tempo also gave me the opportunity to showboat a bit by playing the bass upside down, thumb slapping and other techniques I had developed during my club days as a member of various funk and R&B acts. During the guitar solo Ozzy darted over to Randy's side and mischievously pulled on his golden mane almost lifting him off the ground. Randy retaliated by letting out a wailing sustaining feedback that didn't fade until Ozzy let go of him right before his eardrums shattered. They looked at each other and broke out laughing.

"Mr. Randy Rhoads!" Ozzy echoed, pointing at Randy. All the spotlights converged on him, igniting still another cheer from the crowd. I always looked forward to Randy's solos, dating back to the Quiet Riot days. It was interesting to hear the variations he did on his themes each night depending on his guitar tone and the acoustics of the venues. His solo tonight featured a solid foundation dating back to the Quiet Riot shows, the major difference now was that while spending time in England Randy had taken classical guitar lessons to expand his musical vocabulary. All of the great Los Angeles guitarists from his generation had dipped into the same blues-based musical pool but what now separated Randy from the rest was his ability to build on this foundation and enhance it with his newly acquired European flair.

I believe that a concert stage is a magical place. You get to stand on the same planks your heroes stood on in a different time. That night I saw Randy outshine all his heroes as he embarked on a sonic journey that included lightning fast arpeggio runs, precise double picking, left hand pull offs and such fierce string bends that seemed to wrap the heavy gauged strings around the wide neck of his Les Paul.

As of 1981, only a handful of guitarists had been successful at incorporating classical guitar techniques into metal the way Randy did. I think that it's safe to say that Randy's rhythm guitar and soloing techniques, as well as his songwriting style have served as a major influence on guitarist worldwide. As I stood behind my backline I could clearly see the impact of Randy's performance on the spellbound faces in the audience. As Randy finished his solo I imagined all of the mesmerized listeners gathered around their radios wondering who on earth this new guitar hero was.

"Randy Rhoads! Randy Rhoads!" Ozzy announced proudly as Randy waved and smiled at the adoring crowd. "OK, let's go for 'Iron Man'!" Ozzy yelled prompting an deafening cheer from the audience that nearly drowned out Tommy's quarter note kick drum intro. "We love you all!" Ozzy thrust peace signs skyward as we ripped into the Sabbath classic's plodding chords.

Randy had expressed to me in the past his discomfort with performing Sabbath songs at the end of the set. He felt that after writing and recording two albums with Ozzy, having to perform these songs almost negated his contributions. On the other hand, he also understood that Ozzy couldn't leave the venue alive if he didn't perform a few of these crowd favorites. That night Randy amazed us all with mesmerizing versions of these Sabbath songs; he made everyone at the venue and all those radio listeners understand that a new era of heavy metal had arrived.

"All right! I want everybody rocking and rolling because we're gonna do 'Children of the Grave'," Ozzy roared as Tommy beat out a blindingly fast drum fill and picked up the tempo like a racehorse heading down the final stretch. "Everybody stand up! You guys upstairs ... Stand up!"

In contrast to Randy's distaste of the Sabbath tunes, I actually looked forward to them. Where Ozzy's songs were filled with mid- tempo melodic bass lines, the Black Sabbath material was balls to the walls aggressive and a perfect vehicle for me to let loose on some fast, headbangin' riffs.

"Thank you! We love you all! Goodnight!"

While we waited in the wings for our encore, the crowd chanted relentlessly: "Ozzy! Ozzy! Ozzy!"

"You can't kill rock and roll!" Ozzy yelled as we all re-entered the stage and grabbed our instruments. "All right! We're gonna do 'Paranoid'," he announced as the band aggressively kicked into the Black Sabbath magnum opus.

Of all the songs in the set, "Paranoid" always got the biggest crowd reaction. Maybe it was the fact that the audience was not as familiar with the Blizzard of Ozz record as they were with the Sabbath songs. Whatever the case, this was a huge thorn in Randy's side. Still, that night Randy put his feelings aside and cranked out the most riveting version of "Paranoid" I ever heard him play.

"Thank you! Goodnight! We love you all! God bless you!" Randy, Tommy and I flanked Ozzy, put our arms around each other, and took a bow before the worshipful crowd.

"Hey guys, don't ya'll wanna hear this?"

It was Chuck Weisners' honey-dipped Southern drawl as he poked his head in the front lounge of our bus. He was holding up a cassette tape.

"Give it to me," Sharon said excitedly, grabbing the cassette.

"I don't wanna have to hear that crap now, Sharon!" Ozzy pleaded. "I just got off the bloody stage for fuck's sake!"

"Oh, Ozzy, I just want to show you and the boys how wonderful you all sounded. So if you don't want to hear it just fuck off to the back lounge."

Sharon popped the tape in the cassette player while the bus rolled out of town toward the next city.

"How was your show Rudes?" Randy asked as we removed our sweaty clothing while listening to the tape.

"Oh, I don't know. I'm afraid I had a couple of flubs in the intro of 'Believer,'" I replied.

"We'll soon find out!" Tommy remarked as he poured himself a gin and tonic. For Tommy, a veteran of numerous live broadcasts, tonight was just another great night behind his drum kit. For me, on the other hand, that show was my live recording initiation.

Thankfully, and much to my surprise, the band sounded like an airtight, world-class unit. As we listened to the intro of "Believer" I cringed awaiting my mistakes, but didn't hear any. It's funny that what sounded like a major flub went by so fast that it was totally indiscernible. Halfway into the playback, Ozzy came in the front lounge and sat between Sharon and Randy. Without uttering a word, Sharon put her arms around Ozzy as he laid back, listened and smiled.

7
It's All About the Songs

On the morning of May 12th we arrived in Erie, Pennsylvania. We got out of our bunks still flying high from the previous night's show. Shortly after Sharon checked us into the local Hilton she summoned us to her room.

"Guys, I have some bad news. The promoter has cancelled tonight's show."

Randy posed the first question.

"But doesn't the promoter think that there could be a strong walk-up after last night's broadcast?"

"The promoter doesn't want to take any further risks," she said. "He's afraid he'll be throwing good money after bad. And there's a strong possibility that there will be more cancellations in the next few days." Sharon's tone was understandably strained. Ozzy's tour was one of her first major responsibilities as a manager and her family had put up most of the money to cover the initial expenses so it was on her to make this tour a profitable one. Usually, when a promoter cancels a show, the artist gets to keep the deposit, in most cases 50% of the guarantee. But in the case of this tour that didn't come close to covering our daily expenses.

Most artists try to schedule an average of five shows a week. Two shows on, one day off, three shows on, one day off, and so on until the next tour break. Scheduled days off on tour are necessary, not only to give the artists and crew much needed rest but for logistical reasons as well. Sometimes you need more than 24 hours to get your equipment trucks from one city to the next. But when the shows are cancelled the artist usually spends money instead of making it.

That afternoon in an attempt to cheer the band up, our

bus driver picked up the latest video game console, Intellivision. That evening's bus ride to the next city was an entertaining one. We all gathered in the front lounge playing video games. It was great to see Ozzy and Randy having a good time playing video soccer as the match stick figures moved across the screen.

The next morning, we arrived in Columbus, Ohio. After checking into the hotel, Randy and I headed for the local mall where we were pleasantly surprised when we were recognized for the first time. Some fans had attended the Cleveland show, and others had heard the radio broadcast. Needless to say, their excitement was a promising sign that the band was finally going to get the recognition it deserved. That night's show was at the Veterans Memorial Arena in front of an exuberant crowd.

During our after-show bus ride, we couldn't wait to get out of our clothes and play the video games again. We all got so addicted to them that on some mornings we'd wake up with sore thumbs from playing all night.

"Hey Ozz, it looks like you're finally beginning to enjoy yourself on this tour," I said as we watched Randy and Tommy with their fingers flying on the game pads.

"Rudes, I'm so glad we're on a bus. As long as we can all get along like family, traveling by bus is fine by me," Ozzy said, offering me a swig from a whiskey bottle.

I turned it down.

"I think I'm going to hit the sack soon."

"With Sabbath we used to fly all the time," Ozzy said. "Sometimes I wouldn't know what bloody city I was in. Traveling like this reminds me of when Van Halen toured with Sabbath."

"How was that?" I asked.

"Van Halen was great to tour with," he explained. "Every night they put on a killer show. And once they got off stage they were always looking for fun or trouble, which ever came first. Let me put it this way, Rudes, I just knew that my days with Sabbath were numbered when one night after Van Halen blew us off the stage we came out and Iommi spent half an hour trying to tune his bloody guitar with his back to a booing audience. That was it for me. Fuck it! No more! I fucked off right after that." Ozzy grabbed one of the game pads and challenged Randy to video soccer.

The next morning, we arrived in Louisville, Kentucky. After checking in, I took advantage of having another day off to call my friends in Los Angeles and see how things where going. One of the first things you realize when you go on the road is that compared to the folks back at home it feels like you're traveling at the speed of light. You're covering hundreds of miles everyday, playing in front of thousands of people, while back home things don't change that much, at least for my musician friends struggling back home.

The following evening, May 15th, we performed at the Louisville Gardens before a nearly full house. The rock reviewer for the local paper wrote of that evening's performance:

"Osbourne's new group, Blizzard of Ozz, is integral to his performance. If, and it's a very large if as far as I'm concerned, Heavy Metal is The Next Big Thing Ozzy Osbourne will be there at the top of it all. His music is never boring, never droning. It's often highly colored with light melody or catchy syncopation in the beat. And he has some fairly incredible players helping out, too. Randy Rhoads' checkerboard, flying-V Gibson guitar was made to sound like a harmonica, an organ, even an accordion at one point, and his technique is not all flash. There's depth to it, and lots of influences showing, from Hendrix

to Lennon."

A very perceptive observation. Even though he misspelled Ozzy's name and he didn't fully buy into the rise of Heavy Metal. In a couple of years the launch of MTV would propel the fresh young faces of heavy metal to heights never reached before in the music industry.

The morning of May 16th we arrived in Saginaw, Michigan.

After we checked into another Holiday Inn Sharon once again called us into her room.

"Guys, I got some bad news again. The next couple of shows have been cancelled."

"Shit!" Randy reacted quickly. "The last few nights we've been doing so well. Is there something we can do?"

"Don't take it so hard, Randy," Sharon tried to console us. "It has nothing to do with you or the rest of the boys. It's just that the broadcast hasn't reached all the markets yet. And it's only a few promoters who are pulling the shows. Don't worry. We'll be all right." She forced a smile.

One of the situations Sharon wanted most to avoid was having Ozzy sitting in a hotel room for the next three days with nothing to do but drink. So we kept traveling from city to city as scheduled even though the shows where cancelled.

That evening, on our scheduled after-show bus ride, Sharon excused herself and retired earlier than usual. She was completely exhausted from a long day on the phone dealing with promoters and agents as she tried to keep the tour from falling apart.

Fact: Concert promoters are gamblers by nature. They bet on an artist by putting up the money to produce a show in the hopes of making a profit from the gate and other sources like merchandise sales and vendors in the venue. They take the risk of losing all their investments without any guarantees of significant ticket sales. Also, these gentlemen have a support system where they call and warn each other when a tour is not doing well. It was Sharon's responsibility to put out all the fires by any means possible. One of the alternatives in these situations is for the artist to lower their guarantees with the option of a higher percentage in case of a sell out. Sharon knew all the possible options: she learned the game from one of the most cunning artist managers in the business, her father.

On the morning of May 17th, we arrived in Indianapolis, Indiana.

"Ozzy, Ozzy! Sharon's not waking up!" Rachel cried hysterically as I jumped out of my bunk.

"Somebody call a paramedic! I think she's fuckin' OD'ed!"

Ozzy yelled sending Rachel into the lobby of the nearby Hyatt. Within minutes paramedics stormed into the bus and began to check Sharon's vital signs.

"Is she taking any medication?" asked one of the paramedics. "She takes these to help her sleep," said Rachel as she held an empty bottle of prescription pills.

"We need to rush her immediately to the hospital and pump her stomach." Sharon was strapped to a gurney and carried into the ambulance

"Fuck it, I'm going with her!" Ozzy snapped as he bolted out of the bus and jumped into the back of the flashing ambulance.

A few hours after having her stomach pumped, Sharon recovered, and was back taking care of business as usual. The only effect it had on her was that a piece of mushroom, of all things, got lodged in her sinus cavity during the procedure and for the next few days she sounded like a high-pitched duck. Eventually, she was able to sneeze out the mushroom and her voice returned to normal.

We stayed over in Indianapolis so Sharon could have

a restful night's sleep. Ozzy was pretty shaken up by the incident and he was in his best behavior in the Hyatt bar.

The following day, we left in the early evening to give Sharon a full day to take care of business and keep the tour going. I can imagine how much more of a workaholic she would have been back then if she had a cell phone and a laptop. The next morning, we checked into the Detroit, Michigan, Howard Johnson's. That afternoon I dragged Randy out of his room and we made the pilgrimage to Hitsville, USA, the Motown museum. As we walked through the former studios where all the famous Motown hits were recorded I could still feel the music that was made within those walls, the soundtrack to my teenage years.

"Randy, can you believe that all those great songs with that big Motown sound were recorded in this tiny studio?"

"Yeah, it goes to show that if you've got great songs and great players it doesn't really matter where you make a record. It's all about the song, Rudes."

Randy was right. Ever since I started playing with him in Quiet Riot and now with Ozzy, Randy's priority was his songwriting. Even when he practiced his guitar, he always played songs rather than doodling on scales or finger exercises. Every single time I saw Randy pick up his guitar he played music.

That evening's show was at the Masonic Temple Theater in front of an almost capacity crowd. It seemed that the cosmopolitan cities were more inclined to embrace the band than the rural areas.

The next day we woke up in the parking lot of the Marc Plaza Hotel in Milwaukee, Wisconsin. That evening's performance was at the Riverside Theater in front of a sellout crowd. A couple of hours before the show I walked into the production office and found Sharon in the corner of the room yelling at a man flanked by a couple of the venue's brawny security guards.

"Listen to me. I don't ever want to see you selling your fuckin' bootleg shirts again! You're stealing money from Ozzy! When you fuck with Ozzy, you're fucking with me!" Sharon poked her finger at the terrified man's chest. "And I guarantee you I will make your fuckin' life a living hell if I catch you around us again!" She put her face right up to his as he closed his eyes in a futile attempt to make her disappear. "Look at me! Do you understand?" Sharon yelled as her spit rolled down the frightened man's face. "Get this piece of shit out of here!"

The security guards dragged the bootlegger out of the room.

I had never witnessed that side of Sharon before. I guess the apple doesn't fall far from the tree. Her father would have been proud.

"Oh, hello dear," Sharon asked, in her usual charming demeanor. "Is there anything you need from me?"

"Oh, I just need to add a couple of names to the guest list," I said still a little shaken by what I'd seen.

"Not a problem," she smiled, as if nothing had happened.

That moment I took a mental note, don't ever fuck with Sharon. A local rock reviewer wrote of that evening's performance:

> **"One of the legends of heavy metal rock took Milwaukee by storm Wednesday night with a one- hour blizzard. Osbourne's voice was high and reedy and not very good as usual. When he wasn't singing, he was shaking to the music or urging the crows to clap along. Blizzard of Oz, a quality power trio, was not relegated to back up band status. Its members showed nearly as much personality as Osbourne. Guitarist Randy Rhoads is the**

personification of the heavy metal guitarist, cranking out solo runs in the classic style of Jimmy Page, Tony Iommi and Eddie Van Halen. Bassist Rudy Sarzo, unlike many bass players, was animated. Drummer Tommy Aldridge gripped the audience with a five-minute madman solo."

May 21st. We arrived in St. Louis, Missouri. Faced with another day off, Randy and I went sightseeing as usual after we checked into the upscale Chase Park Plaza. I always found it amusing the strange looks we got every time we stayed at a posh hotel. Maybe the patrons had previously experienced Ozzy's pranks. Late at night, the guests in these old world hotels would leave their shoes outside their doors to be shined overnight. Ozzy was happy to oblige them, only he didn't exactly shine them. How he looked forward to the horrified screams the next morning as his neighbors shoved their feet into poop-filled shoes. The merry prankster!

The following evening, we performed at the Checkerdome. That night's show was extremely important. We were expecting a visit from Bill Elson, a successful booking agent friend of Tommy. Sharon felt that if Ozzy was represented by a more prestigious booking agency he would have a better chance of working with more legitimate promoters. Even though we played in front of a half-filled house, Bill was impressed enough by our performance to accept Sharon's offer to represent Ozzy. Shortly after, Bill became Ozzy's agent.

On May 23rd, we woke up in Rockford, Illinois. It was back to basics as we checked into another Holiday Inn. In those days I felt more at home in the humble accommodations of Holidays Inns than the posh settings of the upscale hotels, where you have to wear a borrowed tie and sports jacket just to get an overpriced bagel. That evening's concert was at the Metro Center in front of another halffull house.

The after-show trip from Rockford to Chicago was a short one so Sharon arranged an early morning check in. Sharon was carrying Mr. Pook inside her oversized shoulder bag as she checked us in. It was about 4 a.m. and Mr. Pook liked to sleep in late. Suddenly, while standing at the front desk, Sharon's shoulder bag starts shaking.

"Is there a pet in your bag, Madame?" asked the clerk. "We have a 'No Pets Allowed' policy in our hotel."

"Oh no," she acted quickly. "I'm just tired and this bag's a bit heavy."

Too late, though. Mr. Pook started barking out of control and Sharon herself joined in the barking in a futile attempt to cover up the noise and fool the clerk.

"Sorry, Madame. I can't allow your party to check into our hotel with your pet."

"Oh fuck it! I wouldn't stay in this shithole even if you paid me." She yelled as she pulled Mr. Pook out of her bag. "Come on, Pook, let's get out of this dump."

As we walked out Sharon put Mr. Pook on the plush carpet where, in true Osbourne fashion, he left his mark.

We spent the next couple of hours driving around downtown Chicago until we found a hotel with a more pet-friendly policy.

That evening, May 24th, we played Chicago's Aragon Ballroom in front of an oversold crowd. It was a hot and sweaty night as we stepped onto the rickety stage. The crowd rushed forward as we started playing, causing it to rock back and forth. I looked back at my amplifiers as my bass tech held them to keep them from falling over.

After our encore I could hear the crowd chanting for more as we left the building. When we drove out of the venue we could see through the open doors the massive pile of debris left by the insatiable fans. It was truly a memorable show from the first to the last note.

A local rock reviewer wrote,

"The place got destroyed by the crowd. Drawing energy from the sardine-like confines of the Aragon, Ozzy ripped off his shirt like a madman trying to escape a straitjacket. He pounced and screeched and glared with evil eyes that could be matched only by the devil himself. Randy Rhoads and his custom guitars were on a constant collision course with destruction. He danced and jammed wildly melting the red-hot strings during 'Suicide Solution.' Bassist Rudy Sarzo and superstar drummer Tommy Aldridge formed a perfect rhythm combination."

The next morning, May 25th, our bus driver took us directly to the venue, The Riverflats Park, in Minneapolis, Minnesota. We barely had enough sleep when we followed Motorhead onstage at noon. There's no wake-up call like having a frantic crowd of 22,000 singing along to the songs.

We checked out of the Holiday Inn the next day and headed for Omaha, Nebraska, to spend a few days off at the local resort, the Best Western Hotel.

"Three days off in Omaha with Sharon and Ozzy," mused Tommy. "Now there's a recipe for disaster if I ever heard one." He walked out of the bus and got into the passenger seat of a sporty convertible driven by a beautiful blonde.

"Good luck guys. See ya'll at sound check." Tommy's car bolted onto the highway as Randy and I stood in the middle of the parking lot surrounded by cornfields.

"That's it. I'll be in my room with my guitar." Randy carried his guitar into the lobby, not to be seen or heard from again until the next day.

After spending the last 24 hours watching the corn

grow outside her hotel window and faced with another painfully boring day off, Sharon dragged Ozzy, Randy and me out to lunch.

"Where do you boys like to eat?"

"I'm so hungry I can eat the bloody asshole of a diarrhea stricken chicken!" Ozzy quipped as the taxi driver waited for a destination.

"I don't know were to find diarrhea stricken chickens, but I can take you to the best steak house in town," the taxi driver interjected.

"Oh, that's too heavy for lunch," Sharon shot down the idea. "How about Chinese then?" the taxi driver suggested.

"That sounds great, Chinese's my favorite," Randy said.

"Is everybody OK with Chinese?" Sharon asked.

"Sharon, I don't give a rat's where we eat as long as there's a bloody bar," Ozzy commented.

"Don't worry," said the driver. "It's got one of the best lounges in town and very popular with the business crowd. I know you'll like it."

A few minutes later the taxi driver dropped us off in front of a nondescript two-story building situated in a shopping mall. All eyes from the tables filled with the business lunch crowd fell on us as we entered the restaurant.

"What can I do for you?" the unfriendly Asian host asked as he gave Ozzy the once-over.

"Table for four please," Sharon requested in her best upper-class demeanor.

"So sorry. One hour wait," the host curtly replied as we looked around the empty waiting area.

"Oh, fuck it. Where's the bar?" Ozzy blurted.

"Go to staircase and make right down hallway, but bar close soon." We all followed Ozzy into the bustling lounge and stood at the bar.

"Bartender! I need a drink!" Ozzy yelled as he tried

to grab his attention.

"This is last call folks, we'll be closing the
bar in a few minutes," the bartender replied.

"Then let me have that bottle of whatever that is and
four glasses," Ozzy ordered while pointing at the biggest
container of Sake I have ever seen.

"I'll have to serve it cold, since there's no time to heat
it up," said the bartender.

"I don't' give a fuck, I'll be pissing it away in a few
hours anyway," Ozzy said, pouring the cold sake into
tumblers.

I declined.

"No thanks, Ozz, I'm on the wagon."

Still, he shoved the brimming glass in front of my
face.

"Don't' be such a cunt, for fuck's sake! One bloody
drink ain't gonna kill ya."

I figured there was no point arguing with him about
drinking so I grabbed the glass.

"Here's a toast."

We raised our glasses.

"To a bloody great Blizzard of Ozz tour. To Randy,
the best musical partner I've ever had. And Sharon,
the best manager in the world."

We cheered Ozzy's toast as we clinked our glasses. It
had been a few days since I had tasted booze and the
awful taste of cold sake made it easy for me to refrain
from finishing my glass.

"Better drink up folks, we're about to close the bar in
ten
minutes." The bartender announced as he delivered
the bar tab.

"Of all the bloody bars in bumfuck Nebraska we had
to come to
the one that shuts down in the middle of the
afternoon," Ozzy complained, quickly downing his
second glass.

Suddenly, Randy grabs a handful of peanuts from a bowl and throws them at Sharon. Sharon grabs another handful and throws them at Ozzy. Ozzy grabs the whole bowl and throws it at a table nearby filled with businessmen.

The host appeared.

"That's it! You must leave now! You pay first! Then you leave
now!"

"Come on, Ozzy, let's get the fuck out of this shithole," Sharon yelled, pulling Ozzy by the arm.

But instead of leaving the lounge I see them wobble up the staircase to the upper level restaurant where they grab a table and start ordering lunch.

"Bring us four of your daily specials!" Sharon ordered without opening the menu.

"Will that be all?" asked the waitress.

"Arrrrgh, bring me more sake!" Ozzy muttered like a drunken pirate.

"Uh, I'll be right back," said the waitress, amused.

There was no doubt about it. My lunch companions were smashed out of their gourd. I guess I would have never noticed it if I hadn't been so sober. It was quite entertaining to see them down glass after glass of sake as they made nasty remarks to the surrounding patrons.

"You pay now and take food to go!" The nasty host reappeared with our food neatly packed inside two large paper bags.

"We ordered our food to eat here and we'll eat it here!" Sharon yelled at the top of her lungs as she stood face to face with the host.

"No! You pay and you go now!" The host was angry. He slammed the bags on our table.

Suddenly, Randy gets up, grabs a couple of containers and runs to a nearby table and smashes them on top of the table. Food exploded in all directions! Following Randy's lead Ozzy and Sharon did the same as they're being chased around the tables by the host and the rest of the restaurant staff. It was the food fight from hell as my companions drop-kicked and hurled containers with Olympic grace.

"What goes on?" asked the puzzled Asian cook, poking his head out the kitchen door.

"Oh, nothing," I replied as I attempted to quietly slip out the door in the midst of all the chaos. Suddenly Ozzy, Sharon and Randy run past me through the parking lot.

"Run, Rudes, they got knives!" Randy slurred.

"What?"

All of the sudden a dozen hands grab me and pull me back towards the restaurant.

"Get your hands off me! I didn't do anything!"

I looked around to see the furious kitchen staff waving cleavers and knives at me.

"Let me go!"

I feared for my life. I had seen every Bruce Lee movie ever made and these angry guys looked like they meant business.

"Let him go, it's not him." I heard the host yell at my assailants.

"I told you I didn't do nothing, asshole!" I snapped at my attackers as I pulled my arms from their hold.

"You tell your friends never come back! Never!" The host yelled at me as I looked over at Ozzy, Sharon and Randy who were by now at the far end of the parking lot hysterically laughing and rolling on top of each other on the ground like demented puppies.

It was a two-mile walk back to the hotel and their hysterics never ceased as we attempted to flag down any car that would give us a ride. Possessed with uncontrollable laughter, Ozzy kept stumbling and taking Sharon down with him as he held on to her. A few of minutes into our walk Ozzy relieved himself on the sidewalk in plain sight of the honking motorists who were driving down the busy main highway. Once we got back to the hotel my inebriated companions crawled back to their rooms to sleep off the excitement of the afternoon and freshen up for the night that lay ahead.

Later, I made my way to the hotel lobby to meet Randy anticipating a big night out in Omaha.

"Is there anybody here from the band?" the desk clerk asked, waving a phone.

"Yeah, I'll take it," I said, thinking it might be Randy calling to say he's running late. "Hello?"

"Who's this!?" demanded the brusk male voice on the other end.

"Ahhh, this is Rudy."

"This is Don. What the fuck is going on over there!" The phone started to throb in my hand as Don yelled at the top of his lungs.

"I got a call from Rachel crying all hysterical telling me that Ozzy and Sharon are beating the holy crap out of each other. Tell me, is this true!?"

Not knowing what to answer I started juggling the hand set like a hot potato.

"Who's that on the phone, Rudes?" I look over and see Randy approaching.

"It's Don!" I panicked and shoved the phone in his direction.

"Hi Don, this is Randy." Randy calmly answered while smoking a cigarette as he patiently listened to Don's rant.

"Well Don, I haven't seen Ozzy or Sharon since we went to lunch this afternoon but I wouldn't be too concerned. Rachel's probably blowing the whole thing out of proportion." Randy stood listening to more of Don's rant as he looked in my direction shaking his head. "OK, Don, I'll tell Sharon when I see her."

"What's going on?" I asked.

"Oh shit. Ozzy's in big trouble," said Randy hanging up the phone.

"So what's gonna happen now? Do you think Don's gonna pull the tour?" I asked Randy with concern as we got in the taxicab.

"Oh no. Don will never cancel it," said Randy. "He's got too much riding on it. Don will probably find a way to deal with the situation." Randy lit a cigarette as our cab headed out into the crisp Nebraska night.

The following morning, May 28th, I headed over to the hotel restaurant to meet Motorhead's guitarist, Fast Eddie, for breakfast.

As I passed the darkened hotel lounge I saw three figures sitting at an otherwise empty bar.

"Hey, Rudes, come over here!" Ozzy shouted. "Blizzard of Ozz

went up the charts. Isn't that great!"

As I approached the darkened bar I could see Randy holding up an issue of Billboard magazine. I was speechless! But not because the Blizzard album was doing so well; after hearing the Cleveland live radio broadcast I knew things had to improve. I was shocked because I saw the purple shiner on Sharon's eye and the red scratch marks and bruises on Ozzy's face. But it was strange. They sat there smiling from ear to ear in the dimly lit room as if nothing had happened.

Randy was right when he told me way back when that Ozzy and Sharon were like no one else I'd ever met and it was becoming more obvious everyday that these two were definitely made for each other.

That evening's performance was at the Music Hall in front of a half-filled house. Before the show, Ozzy went into his usual mantra of "I'm not doing it." And I couldn't blame him. He had a major hangover, bruises, and his voice was shot. What do you expect after three days off in Omaha?

The local rock reviewer wrote about that night's

performance.

> **"Ozzy Osbourne left the stage after performing for 45 minutes, if that long, and did not return, despite prolonged cheers that turned to boos when it became obvious there would be no encore. Osbourne probably didn't hear the crowd. He was too busy being sick to his stomach backstage. He apparently was so sick with the flu that it was something of a feat for him to have performed at all. Osbourne, whose voice was very hoarse, apologized four times during the show for "singing so badly" because of his illness. It's too bad, because the music was interesting, at least by contrast with that of Osbourne's former group, Black Sabbath. The volume was just as shattering, and the drums and bass just as indistinguishably thunderous, but the guitar playing was much more melodic."**

It never ceased to amaze me how Ozzy got away with his antics. Here he was onstage with a major sake hangover from the day before and the reviewer feels sorry for him thinking that he had the flu— praising him for his courage to face the crowd under such conditions! Talk about charmed!

8
And on Bass, Rudy from Cuba

May 29th we arrived in Tulsa, Oklahoma for yet another day off. After checking into the Holiday Inn Civic Center, Sharon called Tommy, Randy and me into her room.

"Here boys, start signing these." Sharon handed us stacks of Ozzy Osbourne's Blizzard of Ozz promo photos and pens.

"What are you doing?" Randy asked, as Sharon forged Ozzy's autograph on the promo photos.

"The publicist has been nagging me about getting these promo pictures autographed and I'm not about to wake up Ozzy. I've left him passed out in the bus and hopefully he'll stay there until show time tomorrow. I can't take another one of his drinking binges like the last one in Omaha. One of us will wind up dead!" She laughed as she signed the photos.

None of us could have foreseen the irony of Sharon forging Ozzy's signature given her own present celebrity status.

The next day, we drove straight to the venue, the Old Lady of Brady, in Tulsa, Oklahoma. After spending nearly seven weeks on the road everyone was looking ahead at the scheduled break the following week.

"Hey Rand, what are you planning to do during the break?" I asked him as he played his guitar in the tuning room before the show. "I'm gonna lock myself up in my bedroom, crank up my stereo, set up my Z scale train set, order some Chinese take-out and hang out with Jody. I'm not leaving my bedroom until it's time to go to the airport." He lit a cigarette. "How about you?"

"I'm going to Miami to visit my folks. It's been a couple of years since I've seen them. I can't wait."

No matter how much fun we were having on the road,

how great the band and our band mates were, after spending a couple of months together in a tour bus we needed to get away from each other and recharge our batteries.

We arrived the next day at the Hilton in Austin, Texas. Though that evening's show was cancelled, we stopped there as Sharon tried to avoid having too many days off in the same city in an ongoing (but futile) effort to keep Ozzy from going on his now daily binges.

The next day we arrived at the Holiday Inn in Kansas City, Missouri, for yet another scheduled day off. By now, Ozzy's voice was beyond trashed; he could hardly speak. No one was sure if it was due to the erratic scheduling or just a simple case of alcohol abuse.

The following evening's performance, the night of June 2nd, was at the Memorial Hall, in Kansas City. When we got to sound check I was surprised to run into a bootlegger from Los Angeles named Rick inside the venue since Sharon's wrath was well known among these merchandise pirates.

In those days, there were basically two types of bootleggers, the regional ones that followed the bands only within a few states and the nationwide ones, like Rick, that followed the bands in their vans from state to state throughout the whole tour. He was eating a meal with the crew.

"Rick," I said, "what the hell are you doing here, man? If Sharon catches you she'll feed your nuts to Mr. Pook for lunch." "Oh, I'm kosher, man," he said as he flashed me his tour pass. "I struck a deal with Sharon where I'm responsible for keeping all the bootleggers away from the gigs. In exchange for that she allows me to sell my stuff and at the end I give her a taste."

I couldn't believe it. Sharon had figured out how to get rid of the pesky bootleggers and put money back into Ozzy's pocket. Brilliant!

After sound check the promoter arranged for a local doctor to administer Ozzy's by now mandatory B12 shot prior to the show. In an attempt to win over the crew and band, the friendly doctor offered everyone he met backstage a bump of his pharmaceutical cocaine. Though not everyone accepted his generous offer, by the end of the show Dr. Feelgood had made a lot of friends.

The rock reviewer for a local Kansas City paper wrote about that evening's show:

> **"While being adored by his simple-minded followers, Osbourne led his three piece band through an 11 song set that lasted almost 90 minutes. Osbourne attempted to put emotion and energy into his vocals, but two thirds of the words were lost in the roar.**
> **Randy Rhoads showed some good flash guitar, and the dramatic lighting was excellent. Osbourne rallied his followers throughout, but it's unbelievable how those fans could adore a fat pretension who is fading into middle age."**

Just another review from a critic who failed to see the deep- rooted connection between Ozzy and his working class fans.

The following morning, June 3rd, we arrived in San Antonio, Texas. After checking us into the Hilton there, Sharon joined Ozzy, Randy and me on an afternoon stroll on the Riverwalk. It was quite amusing to see Ozzy knocking back shots of tequila and posing for pictures with the local Mexican Black Sabbath fans at various sidewalk cafes along this usually tranquil promenade before being hauled away by Sharon.

The next evening we performed at the San Antonio Convention Center. When I got to sound check I couldn't believe how lively the road crew was.

"I've never seen the stage go up so fast and things run so smooth. I guess the crew had a great night out on the town last night," I said to Tommy, as we got on stage to do sound check. "No Rudes," he said, knowingly. "I know what it is. This happens every time it gets close to a tour break. Just like horses approaching the stables, we all pick the pace and just get things done."

So just as Tommy had predicted, the following shows—June 5th at the Will Rogers Auditorium in Ft. Worth, Texas; June 6th at the Fair Park coliseum in Beaumont, Texas, and June 7th at the Sam Houston Coliseum in Houston, Texas—all flew by without any incidents or misbehavior from the crew and band. All in all it had been a very successful first leg of the tour and everyone was going home feeling fired up as part of something that was ready to skyrocket.

On the morning of June 8th we began our first scheduled tour break. I planned to spend the first five days in Miami with my parents and then return to Los Angeles to stay at the Arden's estate until we resumed our touring on the 12th.

While at Houston's International Airport I quickly scanned the magazine stand adjacent to the departure gate as I waited to board my Miami flight. I was elated to find Ozzy wearing a tutu and boxing gloves on the cover of the latest issue of hard rock's most popular publication, Circus magazine. I was about to glance through the magazine when I heard my boarding announcement so I just bought it and ran over to the gate and boarded my flight.

Right after take off I started to read Ozzy's interview, hoping to see my name in print at last. When asked by the interviewer about the band members, Ozzy answered in detail about Randy and explained that the previous rhythm section had been replaced by veteran drummer Tommy Aldridge and on bass Rudy from Cuba.

Though I was aware that Ozzy had done the bulk of the Blizzard of Ozz tour interviews within days of me joining the band, "Rudy from Cuba" was not exactly what I had hoped to see in print.

On the other hand I found the moment to be totally ironic. Here I was reading Ozzy's announcement to the world about my ethnic background as I was bound for Miami, the place where I grew up being told by childhood friends and band mates that because I was Cuban I didn't have a chance in hell of ever playing in a British Metal band. All of a sudden, I was filled with a sense of pride I never had before; I realized that I had beaten the odds and was coming home to share in the celebration with my family and friends. Through the years, Ozzy and Sharon recruited many musicians of various ethnic backgrounds to play in the band. This is just one of the many great qualities I've admired in the couple over the years.

Upon my arrival at the Miami airport my mother and father were waiting for me. We ran into each other's arms and melted into one big tear-filled hug. It had been a couple of years since we had been together and to finally come home—as a member of a successful band—was icing on the cake.

As I dropped my bags in the humble bedroom I used to share with my younger brother Robert, I noticed that my parents had kept the room untouched from the day we left home together. That was back in the fall of 1975 and we were both in search of the rock and roll dream. That night as I fell asleep in my old twin bed I glanced at the Beatles posters that still lined the walls, the '70s rock paraphernalia that filled the room, and thought of the incredible journey I had been on starting back in Cuba.

Shortly after Fidel Castro came to power in 1959 and declared himself a Communist, my mother, Magnolia, and my father, Rodolfo, decided we should leave Cuba and come to Miami to seek political asylum. In the early morning hours of September 1, 1961, we left our home in

Havana bound for the airport with just a few pieces of luggage. We left all of our furniture, electrical appliances and other personal belongings behind because my family didn't want to raise any suspicion regarding our departure. My father was a technician and Castro's government was prohibiting the departure of such skilled workers. That early morning drive through the quiet empty streets of Havana will be forever etched in my memory.

Upon our Pan American Airline flight's arrival in Miami, my parents requested political asylum and the four of us were granted Cuban refugee status. I will always be grateful to my parents for giving up everything they had and journeying to a foreign land so that we could live in freedom.

Adapting to a new language in school was tough for my brother and me, but even tougher for my father. He was constantly turned away from jobs in his field because he didn't have command of the English language. In the early 1960s, Miami was primarily a retirement community with very few employment opportunities outside of the tourist industry. So in the summer of 1963 when my family was given the option to relocate to New Jersey they accepted the offer in hopes of finding better jobs in a more industrialized part of the country.

Moving from Havana to sunny Miami was a mild cultural shock compared to living among the drab brown buildings of West New York, New Jersey and surviving the harsh cold winters. I clearly remember my first day as a 7th grader at Public School Number 5. Upon entering the classroom and being assigned a seat, I heard this name for the very first time:

"Rudy." The teacher called out as I put away my books. "Rudy," the teacher repeated as I completely ignored him and kept about organizing my desk. "Rudy," I heard the teacher call out once more as one of my snickering fellow students tapped me on the shoulder and pointed to the teacher. "Yes, you young man!" He said pointing at me as I stared back at him.

"But, sir, my name is Rodolfo," I said in my best-broken English.

"You're in America now. Your name will be Rudy from now on."

Young Rodolfo Maximiliano Sarzo Lavieille Grande Ruiz Payret y Chaumont was now simply Rudy Sarzo from that day on.

Adopting my new name was the final step to becoming Americanized. In the two years since my family had arrived in the U.S. we had come to accept the sad possibility that we may have to live away from Cuba longer than we had anticipated, and we started to adapt to our new way of life. Having left Cuba at 10 years of age, old enough to understand the changes Castro's communist regime brought to the island, I was extremely appreciative of the American Democratic system and of our then President, John F. Kennedy. We were still living in Cuba during the Bay of Pigs invasion and in Miami during the October Missile Crisis so I was not surprised to hear my parents curse Castro the day John F. Kennedy was shot.

My parents tried to get my brother and me out of our state of depression caused by Kennedy's death by buying us an Old Kraftsman acoustic guitar for Christmas in1963 from a Sears mail order catalogue. Having a guitar in our home for us to share was a saving grace, even though there was not much musical inspiration outside of the sugar-coated American pop music then on the radio and television. But that was about to change.

"Is that man or a woman?!" my father shouted in disgust.

"I don't know what they are, but they sure are ugly!" my mother replied, as we sat behind our TV trays holding our frozen TV dinners.

We were watching the Beatles' first performance

on "The Ed Sullivan Show." I was in awe! They were the like nothing else I had ever seen before: long hair, loud guitars, and hundreds of hysterical girls worshipping them. They had all the cool qualities girls were crazy for. Qualities ,incidentally, that I lacked, since I was a timid, overweight 13-year-old.

"The long hair reminds me of Fidel and his rebels," my dad added. "I bet you they're Communists, too!"

I wasn't about to argue with him but what I heard that night was without a doubt the sound of freedom. I think it's safe to say that every American rock musician old enough to watch the Beatles on the evening of February 9, 1964 would likely claim that as the decisive moment of their musical careers.

After three unbearable New Jersey winters, my family moved back to our old Miami neighborhood in 1967.

"Hi my name is Rudy. My family just moved in from New Jersey and I want to join your band." I barged into the rehearsal of the most popular garage bands in the area, called the Era of Good Feeling. I had my acoustic guitar over my shoulder.

"Sorry, but we already have enough guitar players," said the scruffy kid seated behind a dilapidated drum kit.

"What we really need is a bass player," said one of the three guitar players plugged into the same, single 12" speaker Silvertone amplifier.

"Oh, I can play bass, too," I lied. I desperately wanted to be in the band.

"Come back with an electric bass and amp and you're in," said the chunky singer, holding an old microphone as big as his head plugged into a reel-to-reel tape machine doubling as his p.a. system. I could easily see through their motivation. They needed another amplifier for the singer to plug into as much as they needed a bass player.

It didn't take much to coax my always supportive parents into going to Sears and purchasing (on credit) a

Silvertone bass guitar and a single 15" amplifier with enough inputs for the whole band to plug into. I initially bluffed my way through our song list mostly comprised of Beatles, Rolling Stones and The Who. But it wasn't long before I began to comprehend the role of the bassist: the link between rhythm and melody.

By 1967 I had become infatuated with the bass. I spent countless hours locked in my bedroom listening and playing my brand new Fender Jazz Bass along with any rock record I could get my hands on. Through those early years my bass guitar became the only thing I could depend on as I survived the constant break-up of ill-fated bands and ill-fated teen romances.

Upon graduating from Miami Senior High School in 1969 our band, Sylvester, got its first nightclub job backing up R&B singer Jeb Stewart, the M.C. at the Topless Tomboy Club in North Miami. Performing seven forty-five minute sets six nights a week gave me the opportunity to hone my chops playing R&B and funk. Also, sharing the dressing room with the friendly topless dancers exposed my raging teen hormones to an exhilarating lifestyle. No more Cuban girls chaperoned by overly possessive mothers!

By the early '70s, my brother Robert started looking old enough to lie about his age. So he quit high school and we formed our own band, Mango, and started playing the South Florida club circuit. As our taste in music gravitated towards heavier bands like Led Zeppelin and Deep Purple, we left the commercialized Miami circuit for the rock clubs of Fort Lauderdale. It was during this period that I met future Quiet Riot drummer, Frankie Banali.

"Hi, are you one of the guys from the band Ginger?" I asked the stylish young guy watching a local band performing at the Flying Machine, the city's hard rock mecca.

"Yeah," he said in a thick Queens accent without

taking his eyes off the stage.

"Oh, wow! I saw your band open for David Bowie a few days ago at Pirate's World and I thought you guys were great! Especially your drummer, I thought he was the best thing out of the whole night."

"Thanks, I'm the drummer," he said, amused.

I had confused him for the bass player in his band and my honesty opened the door to a solid friendship and an intermittent but fruitful musical partnership that has lasted for more than three decades. I appreciate Frankie for exposing me to his incredibly eclectic music collection—heavy metal, progressive rock, fusion just to name a few—and showing me how to improve my role as a member of a rhythm section.

One day in 1974, practically overnight, all the rock clubs in South Florida changed over to discos. The club owners went as far as to demand that bands wear matching disco outfits and play only Top 40 songs. This was a total nightmare for a hard rock musician. That's when my brother and I decided to leave Miami in search of more rock-friendly pastures. But we wanted to leave as a band rather than on our own. Trying to convince some of our musician friends to join us was difficult; most of them were quickly adapting and prospering in the hot disco scene.

"Victor, great to see you man," I said, greeting my old band mate as his band took a short break after a disco-filled set at the Castaway Lounge, one of North Miami Beach's hottest clubs.

"Robert and I are leaving Miami in the next couple of weeks and moving to New York so we can keep playing rock. The music scene here's dead. We want you to come with us."

"Man, are you kidding? I'm doing better than ever!" Victor snapped as he turned to the bartender and ordered his usual vodka tonic. "I got me a steady gig, all the hot chicks I want, a new Corvette and my own pad on the beach where the party never ends. I don't ever want to leave Miami. I've got it made here." He knocked back his drink.

"But Victor that's not what you got into music for," I reasoned. "Remember when we used to go and see Purple and Zep play at the Hollywood Sporatorium and we would get all fired up and stay up all night making plans? We were going to be in the next big rock band."

"Rudy, face it," he said. "We're Cubans, we're supposed to play dance music." He turned to the bartender and ordered us both a drink.

"Victor, I'm just as Cuban as you are but I don't want to play this disco shit. It's just like in Cuba, keep the people dancing and drunk and they'll be too fucked up in the morning to see how fucked up things really are." He handed me a drink. "Rock, that's the sound of freedom. You know that if we were still living in Cuba we wouldn't have a chance in hell of playing or even listening to rock. Castro would throw our asses in jail!"

"Look, disco is what everyone expects us to play now. Forget about hard rock, man! You'll never be accepted. You're not from England or even American. Don't waste your time." Victor picked up the round. "You'd better start saving all the dough you can for a roundtrip ticket." He turned and walked towards the stage to begin his next set.

In the fall of 1974, Robert, his wife-to-be Suzie, a singer named Dave, and I all drove up to Utica, New York.

"They'll be back in two weeks, you'll see," my father told my mother as we all waved goodbye.

Just like my parents had done so courageously 13 years before, I left my home with a couple of suitcases in pursuit of a better life.

Sure, it took me seven long years to bring those two

suitcases back home, it felt good to finally be back, if only for a few days.

The next afternoon I called up my childhood buddies and arranged for us to go clubbing that night. I was shocked to see how much the Miami nightclub scene had declined since the influx of delinquent elements from the recently arrived Mariel Boatlift, so accurately portrayed in the film Scarface.

It seemed like everyone I met was carrying some sort of illegal substance and was more than willing to share or sell. The seedy energy of the whole city of Miami in 1981 made any backstage area at a rock concert feel like Sunday School. As we entered the crowded disco in the Coconut Grove district, I was surprised to find my old friend Victor performing onstage. It was depressing to see a promising rock musician going through the motions, performing the same disco songs for going on seven years.

"Hey man, great to see you!" said Victor, coming to hug me. "Your aunt's been telling my Mom how great you're doing." "Yeah, I'm doing all right," I said. "I'm back for a few days to visit my folks. We'll be back playing in the area in a few weeks.
So how've you been?"
"I've been through a lot since the last time I saw you. I got one of my girlfriends pregnant. We got married and she took me to the cleaners, man. She took the kid, the condo, my Corvette. Everything." He took a sip of his drink. "Gigs got thin and I was really broke so I started dealing and got popped. I'm still paying my attorney bills."
"Man, I'm sorry to hear that." Not only did I feel bad for him but I also felt uncomfortable about my own success.

"You know sometimes I wonder, what if I had taken you up on your offer to leave Miami? I don't know, maybe things would have turned out different."

"Well, you're still a young guy. You can go back and play rock again. You know, I hear from Randy and Ozzy that it's really happening in England," I said as I ordered him another round.

"I can't leave. I got child support payments and a bunch of bills. I'm stuck in Miami." His band gathered on stage for the next set.

"Here, I'll get these," I told the bartender as Victor knocked back his drink.

"Thank you, my friend," Victor said as we hugged before he ran up onstage to join his band mates for the next set.

Just as Victor imagined what it would have been like if he had left Miami with me, I could see what I would have become had I stayed.

As the night came to a close and the House DJ announced "Last Call" I realized that my friends had left me stranded, just like when we were kids. I must have looked abandoned and helpless when one of the pretty young waitresses offered me a ride home. During the short ride to my parents house "Crazy Train" came on the radio.

"Oh, that's our band," I said as I turned it up.

"Isn't that the singer from Black Sabbath?" she asked.

"Yeah, that's him. But now he's got a new band and I'm the bass player."

"Wait a minute. That's you playing bass on the radio?"

"Well, that's not really me playing on the record," I clarified. "They had another guy in the band before I joined."

"Oh, really?" she sneered. "I can tell by your accent that you're Cuban." She had a confrontational tone of voice.

"Well, yeah. So?"

"So how can you be playing in an English band? That's impossible!"

We pulled into my parent's driveway.

"It's a long story and I would love to tell you all about it, but I don't want to wake up my folks. Let me have your phone number and I'll tell you over dinner."

"Forget about it. All you local wannabe rock stars are all the same. You're all so full of shit." She leaned over and opened the passenger door. "You're cute and you seem like a nice guy. Let me give you some advice: You'd better get it together, move out of your parent's house and get a life!"

She slammed shut the passenger door and sped out of the driveway. I dusted off, staring at her rear lights as they disappeared into the Miami night.

9
Boys, I Want You to Meet Harry

Upon my return to Los Angeles, I moved back into the Arden's Estate. As soon as I settled in, I grabbed the keys to one of the half dozen Mercedes 450 SLs that were at the disposal of all houseguests and drove to Randy's Burbank home to catch up on things. As I rang the doorbell I could hear music blasting from his room.

"Hey Rand, is that what I think it is?" I asked as I entered Randy's bedroom.

"Yeah it's the final mix of Diary of a Madman," Randy shouted over the music as he cranked the towering speakers situated on opposite corners of his cluttered bedroom. "Ozzy hates all the reverb and the way his vocals were mixed. He thinks it sounds like he's singing with his head inside of a toilet."

"Well, what do you think?" I asked Randy as I stepped over the train set that was set up on the floor near his bed.

"It's definitely different from Blizzard. I don't know, I kind of like it." He said as he paused the cassette player. "Maybe it's good that they both sound so different since they were recorded within months of each other."

"This is really different from anything I ever heard you write before. What inspired you?" I asked as I sat on the edge of the bed.

"One night while we were all in England writing for the second album this documentary about the Holocaust came on the TV. It had this melancholic soundtrack with an odd meter motif running through it. That's how I got the inspiration to write Diary of a Madman. Ozzy and Sharon liked the way it came out so much that they want to use it as the intro for the

105

next tour instead of 'Carmina Bruana,'" he said, enthused.

"You should be very proud, Rand. You've come a long way in such a short amount of time. I can't wait to hear what you'll come up with for the next record," I said.

"Oh, I've got some ideas already floating around my head. Do you want to hear the rest of the album?" Randy asked as he pressed "Play."

I listened in awe as one amazing track after another pumped from the speakers. I had already heard the rough mixes during the rehearsals for the tour but I hadn't heard them within the context of a finished album. It was a short but musically flawless record that left me speechless once it ended.

"So do you like it?" Randy's voice broke the silence.

"Yeah," I muttered, feeling humbled by his performance.

"You sound thirsty. Let me get you something to drink." He went into the kitchen.

While he was gone, I glanced around his bedroom in the house he shared with his family.

"You know Rand, it's funny how after all the years we've been playing together there's still so much that we don't know about each other." He handed me a frosty glass of iced tea.

"What do you want to know?"

"Who are those kids in the picture with you and your mom?" I asked.

"That's my sister Kathy and my brother Doug, sometimes he goes by Kelly. He's a musician, too."

"I didn't know you had any brothers or sisters. I never see them around."

"Oh, yeah. They keep a low profile."

"How about your Dad?" I pried.

"His name is William. He's also a music teacher like my mom. When I was just a baby, my father left my

Mom on her own to raise the kids and run the school all by herself. He moved to the East Coast and remarried. I now have two half-brothers from his marriage, Paul and Dan." Randy paused. "Now that I'm playing with Ozzy all of a sudden my Dad's been calling me and wants me to come and get together with his family when we play in New England. I don't know Rudes. It's going to be hard after all these years."

"Well, I know you'll do the right thing," I told him. "Tell me more about yourself," I said, trying to lighten up the mood. "Well, if you really want to know," Randy said as he lit up a cigarette, "I was born Randall William Rhoads on December 6, 1956 at St. John's Hospital in Santa Monica, California."

"No, no," I cut in, laughing. "I meant, like, how did you get started playing music?"

"Oh! Well, then, let me see ... I started playing the guitar and taking lessons around the age of 6 or 7. My first guitar was an old Gibson acoustic that had been in the family for quite some time. Later on my mom insisted that I take piano lessons so I could learn another instrument and to read music. I'm glad she did. Even though I only took piano for a short while, I still retained the theory and sight reading that I learned then, which has helped me a lot now that I'm studying classical guitar."

Randy took another sip of his tea.

"So how old were you when the rock and roll bug hit you?"

"Oh, when I was about twelve I started playing this old semi acoustic guitar," he said. "This thing was huge, almost bigger than me!" We laughed. "I took lessons for about a year from Musonia's guitar teacher until he ran out of stuff to teach me. By the time I was 14 I began to feel confident enough with my playing to start a band. My first band was with my brother Doug. I played rhythm guitar and he played drums. We named the band Violet Fox and it lasted just a few months."

"I grew up playing with my brother also," I said. "I think it's great especially when you both have the same taste in music."

"I know what you mean, because my other alternative was to play folk music with Kathy. I think I would have been just a bit too loud to play 'Kumbaya'!

"After that I was in a couple of local bands playing kegger parties around Burbank until we formed Quiet Riot. I think you pretty much know the rest." Randy puffed his cigarette. "So tell me about yourself, Rudes." We heard a knock on the door. "That must be Jody. She's bringing over some Chinese take out. Do you want to stay for dinner?"

"Hey Rudy!" Jody gave me big hug at the doorway after kissing Randy. "I haven't seen you since you all started the tour. How's the road been treatin' you?" she asked.

"Hasn't Randy been telling you about all the crazy stuff that's happened?"

"Oh yeah, some pretty funny stuff," she laughed.

"Well, if it wasn't for Randy at the beginning showing me the ropes I would have gone insane," I admitted. "Sharon and Ozzy are real nice people but they sure are unpredictable. There's never a dull moment." We all laughed.

"I know what you mean," Jody smiled. "When I went over to visit Randy at Ridge Farm during the recording sessions they pulled some crazy pranks on me. I guess it's their way of welcoming you to the family."

"If that's the case then I'm officially adopted!" I joked.

"So are you staying for dinner?" Randy asked. "There's plenty for all of us."

"I'd love to but I can't stay. I'm meeting Kevin for dinner at the Rainbow later. It's my first night back in town and I'm feeling lucky," I said as I got in my car. "Great seeing you again Jody. Rand, if I don't see you before I guess I'll see you at the airport in a few days." We waved goodbye as I backed out of the driveway and headed for the Sunset Strip.

Sharon ran an extremely tight ship on the road. There were no groupies allowed backstage so my only chances for "socializing" were during days off on the road or tour breaks. Word of mouth had already created a buzz about the Blizzard of Ozz on the Sunset Strip so for the remaining of the five summer nights in Los Angeles I was given the royal treatment by the colorful cast of characters at the Rainbow Bar and Grill.

On the morning of June 18 th we all gathered at the Los Angeles airport to board our flight to Denver where the bus would meet us to get us to the gig in time for sound check.

"Boys, I want you to meet Harry. He'll be helping me with some of the tour managing chores," Sharon said. Randy, Tommy and I exchanged pleasantries with him.

Harry Mohan was a brawny, middle-aged Englishman with a vice grip for a handshake. After some casual conversation I learned that he was a former British boxing champ, which explained his broken nose, and that Don Arden had sent him over from England. As I began to put two and two together I realized that Harry was here not only to help Sharon with the tour but also to keep her and Ozzy from killing each other.

When we arrived at Denver's Rainbow Musical Hall for sound check we were disappointed to see how small the venue was. Our tour was beginning to draw some good crowds and this venue, with a maximum of 1,500 capacity and unusually small stage, was not the best way to kick off the next leg of the tour. Nevertheless, the combination of a re-energized band and an enthusiastic

109

crowd made for a great show.

The following morning we arrived at the Hilton in Colorado Springs, Colorado. That evening's show was at the City Auditorium.

After an unusually long overnight drive we arrived at the Sheraton Hotel in El Paso, Texas the afternoon of June 20th. This was our first day off after the break and Ozzy had missed hanging with the crew, so instead of Sharon trying to keep them apart she let them carouse, with Harry keeping a close watch on Ozzy.

The next evening's performance, on June 21st, was at the dusty and cavernous El Paso Coliseum. The first thing that hit us upon arriving at sound check was the stench left behind by the rodeo from a couple of days before.

Even Ozzy, who had worked at a slaughterhouse in his youth, was appalled by the smell. After sound check we were greeted backstage by the Official Japanese Ozzy fan club. These genuinely devoted fans had paid for their own travel expenses and were grateful to be allowed to interview and take photos of the band for their fanzine. They had been especially excited to see Randy, whom they had been following since Quiet Riot released their first album in Japan.

During the show I witnessed the most awesome display of pyrotechnics, courtesy of the crowd, mostly made up of Mexican fans from Ciudad Juarez, right across the border from El Paso. The spectacle consisted mainly of blazing, gasoline-soaked rags hurled through the air that burst in mid-flight, and spouting hair spray cans ignited with lighters resembling flamethrowers. Not to be outdone by the rowdy fans, the band displayed some sonic pyrotechnics of its own.

A local rock critic wrote of that evening's performance:

"Musically, Osbourne has advanced writing more intelligent lyrics, wrapping them in a tightly-executed metallic

insulation provided by guitarist Randy Rhoads, England's answer to Eddie Van Halen, bassist Bob Daisley and drummer Tommy Aldridge."
By misidentifying me for Bob I suspect that the critic read the album press release and skipped the show.
Maybe he was afraid of the rowdy pyromaniacs in the crowd.

The next morning we arrived at the Marriott in Tucson, Arizona for a day off. Randy and I spent most of the afternoon rummaging through the Tucson music store called the Chicago Store for any vintage instruments we could find. Unfortunately, we had little success. Later that evening we joined the crew for a rowdy night out at a local Mexican restaurant complete with Mariachi bands and table top dancing courtesy of our fun-loving, inebriated road crew.

The following day, June 23rd, I woke up with the worst case of food poisoning imaginable. That evening's show at Tucson's Community Center Arena was unforgettable by the mere fact that I was so deathly ill. When you're on the road and the show must go on, your health is one of your top priorities. After all my years of touring I've come to view a good meal not by its taste but how well I feel after it's digested.

As a rule I always have my main meal of the day at least eight hours prior to show time. That way I avoid going onstage feeling bloated. After the show Sharon decided as a precaution that I should stay behind and travel with our tour accountant to the next city just in case my symptoms were from a stomach virus and not food poisoning. We were about to hit the Los Angeles area in a few days and she wanted to avoid the possibility of me spreading the bug to anyone else in the bus, especially Ozzy, our resident hypochondriac.

The rock critic for one of Tucson's newspapers wrote

of that evening's performance

"**The fact that Ozzy Osbourne's music is excruciatingly loud, noisy, and unimaginative is not the issue here. The fact that Ozzy Osbourne can't sing and can barely shout, is not the issue here, either.**
The issue that was raised at the Blizzard of Ozz concert last night at the Tucson Community Center Arena was that of the power of a rock star, term used loosely, has over his followers." Another rock critic wrote, "Osbourne is in his onstage temple, encouraging the faithful to keep smoking that good weed. The stage design for this symbolic setting is centered on Tommy Aldridge, sitting behind his drums on an altar-like platform above the stage.
Looking monolithic as time itself, he provides the rhythm. Out front with Osbourne, at his right hand and left respectively, are bassist Rudy Sarzo and guitarist Randy Rhoads. Both slender figures dressed in tight-fitting red jump suits. They could represent the surrounding powers of Satan, or the blood of life, or the wine of communion."

I wonder if this reviewer considered that maybe Randy and I were wearing these clothes because they were easy for Rachel to care for.

The following day, June 24th, the tour accountant and I took our commuter flight to Phoenix, Arizona. By the time we boarded our flight I was beginning to feel normal again. As the accountant and I engaged in small talk I took the opportunity to learn exactly what his function was on the tour. I learned that a tour accountant's main responsibility was to collect all the monies that were due to the artists from the promoters and vendors after each show. In the precomputerized ticket system days, the accountant would stay after the show and count each ticket by hand in front of a promoter rep and make sure that there was an accurate ticket sale count.

This is a very important issue when there is a sellout and the artistreceives a bonus that could add up in the tens of thousands.
The tour accountant would usually travel separate from the band, since they usually finished their job hours after the band had left town, and then go to a local bank and wire transfer the previous night's profits back to the artist's management bank account.

They can also be responsible for other financial duties, such as the handling of per diems to the crew and band members, weekly salaries, hotel bills, and any petty cash situations that arise.

When we got to Phoenix we found out that the show had been cancelled due to a three-inch crack in the roof of the Veterans' Memorial Coliseum. It was then rescheduled for June 28th and moved to the Grady Gammage Memorial Auditorium in nearby Tempe.

The following day, June 25th, we arrived in Las Vegas. That evening's show was at the Aladdin Theater situated in the Aladdin Hotel. Traditionally, when artists perform in a Vegas hotel the management provides the lodging in the hopes that the artists goes to the casino and gambles away their performing fees. So, in an attempt to discourage Ozzy from getting into trouble, Sharon booked us in the only hotel in town that didn't have a casino, the Jockey Club.

That afternoon Randy got together with his old friend and former Quiet Riot bass player, Kelli Garni. Randy hadn't seen Kelli since his move to Vegas so there was plenty of catching up to do. Neal Preston, the veteran rock photographer, flew over from Los Angeles to shoot a pictorial of Ozzy for People magazine that included

Sharon and Mr. Pook. He also set up a pre-show photo session with Randy and his guitar collection in the dressing room. After the show, Randy and I hung out at the game arcade at Circus Circus and skipped the casinos since neither one of us gambled. I believe life itself is a gamble and I had just hit the jackpot when I joined the band. The following morning, June 26th, we arrived at the Plaza Hotel in San Diego. That evening's performance at the Fox Theater was electrifying, partly due to the exuberant fans and the anticipation of the next evening's homecoming show.

A local rock critic wrote about that night's performance:

> **"Rock music for people without brain cells hit San Diego Friday night. The heavy metal concert featured the mindless, raunchy, crunching sounds of Ozzy Osbourne and Motorhead, don't try to make sense of either band. You'll hurt yourself. Lightning fast Rhoads delivered a scorching three-minute guitar solo on 'Suicide Solution.' Rhoads played riffs on that song and 'Mr. Crowley' that would make most lead guitarists blush."**

Immediately after the show we traveled to Los Angeles where all of us except Randy, who went home, stayed at the Arden's estate.

The following evening's show, June 27th, was at the Long Beach Arena, in the city of the same name.

"Hey dude, you must be really excited to be playing back home for the first time," said the leather-clad young man as we washed our hands, glancing at each other's reflection in the mirror of the backstage bathroom.

"Yeah, I can't wait," I said, drying my hands.

"Dude, there's a huge buzz about you guys and everybody in town is here tonight to see if you guys

114

are as good as everyone says." He pulled out a vial filled with cocaine.

"Really?" Anxiety and apprehension came over me. What if I suck tonight? No way! That's it! I was determined that tonight was going to be the best show I had ever played.

"Do you want a bump, dude?" he asked.

"Are you kidding? Now you got me so tense I'm about to self- combust." I walked out of the bathroom and headed for the dressing room to start warming up.

That evening I hit the stage like a caged tiger, trying to play harder and faster than ever before. But with each song I found myself playing worse as I tried to reach a level of performance beyond my normal watermark. It took me a few songs to settle in as I realized that just like athletes, performers have their own personal best. This is a certain level of performance that can rarely be improved on and at best matched. But then again I've done some of my best work when I've least expected to, in small towns, or when I've had a cold and I talk myself into taking it easy. As soon as the music starts and the adrenaline starts pumping I forget about what's ailing me, catch the groove and go for it

The celebration after the show at Arden's was the icing on the cake. I was amused to see Lemmy reading a paperback novel at the bar, ignoring all the Hollywood celebrities surrounding him. Sharon spent most of the night ejecting scantily clad female gatecrashers from the premises. Despite her vigilance, a good time was had by all.

A local rock critic wrote of the Long Beach performance:

"Osbourne's debut as a solo act on Saturday night at the Long Beach Arena showed that while unorthodox approach to heavy metal is still evident, it's been

115

refined to a thin shadow of its former self. Osbourne calls his act Blizzard of Ozz, and its main problem is the way it smoothes heavy metal's rough edge, this genre's reason for being." Another critic wrote:

"Surely an unlikely candidate for career longevity, former Black Sabbath vocalist Ozzy Osbourne staged a comeback of sorts before a sellout crowd at the Long Beach Arena on Saturday.

Neither a standout singer nor a particularly captivating showman during his 11-year stint with Sabbath, the chunky Osbourne is nevertheless riding the crest of a hit solo album, Blizzard of Ozz."

Backed by a trio of young hotshots, including ex-local metal mongers Quiet Riot guitarist Randy Rhoads whose playing is strictly state of the cliche."

By now I've come to realize that the ones who can actually play go on to become real musicians, while the ones who can't go on to become critics.

The following morning, June 28th, we flew to Phoenix to perform the rescheduled show at Grady Gammage Memorial Auditorium in Tempe, Arizona. We skipped hotels and went straight to sound check from the airport. We were all a bit tired from the night before, but nevertheless the band shone in the afterglow of the previous night's performance. After the show we took the last flight out of Phoenix back to Los Angeles.

A local Phoenix critic wrote of the evening's show:

"Ozzy Osbourne is not what God intended lead singers to be. For a start he has a round, merry face and then there's the sturdy earnest figure he cuts on stage. Osbourne and his band, Randy Rhoads,

116

Bob Daisley and Lee Skerslake gave their audience an energetic and highly appreciated set that lasted about 75 minutes. Neither Osbourne nor his accompanists have a particularly distinctive sound. But the songs they have composed are a cut above the usual heavy- metal subject matter."

Once again I suspect this critic never made it to the show and only read the Blizzard of Ozz record's press release.

The day after, June 29th, was a scheduled day off back in Los Angeles. I took it easy and tried to replenish my batteries for the big upcoming shows. On June 30th, we flew to Fresno, California, for that evening's show at Selland Arena. When I met Randy at the Burbank airport I couldn't help but notice how unusually quiet he was.

"Hey Rand, what's wrong?" I asked him as he sat quietly at the gate with an ice pack on his cheek.

"Oh, Rudes, I've had this toothache since yesterday and my

dentist is out of town."

"How bad is it?" I asked.

"It's killing me, I just hope the cabin pressure doesn't make it

worse," he said as we boarded the plane.

As soon as we got to sound check Randy was rushed to an emergency room. Just as he feared, the cabin pressure had worsened the pain. The doctor performed an immediate wisdom tooth extraction. Between the pain killers and the surgery Randy was incapable of performing so the show was cancelled and we returned to Los Angeles.

July 1st was, fortunately, another scheduled day off, since Randy didn't have enough time to recuperate from the oral surgery.

The next day it was back on the tour bus as we drove

from Los Angeles to nearby San Bernadino to perform at the venue where we did the pre-production rehearsals, the Swing Auditorium. After being on the road for a few months and playing in various large venues the once seemingly huge auditorium suddenly didn't look as ominous as it did that first day of rehearsal.

On the 3rd, we headed north to Bakersfield to perform at the Kern County Auditorium. After checking in at the Hilton we all drove to the venue for an early sound check. While there Ozzy befriended a local biker and spent a couple of hours riding his Harley though town. A couple of hours before show time Ozzy started complaining to Sharon about a pain in his lower back.

"I told you not to go riding on that bloody bike!" Sharon yelled. "Look it's too late now to start yelling at me. I'm in fucking awful pain. I need a doctor."

"Ozzy, we're in bumfuck Bakersfield on a 4th of July holiday weekend. Where am I supposed to pull a doctor out of? My twat?!"

"I don't think I can do the show tomorrow morning," Ozzy moaned.

"Oh, no you don't! You are not pulling a runner out on this one. This is the biggest show of the tour and Bill Graham will have your balls for breakfast! That's it!" She shouted. "We're going to San Francisco right now. Get the boys on the tour bus right away!" she hollered at the tour manager, 'And don't make any announcements to the crowd until you hear from me."

We all quickly piled in the tour bus and headed for the freeway. As we reached the Bakersfield city limits Sharon grabbed the tour bus citizen band radio and reached our tour manager who was standing on stage waiting to make the announcement.

"Can you hear me?" asked Sharon. "Go ahead. You can tell them the show has been cancelled."

The next morning, July 4th, I had the earliest wakeup call I've ever had for a rock show: 7 a.m. We had a lobby call of 8 a.m. since we had to drive Knob Hill area of San Francisco to Oakland Coliseum and fight bumper to bumper the traffic all the way. Our set time for that years' Day on the Green, a big rock festival, was 10:50am to 11:35am. These shows run like clockwork and if you're late getting on stage it goes off your set time. Since we were only doing a 45-minute set it was decided that we drop a few songs, shorten the solos, and skip the encore.

Before the show, Ozzy was in fine form backstage as he engaged in compromising positions with decorative plastic elks and reindeer for the photographers of Sounds, the British journal that had come over to cover the event. It seemed that running into his old mates was the best cure for Ozzy's ailing back.

Though I was still yawning as we waited to go onstage once I heard the roar of the crowd it was like a rush of caffeine through my veins. It was amazing to see the 40,000 hands raised skyward through the whole show in the early morning sunlight. Ozzy was inspired to new heights as he showered the crowd with such sentiments as "I wanna fuck you all!"

After we ended our set, we ran up the long tunnel that connected the stage area in the baseball field with the dressing rooms. I was half undressed as I reached our dressing room when I heard the event's stage manager yelling, "You guys have to come back for an encore, the audience is going wild and we're afraid we might have a riot on our hands!" When we went back onstage and looked out into the Oakland Coliseum we knew that we were witnessing a defining moment in the band's short history as the crowd erupted with a deafening chant of "Ozzy! Ozzy!"

10
Ozzy Comes Home to Save the Day

The afternoon of July 5th we rode to nearby Santa Cruz, for that evening's performance at the Civic Auditorium. Since we were taking the bus back to Los Angeles right after show Sharon decided to skip the hotel that day and drive straight to the venue for sound check. Upon our early morning return to Los Angeles I opted to stay at a friend's house in the Hollywood Hills area to spend the next day off. The following afternoon, July 6th, I got a call from Sharon. "Rudy, Ozzy's a bit under the weather so we have to cancel the next few shows. I'm running out of excuses to give the promoters regarding his health so I've told them this time that you're not well."

"OK," I agreed. "So what am I sick with?"

"I've told them that you fell, got hurt and your arm's in a sling." "Oh, really!?" I laughed.

"So don't go out. You must not be seen in public. You'll have to stay in for the next few days," Sharon said.

"OK, no problem," I assured her.

As I hung up the phone I realized that I was going to miss out on a substantial amount of hedonist Hollywood nights. Then it dawned on me; if Rudy can't go to the party then the party must come to Rudy. I spent the next five nights entertaining my crazy Sunset Strip friends and savoring all the delights that a member of the hottest new band can enjoy.

Meanwhile the next four shows: July 7th at the Civic Auditorium in Redding, California, July 8th at the Nevada State Fairgrounds in Reno, Nevada, July 9th at the Performance Hall in Eugene, Oregon, and July 10th at the Yakima Speedway in Yakima, Washington were all cancelled.

On the afternoon of July 11th, we arrived in Portland, Oregon, to perform that evening at the Paramount Theatre. After checking into the Hilton Randy and I went out for lunch and a bit of sightseeing, as we were thrilled to be back on the road. It seemed like the longer the tour went on the more time we spent in Los Angeles and the less time we spent on the road. We really needed to get back on a performing groove once again by playing more consecutive shows. That evening's performance was filled with plenty of musical angst, as we tried to shake the cobwebs off our fingers.

A local rock critic wrote of that evening's performance:

> **"Osborne and his band made their Portland debut Saturday night at the Paramount. Instead of Black Sabbath monotone vocals, the material from Blizzard of Ozz actually contained melodies of sorts. The new band is just as heavy as Black Sabbath and features the same instrumentation, but rocks in a more uptempo vein. The audience either didn't notice the monotony of the band, or didn't care. The sold-out Paramount was a mass of screaming, avid fans, cheering every move and solo."**

The next morning, July 12th, we arrived at the Washington Plaza in Seattle. It had become the norm by now that if the distances between cities were less than 200 miles, we would then spend the night over at the hotel instead of sleeping in the bus. That evening's sold out show was at the Paramount Theater. It was a quite disturbing to watch from the stage the flimsy protruding balcony dangerously bouncing as the fans banged their heads to the beat of our music.

A local rock reviewer described that night's

performance:

> **"Like a fire engine with all its horns and
> sires stuck, Osbourne and his band
> trounced their newfound fans last night
> and blew them away like soldiers who got
> too close to an atom bomb test. Beneath
> all the noise and rubble lies some decent
> rock and roll in need of a permanent
> audience. Osbourne's band is guitarist
> Randy Rhoads, bassist Bob Dasiley and
> drummer Lee Kerslake. Kerslake,
> formerly with Uriah Heep, also plays
> tubular bells and timpani drums. Rhoads
> and Kerslake showed off their special
> talents during solo performances last
> night."**

This was quite a good review especially for Lee who wasn't even in the band by then. Also, Tommy never played timpani drums or tubular bells during that tour.

The following morning, July 13th, was a travel day. We rode our tour bus early that morning to the nearby Puget Sound landing where the tour bus boarded a ferry that took us to Victoria, British Columbia to begin our Canadian tour. It was a most pleasant ferry ride. The band and crew climbed to the upper deck—except for Ozzy who remained asleep in the locked bus—to enjoy the breathtaking views and soak up the sun. As soon as we arrived at our hotel, the Chateau Victoria in the heart of the city, Randy and I grabbed our cameras and went sightseeing.

Later that evening Randy and I went out for a short walk to meet the crew for our by now traditional boys night out at a nearby club. A teenager carrying a cardboard guitar case approached us as were about to enter the nightclub.

"Excuse me, but are you Randy Rhoads," he asked, shyly.

"Yeah, that's me," Randy replied with a smile, acting surprised at being recognized.

"Wow! I'm a big fan of yours! I love your playing on Blizzard of Ozz. I haven't stopped listening to it since I got it!"

"Gee, thanks," Randy bashfully replied.

"I'm looking forward to the show tomorrow night. I can't wait to see you play!"

"Well, I hope you enjoy our show," Randy graciously responded. Suddenly there was an uncomfortable silence as the young man tried to gather his words as he stared at the ground.

"Mr. Rhoads, I feel kind of awkward asking you this in the middle of the street." He stared at the ground.

"Oh, don't worry. What is it?"

"Well, I've been trying to learn the solo on 'Goodbye to Romance' but I'm having difficulties making out some of the riffs you're playing," he explained. "I was wondering if you could show me how you played the solo." He pulled a beat up old guitar out of the cardboard box.

"Well, it's been a while since I played that solo. You see, we're not performing it on this tour so let me see if I can remember how it goes." Randy crouched on the sidewalk and tried to tune the guitar. "If I remember correctly it goes something like this." Randy struggled for a couple of minutes to remember the same solo he had recorded.

"Oh no, Mr. Rhoads, let me show you. It goes like this."

The young man took the guitar from Randy and proceeded to play the solo perfectly note for note. Randy and I looked at each other in disbelief and laughed.

"Oh, yeah, that's about right, Randy said with a grin as he shook the young man's hand and walked away.

"Rudes, that's the last time I'm giving anybody a guitar lesson in the middle of the street!"

We both laughed about the incident and entered the nightclub to carry on with our boys' night out.

The next evening, July 14th, we performed at Victoria's Memorial Arena. A Canadian band by the name of "Queen City Kids" was added to the tour. After some casual backstage conversation with the members of the band I learned that the Canadian government is very supportive of their native artists. As a rule, at least half of the play list played on Canadian radio stations must be of national origin and any non-Canadian headlining artists must include at least one national act on their bill. This kind of support has established Canada as a creatively fertile ground for some of music's greatest artists.

The following morning, July 15th, we took a ferry ride from Victoria to Vancouver. I was swept away by the natural beauty of the city's landscape and impressive skyline. After checking into the Four Seasons Hotel, Randy and I went on a long sightseeing trip before sound check. Upon our return to the hotel we found out that Sharon had left a message for us to come to her room.

"Come in boys," Sharon said as she let us into her suite.

"What's up?" Randy asked.

"Thelma, Ozzy's wife, will be joining the tour. She'll be traveling with Ozzy on the bus, and I just don't feel comfortable with the whole thing, so I'm going to let them and Harry have the bus."

"You boys and I will be flying the rest of the tour until Thelma goes back home." Sharon grinned wickedly.

"I don't know Sharon," Randy said, concerned. "That's a lot of flying and you know how much I hate to fly."

"Well, look at the alternative. Once we get to Calgary we have a few, 900-mile drives. Would you rather be stuck with Ozzy on a bloody smelly bus driving across Canada for days or would you rather fly with me?"

"Nope, I'll fly!" said Randy quickly.

"Yeah, me too!" I said, raising my hand as we all laughed.

That evening's show was at the Kerrisdale Arena. The reaction from the mostly male urban crowd seemed out of hand in comparison to the sedate response from the rural audience the night before.

A critic for a local publication wrote of that evening's performance:

> **"It's easy to understand why the crowd likes Osbourne. Slightly paunchy, certainly less pretty than his sidemen, Osbourne's out to have an entertaining good time and you get the impression that if he hadn't drifted into performing so many years ago he'd be down in the front row cheering on somebody on stage who looked just like him and played his kind of music. The Osbourne band drummer— Tommy Aldridge, bassist Rudy Sarzo, guitarist Randy Rhoads and an occasional, nameless keyboard player who was inaudible anyway—fared slightly better than Motorhead, suggesting that by hard rock standards the group could have been dynamite."**

The following morning, July 16 th, Sharon, Randy, Tommy and I flew from Vancouver to Edmonton, Alberta, on one of our numerous flights during the Canadian Tour. While checking into the Four Season's Hotel I scanned through the pages of the local entertainment guide and to my surprise I found an ad for Motley Crue's show later that same evening.

After a couple of phone calls, I arranged for the band and road crew to get in the show in anticipation of another wild night off.

"Hi, we're on the Motley Crue guest list," said Tommy to the menacing looking bouncer.

"What's your names?" he growled as he scrutinized our rowdy entourage.

"I talked to one of the guys from the band earlier today and he said he would put us all on the list under the 'Ozzy Osbourne Band.'" I told him.

"It's downstairs, just follow the noise," he said, after taking a long look at the short guest list.

We descended a long steep staircase that took us inside a small bar with a ceiling so low that some of our guys' heads were scraping the ceiling.

Giving their best to put on an arena-type performance, Motley Crue were in the middle of an angst-filled set as most of the small crowd danced in front of the stage. When their set was over, Randy and I followed the guys to their room in the skid row hotel.

"I hate this fucken shithole! They're just a bunch of line dancing yahoos," yelled a pissed off Mick Mars as Nikki, Tommy and Vince scattered across the messy hotel room crammed with heavy metal regalia.

"Those mother fuckers at customs took my blades and all my studded shit. Can you fuckin' believe that!" Nikki yelled as he offered Randy and me a couple of beers.

"Yeah, this asshole came in the toilet when I was taking a piss and started harassing me so I just knocked him out," added Tommy as he punched the air.

"Man, we've been playing in this dump for almost a week and this fucking gig's getting worse," Vince said.

"Don't worry guys, things will get better," I said attempting to cheer them up.

"Hey man, how about you putting in a good word for us with Ozzy so we can get on the tour?" Nikki asked Randy and me.

"Yeah, that will fucking definitely make things better!" Tommy added jumping to his feet and grabbing a beer.

"I'll see what I can do," said Randy.

"Yeah, I'll definitely tell Sharon, Ozzy's manager, and see what happens." I said, clinking Nikki's beer bottle.

As fate had it, Motley Crue finally got their wish in 1983. After the release of Shout at the Devil, they opened up for Ozzy during the "Bark at the Moon" tour.

The morning of July 17th, I got a call from Sharon asking me to meet in her room.

"Boys, I got some wonderful news!" she said as she bounced up and down like a schoolgirl. "Black Sabbath pulled out of the Port Vale show at the last minute and Motorhead asked Ozzy to take their place."

"That's the festival in England, right?" I asked, charged by Sharon's enthusiasm.

"When's the show? Randy asked.

"It's August 1st." Sharon replied.

"Damn! That's less than two weeks away," Tommy interjected. "Right, so you boys better give me your passports so we can get all the visas ready."

"Wait, Sharon, I don't have a passport. You see I'm still a Cuban citizen and all I have is my green card," I said, as my excitement turned into a major concern.

"Don't you worry," she reassured me. "Let me call Jet Records' attorneys and they'll sort it out. Boys, I can just see the headlines: Ozzy comes home to save the day!" Sharon said her eyes gleaming.

That evening's show was at Kinsman Auditorium in Edmonton. Backstage I tried to avoid being around Thelma, even though she seemed like a quiet and unassuming person. I just sensed that Sharon would have frowned upon it and I didn't want to wind up back in the bus. But being Ozzy's wife, Thelma's presence could not

127

be ignored, especially in the dressing room before the show.

"Hey man, look at what Thelma made me," Ozzy said as he pulled out of a garment bag a black, polyester, lace-up shirt with an awful wide-winged collar, white fringe on the sleeves and "OZZY" embroidered in silver sequins across the front of the shirt. It was hideous, even by Ozzy's stage apparel standards.

"Is she bloody talented or what?"

Out of the comer of my eye I could see daggers flying from Sharon's eyes as Ozzy leaned over and hugged Thelma. If looks could kill Thelma would've been in a body bag on the next flight back to Birmingham.

"I hope she made him two of those—one to shit on and the other one to cover it with," Tommy whispered in Sharon's ear as he passed by twirling his sticks.

The following morning, July 18th, we flew to Calgary, Alberta, for a much needed early afternoon check in to the Calgary Inn Hotel. All the flying was beginning to take a toll on us, since we usually had to leave the hotel very early in the morning, at least a couple of hours before the flight. In comparison, traveling by tour bus was a more relaxing and practical mode of transportation.

With a few exceptions, such as that evening's performance at the Max Bell Auditorium, most of the Canadian shows were performed in huge hockey arenas in contrast to the intimate theaters and occasional basketball arenas that we had been performing at in the U.S. From the impressive turnouts at the sold out shows we felt that Canada was more receptive to our brand of music than the U.S., but it was hard for us to tell by the dumbfounded response from the mostly male audiences.

The next day, July 19th, we flew to Winnipeg, Manitoba for another day off. After checking into the Winnipeg Inn I met Randy at the hotel lounge for a drink.

"Randy, if I didn't know any better I would say that Sharon's got a crush on you," I said as we ordered a round of drinks.

"No way Rude's," Randy said. "She does this every time Thelma's around. She's only trying to make Ozzy jealous. There was this one time at Ridge Farm when —" Randy held back as a devilish gleam sparkled in his eye.

"When what?" I pushed.

"Never mind," Randy said as the waitress served his drink.

"Is there something going on between you two?"

"Look. This is what happened. Thelma came over to visit Ozzy during the recording sessions. Sharon had been staying with him and since there were no other rooms available I offered to let Sharon stay in my room." Randy paused to take a long sip. "We started drinking." Randy was carefully choosing his words.

"And the next thing you know we were making out and ... "

"You guys did it, didn't you?!" I yelled as I almost fell off my chair.

"Look, I respect Ozzy and Sharon and I don't want to be in the middle," Randy snapped. "Anyways, I won't be surprised if they wind up getting married someday." Randy paused to take a deep drag of his cigarette. "I don't think things are so good between Ozzy and Thelma. You can tell by how miserable he's been since she's been on tour with us."

"I hear you," I agreed. "He's usually pretty hammered but this is the worst I've seen him."

"And besides, I love Jody," Randy said.

"So you and Jody have plans to get married?"

"We're still both very young and I need time to focus on my music. But you never know, maybe someday." Randy's smoke circles drifted through the air.

The following dates—July 20th, at the Concert Bowl

in Winnipeg, Manitoba, July 21st and 22nd, days off in Kitchner, Ontario, July 23rd's performance at Kitchner's Center in the Square, July 24th's London Gardens show in London, Ontario, July 25th performance at the Place Theatre in Hamilton, Ontario and the July 26th show at Jacques Hardy Arena in Kingston, Ontario—all went without any major incidents. By now we were back in the tour bus since Thelma had returned to Birmingham to prepare things for Ozzy's homecoming show in Portvale.

On the afternoon of July 27th we arrived at the Hilton Harbour Square in Toronto. As I was heading out the door to meet Randy for lunch I got a frantic phone call from Sharon asking me to come to her room immediately.

"I just got off the phone with the legal department at Jet Records in London," she explained, "and they've informed me that you must appear in person at the British Embassy to acquire the proper documentation that will get you into England and then back into the U.S. without any danger of being deported back to Cuba!"

"You're joking, right!?"

"Nope," she said. "I've never been so bloody serious in my life." I pondered the possible consequences.

"So here's what you're going to do," Sharon continued. "Wednesday, the day after the Montreal show, you're flying back to Los Angeles. Then Thursday morning as soon as they open the doors to the British Embassy you get your Cuban butt in there and meet with the attache that will be waiting to hand you over all the documentation you need. Immediately after you're done, you get back to the airport and catch the next flight to London. It should get you into Heathrow the morning of the 31st with plenty of time for you to get over jet lag for the show the following day."

"Wow Sharon, sounds like there's little room for fuck ups." "Little? There's absolutely no room for fuck ups. But don't worry, I'm sending Harry with you. I just want to make sure that you don't get lost in Los Angeles or deported at British customs. Rudy, you've got to make this work. This show is very important for Ozzy's career. Just do me a favor, don't tell Ozzy about your situation, he's got enough on his mind with tomorrow's live recording in Montreal."

That evening's show was at Toronto's legendary Maple Leaf Garden. I can honestly say that every single show that I saw Randy perform with Ozzy was outstanding, but there was always something extra special about his performances when the audiences understood and reacted to his remarkable musicianship. This night was no exception as Randy's soaring guitar inspired all of us to perform one of the most high-energy shows to date.

A local rock reviewer wrote about that evening's performance:

> **"About 12,000 mostly high school age heavy metal rock fans turned up at Maple Leaf Gardens last night to worship a rock fossil named Ozzy Osbourne, who is so old that he could be, and might be, their father.**
> **Ozzy doesn't move much on stage. He claps his hands and throws double peace signs. He frog leaps and shakes his hair. Once, he pulled down his pants.**
> **But he doesn't move much. The band blasted out two new numbers and offered the songs from the Blizzard debut at a decibel level sufficient to blow dry your hair. Blizzard of Ozz lead guitarist Randy Rhoads proved he has all the parts to become a true heavy metal guitar hero. He has the long blond hair to whip around, and the red pantsuit to posture in. His fingers blur along the neck of his Gibson Flying Vee with just the right flash and ostentation. His solos soar."**

Another local reviewer wrote,

"Ozzy's retreating is strictly a cash deal. He did his cheeky, conceptual, occult bit the last time out and now he's just exploiting a reputation reborn in the current head banging renaissance. Sure Ozzy was into it, thrashing around on stage in front of a mercilessly loud and unimaginative power trio, a keyboard player was hidden off stage. But up close Ozzy could be seen laughing behind those plying, sweaty locks.
Maybe it was the sight of 7,000 neanderthals mistaking self-parody for the real thing, whatever that was. Or the luck of an old geezer given up for dead two years ago. Whatever, he was having a good time."

The following morning, July 28th, we arrived at the Meridien Hotel in Montreal. Playing in cosmopolitan cities such as Toronto and Montreal back to back was a rare treat after trekking for a couple of weeks across the rural areas of Canada. The emphasis that afternoon during sound check at the St. Dennis Theatre was on that evening's live recording for a future radio broadcast. It's odd how sometimes you can go from playing a great show one night and then less than 24 hours later the band's on stage struggling with their performance. Maybe it was the unusually unflattering acoustics that made Randy feel like he wasn't getting the right tone or the possibility that Ozzy didn't have much energy left after his spirited performance the previous night, but we all felt that evening's performance was one of the low points on the whole tour and to make matters worse it was being recorded.

A local reviewer described that night's performance like this:

"Ozzy Osbourne is the musical equivalent of the charismatic circuit preacher. Impressionable young lives are changed during his performances. Osbourne's still singing the same belligerent garbage he was five years ago. The names behind him have changed, but the music has become, if possible, simpler and more bothersome than ever before. With all due respect, Osbourne's backing trio was as efficient as these bands come. Drummer Lee Kerslake and guitarist Randy Rhoads both managed to commit suicide in tedious solos but their work elsewhere was to the point. Not that there was much of a point."

I think the review would've had actually been worse if the journalist had bothered to attend the show.

In order for us to make the Portvale concert, Sharon had to cancel the following evening's performance, July 29th, at the Civic Center in Ottawa. Instead, Sharon, the band and crew took an early morning flight from Montreal to London while Harry and I took our flight to Los Angeles. Since our flight was booked at the last minute we were crammed into the last row of the plane and made to endure all the annoyances a six-hour flight can to offer. Fortunately, Harry turned out to be an excellent traveling companion as he shared with me colorful stories of his boxing days. As an added bonus, the marriage of His Royal Highness, Prince Charles, The Prince of Wales to Lady Diana Spencer was being shown live on the in-flight television monitors. What better way to put me in the right mood for my first visit to England?

The following morning, July 30th, Harry and I fought the Los Angeles rush hour and made it to the British Embassy as the doors opened.

"Here's your document, Mr. Sarzo," said the

distinguished embassy attaché.

"It doesn't look very official, does it? Are you sure this will get me into England and then back into this country?" I inquired. "Yes, Mr. Sarzo. The document you're holding is called a reentry permit. Since you're not an American citizen and neither the U.S. or England has ties with Cuba, your citizenship status is regarded as stateless."

"You mean, I'm a man without a country?" I asked in disbelief. "Precisely, Mr. Sarzo. If I were you, I would consider applying for American Citizenship in the very near future."

"I don't know," I said, "I kind of like being a Cuban. That's who I am."

"May I warn you that with the current state of threats from hijackers, you are running a very high risk of being deported upon entering through customs in Europe without a passport," the attache cautioned.

"Well, in that case I'll definitely consider it. Thank you very much, sir, for all your help and advice." We shook hands.

Later that afternoon Harry and I took a British Airways flight bound for London. Once again we were crammed into the very last row.

I was so tired from all the flying that I didn't wake up until our plane landed at Heathrow airport the next morning. Much to my surprise I went through customs without any problems and since I was traveling with a British citizen they hardly looked at my dodgy traveling documents. When we got to the Portobello Hotel Randy and Chuck were sitting at the lobby bar.

"Hey, guys, great to see you!" I said dragging my suitcase into the lobby.

"Hey Rudes, how about a drink?" asked Chuck.

"I'll have the usual," I said.

"One Vodka tonic for my Cuban friend," Chuck told the bartender.

"So what's going on?" I asked expecting to hear good news. "Oh, you don't wanna know," Randy said in disgust as he pulled his blond bangs back.

"Ozzy's been throwing a major wobbler since the Montreal show. Chuck played him a cassette from that night on the flight here and Ozzy almost jumped off the plane." Randy lit up a cigarette. "All I hear from him is how much he hates the sound and his performance. To be honest I think it's all in his head. So if he asks your opinion just tell him that it's fine." Before I could finish my drink Ozzy came down to the lobby and dragged us up to his room to play the Montreal cassette tape.

"It's absolute rubbish! Listen to it. The band sounds awful and my voice is shot!" Ozzy raged. "Tell me Rudes, what do you think?"

"Well, I don't think it's too bad," I meekly replied.

"Oh you're fuckin' daft!" Ozzy yelled as he yanked the cassette out of the boom box. "That's it Chuck. Shelf this! I'm gonna call Sharon and schedule another live recording date." Ozzy grabbed the phone.

And just like that the Montreal live recording was shelved and not heard of again until it was released in 1987 as the Ozzy Osbourne Randy Rhoads Tribute album. I believe that the major reason the Montreal live recording was finally released was because it was the only remaining recorded work of Randy's that had not been heard by the public.

The following morning, August 31st, we traveled to Portvale to perform at the Heavy Metal Holocaust at that city's football grounds. Ironically, that afternoon we got to open up for our friends and former support act Motorhead who were the show's headliner. Before we went on stage, Lemmy came on and introduced Ozzy and the band and later Ozzy returned the favor by doing the same for Motorhead. I'll never forget the pounding of my heart as I heard 30,000 mostly male voices chanting in unison to every song we played. Another memorable moment was that of watching Motorhead during their headlining set that included parachutists jumping off a plane over the football grounds and a life-size bomber that came down from the lighting truss and hovered just inches above Lemmy's head as they performed "Ace of Spades."

A London journalist wrote of our performance:

> "Ozzy the man is a phenomenon. He sidled on stage in a purple shirt with white fringes down the arms, raised his hands and shot a brace of peace sings at the audience. Every arm in the place responded in kind and for the first time the festival really got into gear.
> Ozzy and his band played an enormously powerful set mixing in tracks from their new album " Diary of a Madman" with old Black Sabbath classics like "Iron Man". The latter was a startling piece of power driven heavy metal, completely compulsive. "Mr. Crowley", presumably a tribute to the late, great Aleister Crowley, was a chilling little tome with Randy Rhoads ripping the most extraordinary sounds from his guitar and Ozzy whirling and leaping around like a crazed frog. Finishing off the set with "Children of the Grave" Ozzy left to the reaction of the day. A minute late he was back with a piece of advice to the crowd.
> "I want you to go crazy," he shrieked. They duly obliged when he and his band lurched into "Paranoid". If there was ever a definitive heavy metal anthem this must be it, and if there ever was a better performance of "Paranoid" live or on record I'd be surprised. To put it succinctly, Ozzy is back, bigger and better than ever."

Sharon's foresight was correct, Ozzy had come home to save the day.

11
Hi, I'm Randy

In the early morning hours of August 2nd our whole entourage traveled through the quiet streets of London bound for Heathrow Airport to board the 9 a.m. Concord flight, arriving in New York's JFK Airport at 8 a.m., one hour before we left Heathrow. The extra expense of taking this supersonic flight was justified by the fact that we were starting the 2nd leg of the Blizzard of Ozz U.S. Tour that same evening in New Haven, Connecticut, and it would had been impossible to make sound check had we traveled on an average commercial airline.

During the flight, Ozzy was in a complete state of depression. After spending a few days back in England with his family, he was not ready to get back on the road. So he spent the whole flight sobbing and drinking, much to the disgust of the uppity fellow passengers who had paid a hefty sum of money for the luxury of traveling at the speed of sound. About an hour into the flight I made my way down the aircraft's narrow aisle to the lavatory area where I found Ozzy wobbling in front of the occupied toilets and pissing in the hallway. The horrified passengers nearby pretended not to notice.

After a two-hour tour bus ride from JFK, we finally arrived later that morning at New Haven's Sheraton Park Plaza in time for a much needed catnap to shake off the jetlag. When we got to our sound check at the New Haven Coliseum, Def Leppard, the new up and coming British group, was waiting anxiously to get their sound check. This U.S tour, their first, was in support of their new album, High and Dry. Randy and I made a point of greeting the excited wide-eyed young musicians.

"Hey, welcome to the tour," I said as we approached them backstage.

"Hi mates. I'm Joe the singer, this is Sav our bass player, Rick our drummer, Steve and Pete our

138

guitarists."

We all exchanged "hellos" as Joe Elliot, the lanky, baby-faced
singer introduced us to his band. They were all in their
teens and had the kind of gleam in their eyes that kids get
on their first trip to Disneyland.

"Hi, I'm Randy." He said as he stretched out his hand
to Pete Willis, the only guitarist I've ever met diminutive
enough to look Randy in the eye.

Suddenly, Pete dropped his beer and ran away
horrified.

"What was that all about?" asked Randy as he stood
with his handshake still extended.

"It's just a misunderstanding, mate." Joe laughed,
"Where we come from Randy means 'horny.' He
thought you were puttin' the make on him!"

"I better find him and explain things to him," Randy
said.

"Don't bother. He's pissed as a parrot and he ain't
gonna make any sense of it. Better wait until he's
sober."

Randy never found the right moment to clear up the
misunderstanding with Pete since the young guitarist from
Sheffield, was inebriated throughout the rest of the tour.

Up until that evening, Ozzy's pre-show dressing
room chants of "I ain't doing it!" had been sporadic. But
things quickly changed as Ozzy's state of depression got
more severe which each passing day.

The following afternoon, August 3rd, we arrived at
the Sheraton Inn in Glens Falls, New York. Later that
evening Tommy, Randy and I were riding a cab looking
for the hot spot in town to spend our night off as we ran
into Pete Willis who was alone roaming the streets. We
asked the driver to stop so we could ask Pete to join us,
but as soon as we came to a halt we saw Pete standing in
front of an office building looking as if he had picked a
fight with it. After a brief moment of disbelief, we rode

off as Pete's small, intoxicated figure challenged the massive wooden door like Don Quixote battling the windmills.

At the following evening's show, August 4th, at the Glens Falls Civic Center, I decided to feed my curiosity and see what the buzz for this young chart busting band was about.

The first thing I noticed about Def Leppard was that in comparison to Motorhead they added a considerably younger audience to our show. For a change, it was refreshing to see a sizeable amount of young females in the audience. The next thing I noticed was that the charismatic Sheffield quintet had plenty of youthful energy to grab the attention of the audience throughout their set. But musically, in spite of having a couple of major record label releases under their belts, they were still very green even by Sunset Strip band standards.

Nevertheless, Def Leppard was riding high on the crest of the New Wave of British Metal that was beginning to reach the U.S. and their alcohol-driven, sloppy and out-of-tune performances made me feel optimistic that the bands back home would sooner or later get the same recognition by the record labels. But just a couple of years later, after making a member change, Def Leppard proved me wrong. They soon became a world-class hit machine with a string of multi-platinum albums and sold out headline tours.

The next morning, August 5th, we arrived at the Howard Johnson's in Portland, Maine. That evening's show was at the Cumberland Civic Center. We always looked forward to playing at this venue and enjoying the sumptuous Maine lobster dinners served by the local caterers. When you're on the road for months at a time, especially for the road crew, it's indulgences like these that keep everyone going.

Even though Ozzy always managed somehow to pull out a good performance, it was becoming more evident with each show that his depression was taking a major toll on him. Subsequently, this forced the band, especially Randy, to pick up the slack, which most of the times was futile since Ozzy was the star of the show.

A local rock journalist wrote about that evening's performance:

> **"I liked the album a lot, but many of the nuances I liked on the album were bludgeoned into a solid, high level of noise in concert. Although there were keyboards and organs apparently on tape as no such instrument were stage. Osbourne and cohorts, guitarist Randy Rhoades, bassist Bob Daisley and drummer Lee Kerslake, opened with their best number, 'I Don't Know,' whose refrain is very ironical and seems aimed at the same people in his audience who look to him as some kind of satanic leader. The fact is Osbourne is short, appeared overweight and tended to flap his arms or clap his hands over his head constantly when not pumping out a peace sign, hardly the stuff that makes for pop idolatry."**

I really doubt that this writer bothered to attend the show by the textbook critique of Ozzy's performance and the mistaken identity of the rhythm section.

On the other hand, I believe the following writer made it all the way to the encore when he wrote,

> **"In an entirely uninspired performance before about 4,0   hard-core fans, Ozzie Osbourne and his band 'The Blizzard of Ozz,' demonstrated why heavy metal actually died with Led Zeppelin. Osbourne has failed to realize that Black Sabbath**

folded mainly because only 15-year olds are still taken in by that sort of pretentiousness. Anything he and his group do was done infinitely better a decade ago. He seems determined to hang onto a tired-out style. The young audience booed the band because of an unusually short set topped off by a five-minute encore, but considered it a much needed relief."

Late in the afternoon of August 6th we arrived at the Hilton Inn in Bangor, Maine. That evening's performance was at the 6,500 capacity venue, the Bangor Auditorium, in front a small crowd of 1,400 fans.

As the 2nd leg of the tour progressed, Ozzy's depression was beginning to strain his relationship with Sharon. She feared that Ozzy's behavior would cause the cancellation of the tour, prompting catastrophic consequences for both artist and management. One of the ways that Sharon relieved her stress was by laying down the law to the opening band's groupies backstage.

"Hello, dear, what's your name?" Sharon asked the young girl backstage who was flirting with Randy during Def Leppard's set.

"Ah, it's Stacey," she answered shyly.

"That's nice. Now Stacey, I've seen you hanging around backstage for the last couple nights. You wouldn't happen to be traveling on our crew bus, would you?" Sharon inquired.

"No. I'm traveling in Def Leppard's tour bus. I'm with Rick, their drummer," she explained.

"Good. Now do me favor and stick with your friends. I don't want to see you roaming backstage all alone. You might wind up in the wrong bus. Are we clear?" Sharon looked her straight in the eyes.

"Yes ma'am," she replied and then quickly left the backstage area.

A few weeks before, a runaway girl had been traveling on the crew bus, unbeknownst to Sharon. By the time her parents reported her disappearance to the authorities the tour had crossed the state line. When her parents found out what she was up to they contacted Sharon and demanded their daughter's immediate return. Sharon promptly obliged by covering the expenses for the girl's safe trip back home.

The following morning, August 7th, we arrived at the Marriott Inn in Providence, Rhode Island. Moments after checking in, Randy and I met in the lobby for our traditional afternoon lunch and sightseeing.

"Rand, you look like you've got something on your mind."

"I got a call from my Dad," he said. "He wants me to get together with his family and come to the show."

"So are you?" I asked.

"I don't know Rudes. I've got a lot of mixed emotions. I've got to think about it." He gazed at his burning cigarette."

That evening's show was at the Ocean State Theater in front of a half-full house. By now Def Leppard had begun to polish their show and consistently deliver high-energy performances every night. Energized by the boys, we welcomed their challenge by elevating our own performances.

After the show I sat with Randy in the back lounge of the bus. "So, did you see your Dad?" I asked.

"Yeah. You know, it wasn't as weird as I thought it would be after all."

The following two shows, August 8th at Music Mountain in South Fallsburg, New York and August 9th at the Cape Cod Coliseum in South Yarmouth, Massachusetts went without any significant incidents.

On August 10th Sharon decided to cheer Ozzy up by taking the band sailing. The young, hospitable boat captain greeted us as Sharon, Ozzy, Randy and I boarded the fifty-foot schooner. It was a picture-perfect mid summer's day as we sailed the waters off the coast of Massachusetts. I hadn't seen Ozzy so happy since our return from England as he cavorted with Randy around the boat and even took a turn behind the ship's steering wheel. This was a welcomed relief from all the tension that had been building lately between Ozzy and Sharon.

The August 11th Stanley Theater in Pittsburgh, Pennsylvania show and the August 12th performance at the War Memorial Auditorium in Utica, New York were two of the most outstanding performances of the tour's second leg as an invigorated Ozzy unleashed his raging energy onstage. It was great to see him back in top form.

The August 13th performance at the Broome County Arena in Binghamton, New York was cancelled at the last minute. Sharon quickly made plans to check us into the Parker Meridien Hotel in New York City for a full day of fun and frolic in the Big Apple.

The following evening's show, August 14th, at the Nassau Coliseum in Uniondale, Long Island was one of the most chaotic shows I've ever been involved in. Sharon had been at odds for a while with TASCO, the company that supplied our tour's sound equipment, so that afternoon she decided to flex her muscle by firing them and hiring another sound company from Canada. When Def Leppard, the opening act on that night's triple bill, started their show it was evident that the Canadian sound company was not equipped to deliver the thunderous heavy metal British sound that TASCO was known for.

A couple of songs into the openers' set Ozzy panicked and pleaded with Sharon to rehire TASCO who's crew chief was backstage packing up their gear into the semis to transport it back to Los Angeles.

During the Joe Perry Project set, the middle act of the evening, Sharon reached an agreement with TASCO's crew chief and re-hired them and fired the Canadian sound company on the spot. So the confused audience got to watch the Canadian's sound equipment being replaced by TASCO's gear during the break between Joe Perry's and our set. This pushed our show a couple of hours back and added the costly extra expense of the local union's stagehands load-out overtime. Nevertheless, in the end everybody was happy as we got TASCO's earsplitting audio system restored and Sharon got to show everyone just who was in charge.

On August 15th we performed at the legendary Convention Center in Asbury Park, New Jersey. During the particular weekend, from the 14th-15th, the concert that was recorded at the Music Hall in Cleveland on May 11th, 1981 for the Source Network was broadcasted on more than 200 radio stations throughout the country. So after our sound check Randy and I went for a stroll on the nearby boardwalk and were pleasantly surprised at the number of fans who had already heard our live broadcasts on the radio and were anticipating the same kind of high energy performance that evening.

The following morning, August 16th, we had a most welcomed early check in at the Hilton in Baltimore, Maryland as we still hadn't quite recovered from the late show a couple of nights before at the Nassau Coliseum. After all, the coffin-like bunks in the tour bus are no substitute for a good night's sleep in a comfortable bed.

That evening's performance was at the Merriweather Post Pavilion in nearby Columbia, Maryland. At sound check I was surprised to see that the venue was still under construction. My biggest concern was that the unfinished roof might have not been able to support our lighting rig. Needless to say I spent most of the show looking up at the ceiling making sure nothing fell on us.

The following day, August 17th, we spent most of our day off at the majestic beachfront Cavalier Hotel, in Norfolk, Virginia. Sharon's opulent upbringing gave her a craving for the finer things in life, especially on the road.

During my time with the band I got spoiled by a lifestyle I had only dreamed of, compliments of Sharon and Ozzy.

On August 18th, we performed at the intimate former vaudevillian palace, the Premier Theater in Norfolk. Booking heavy metal acts into larger venues remained a tough sell for promoters and we continued to perform in 2,000 seaters like this one to keep the tour going. Things starting changing a couple of years later when MTV at last began airing heavy metal videos, almost exclusively.

A local rock reviewer with an insight on the touring situation at that time wrote of the night's performance:

"While albums by groups like AC/DC sell like hotcakes, attendance at the slugfest like the one at the Premier Theatre Tuesday night continues to dwindle.
A few short years back the show would have been in a large hall. Ozzy himself hasn't changed a bit since the halcyon days of Black Sabbath in the late '60s and early 70's. In fact, his image is such that if he ever took off his fringed jacket, nobody would recognize him. Lead guitarist, Randy Rhoads wowed the crowd with his fiery runs. He quickly showed why he's been hailed as a new superstar in guitar circles. Drummer Tommy Aldridge poured it on during his solo as he pitched his drumsticks into the audience to finish off his stunning display by playing with his hands. Rudy Sarzo used his open palm as a slide providing a thundering bottom throughout the entire set. Tied together the Blizzard came near to an enclosed sonic boom."

On August 19th, we had a late afternoon check-out

from the Cavalier Hotel and rode our tour bus straight to Indiana since that evening's show at the 11,000 capacity Civic Center in Roanoke, Virginia, was cancelled at the last minute.

The next morning, August 20th, we arrived at the Ramada in Evansville, Indiana to spend another lazy summer day off. By now Randy and I were getting pretty bored with our daily sightseeing excursions so we decided to give our trips to the local malls a rest and concentrate on our poolside tanning. In retrospect, our daily tour routines were quite trivial in comparison to what we are now able to accomplish in the today's high tech era. (Today, Randy would've been in his hotel room composing music on his laptop.) That evening we got to hobnob at the bar with the members of Def Leppard while both our road crews took over the Ramada piano lounge.

"I got to be honest," I said to Joe as our band joined Def Leppard at their table. "You guys have really improved since the first night of the tour."

"Well, cheers, mate!" Joe held up his beer and smiled. "You know, it's our first trip to the States and that night we were really scared. But we've been watching you guys and we've picked up a couple of things here and there."

"You guys are definitely quick learners," I said, raising my glass. "You've really given us a kick in the butt."

"Thanks, but we still have some member's issues we need to resolve, " Joe said as he looked over at Pete, his guitarist, who was passed out with his head on the table. "But we'll deal with that before we go in the studio for our next record."

On August 21st we performed at the Mesker Music Theater in Evansville, Indiana. The 6,000 capacity venue looked even emptier as the 2,800 fans attendance crowded the stage to get a closer view of the show.

The following morning, August 22nd, we arrived at

the Whitehall Hotel in midtown Chicago. In contrast to the previous night's performance, that evening's Poplar Creek show was a near sellout with 6,863 in attendance. It was becoming obvious that the band was most popular in metropolitan areas. This was a circumstance Sharon did not ignore when the following U.S. tour dates were booked.

Early the next day, August 23rd, Ozzy celebrated the previous evening's near sell-out show with a shopping spree at Chicago's posh Water Tower Plaza.

"What the fuck does he have on?" Tommy shouted as he spotted Ozzy approaching the bus wearing a Buffalo hide winter coat in the middle of a sweltering Chicago afternoon.

"What do you guys think? Doesn't he look handsome?" Sharon asked as they both climbed aboard the bus.

"And look at the watch she bought me," Ozzy said as he flashed a diamond encrusted solid gold Rolex. "I saw it on the jewelry store window and it had Ozzy written all over it," Sharon said with a smile.

The high-spirited mood carried over into that evening's performance before the biggest crowd of our headlining tour at the Alpine Valley Music Theater near Milwaukee, Wisconsin.

A local rock reviewer wrote:

"Few rock performers are able to send an audience to its feet before uttering one note; the former lead singer for Black Sabbath had no trouble in doing so with the more than 13,500 fans and that was before the curtain went up."

The morning of August 24th we arrived at the Ramada in Green Bay, Wisconsin. That evening's performance at the Brown County Arena before a nearly full house benefited from the afterglow of the previous shows as the band put on another solid performance. Randy, Tommy and I always took advantage of the good mood factor since we knew that things could change as quickly as the English weather.

A local journalist wrote.

> **"The Blizzard of Ozzy Osbourne isn't a snow job.**
> **Osbourne's not the wild man he used to be or is still supposed to be but his show is exciting enough, what with the talents of the three other members of his band. Randy Rhoads on guitar has flying fingers and real talent, while Rudy Sarzo on bass shows a fancy style, playing over and under the guitar neck. Tommy Aldridge, sitting like a king on a throne of drums and cymbals, probably drew the most response, especially when he tossed his sticks into the crowd and played a solo with his hands."**

On the morning of August 25th we checked into the Ramada in Davenport, Iowa. That evening's show was at Palmer College before a near capacity crowd of 4,150.

The local rock critic wrote:

> **"The master of cemetery heavy metal is back with a new band, the Blizzard of Ozz, which unleashed its fury on a packed house at Palmer Auditorium this week. Ozzy's new band features the bassist and guitarist from Quiet Riot, an obscure Los Angeles outfit which was starving along with every other band on the Strip until the Blizzard of Ozz**

happened. The bass player constantly amazed the audience by playing with his left hand over the neck of his guitar as well as with the traditional underhanded approach, while an array of fancy guitars provided screaming harmonics from his lead man. On drums was Tommy Aldridge, one of the most important rock drummers today.

The following day, we remained at the Davenport Ramada to spend a relatively quiet day off in the Quad Cities area.

On the afternoon August 27th we checked into the Holiday Inn in Ft. Wayne, Indiana. Before our evening's performance at the Foellenger Theatre there were major storms brewing in our dressing room as Ozzy and Sharon battled over issues regarding the following night's rescheduled live recording. In an attempt to show Sharon how he felt about the situation, Ozzy bit into his new Rolex watch and crushed it between his teeth. That night Ozzy went on stage with chunks of diamonds stuck between his teeth, producing a banshee like whistle every time he sang.

The next morning, August 28th, we arrived at the Hilton in Indianapolis, Indiana. That evening's show was the shabby Circle Theater in downtown Indianapolis. Ironically, we were more excited about going to see the Jackson 5 perform that evening at the nearby Market Square Arena than we were about re-recording our own live broadcast. We pushed our showtime forward and blazed through the set so we could at least catch the last few songs of their set. Sharon's main motivation for seeing the Jacksons was to go and see what their stage production was like since she was already thinking ahead about the Diary of a Madman tour.

Immediately after our show, still wearing our stage clothes, we ran across the street to the back entrance of the Market Square arena where the Jackson's tour manager waited for us. I stood in awe as we watched their lavish production from the side of the stage.

"What's all the bloody rubbish on stage!" Ozzy yelled at Sharon as giant mechanical spiders crawled across the Jackson's stage.

"Oh, Ozzy, this is the kind of stuff kids eat up," Sharon insisted. "You can't expect to reach this level of success by just going out there wearing your silly white fringed shirts and your peace signs."

After the Jackson's last number the house lights went up to reveal an empty stage.

"That was brilliant!" Sharon said. "Ozzy, next tour there will be no encores. We'll just do our show and then fuck off."

"For fuck's sake, Sharon, we've got to do a bloody encore. It's tradition!" Ozzy maintained.

"No," said Sharon, "we'll be the ones to educate our audience. After all it's already the '80s and we can't keep doing the same old thing over and over."

During our after-show bus ride Ozzy was back to his usual sulking and boozing as he sat alone in the front lounge staring out at the open road. After a short trip to nearby South Bend, Indiana, we checked into the American Inn at 2 a.m. As I lay in my bed I heard a rumble coming from the hallway outside my door. I quickly got up and cautiously opened my door with the security chain fastened and saw Ozzy with his hands firmly wrapped around Sharon's neck choking her.

"Harry! Harry! Hit 'im!" Sharon barely uttered while gasping between breaths.

Suddenly Harry stood in front of Ozzy and delivered an upper cut to his nose. Stunned by the blow, Ozzy immediately loosened his grip on her neck and staggered down the hallway towards the elevators.

"Get me a cab, I've been mugged!" Ozzy yelled at the confused hotel clerk as blood poured from his swollen nose down his shirt, while Mr. Pook followed him out of the elevator barking and peeing on the lobby carpet.

The next morning, August 29th, I got a call from Sharon to come to her room for an emergency band meeting.

"I guess you boys heard what happened last night," she said.

"Are you kidding? I thought a war broke out outside my room," Tommy quipped.

"Well, it did," Sharon said solemnly. "Anyways, afterwards Ozzy took a cab to the venue and spent the night with the crew drinking and doing blow. And now he's threatening to go home.
I don't even know if he can do the show tonight with a busted up nose." Sharon brooded about the situation. "I guess we'll find out when we get to sound check."

"What about Harry?" Randy asked.

"I had no choice but to send him home," said Sharon, regretfully. "I'm afraid Ozzy might kill him in his sleep."

When we got to sound check Ozzy refused to leave the tour bus and remained there right up until show time. That night the tension backstage at the Morris Civic Auditorium was soaring as we waited for our intro cues to go onstage.

Everything seemed to be normal as we charged into our first song, "I Don't Know." But when we got to the solo, Ozzy ran off stage towards the wings where Sharon was watching. Next thing I see is Sharon beating the living daylights out of Ozzy while stagehands, crewmembers and Def Leppard watched in amazement.

"You get your bloody ass back on stage right now or I'm going to fuckin' kill you!" Sharon emphasized each of her words with a flurry of body blows.

As the guitar solo section ended, there was no sign of Ozzy anywhere so we just continued playing the song without vocals. As soon as the song ended, Randy, Tommy and I looked at each other not knowing what to do next. A few seconds later I followed Randy's lead and walked behind my back line and waited. All of a sudden, I could hear the sold-out crowd getting boisterous and infuriated by the unusual situation.

"Sorry, but I had to take a shit!" Ozzy yelled into the mike, as he appeared out of nowhere reversing the boos from the crowd into cheers. "Believer!'" Ozzy yelled into the mike as Randy, Tommy and I quickly got back onstage and continued with our show as if nothing had happened.

12
But the Singer I'm Not Sure

The morning of August 30th we arrived at the Hilton in Grand Rapids, Michigan. The previous night's bus ride had been an eerily quiet one. Everyone tried to avoid getting in Ozzy and Sharon's line of fire. Fortunately, Ozzy was so exhausted from the events of the last 24 hours that he went straight from the stage into his bunk.

During the bus ride to sound check Ozzy kept nodding out on the front lounge.

"Oh, my God. Look at Ozzy's nose," Sharon whispered to me as we sat across from him. "It's all crooked. I think Harry broke it. Just don't tell him. You know what a big hypochondriac he is."

That evening's performance was at the Civic Center in front of an over-sold crowd of 5,600. In contrast to the previous evening's performance everything went smooth with the exception of a couple of Ozzy's failed attempts to execute some of the more challenging vocal lines.

A local rock reviewer wrote of that evening's performance,

"If Osbourne is the lifeblood of the band, then Aldridge sure is its heartbeat. Randy Rhoads whipped the crowd into frenzy with his fiendish guitar playing and Rudy Sarzo was a whirling dervish on bass. The trio sounded so good alone, they should have told Osbourne to take his wing-like costume and fly away."

About an hour into our after-show bus ride I went in the dimly lit front lounge to get a drink out of the fridge and found Ozzy sitting all by himself staring into space with a half empty bottle of scotch on his lap. He looked painfully lonely and in need of someone to talk to. "Hey

Ozz, that was a good show tonight," I said as I tried to cheer him up.

"It was bloody crap," he snapped. "My nose hurts every time I reach for a high note. I think the bastard broke it." He took another swig of scotch. "You know, Rudes, I've been on the road since I was 18 bloody years old. You know what that means? It means I never get to see my missus. I never get to see my kids. The few bloody times that I go home they hardly even know me. I'm like a bloody stranger in my own home. And all for what? So I can keep doing these bloody tours over and over again until the day I drop fuckin' dead!?"

"But isn't this what you've always wanted? You know, being a rock star?" I asked.

"When we put Sabbath together all we wanted to do is find a way out. We didn't want to spend our lives slaving at the same factories and doing the same miserable jobs like our old men did. You wanna know the fuckin' truth, man? I started singing in a rock band so I could be free, but at the end of the day I'm still a fuckin' slave. I've been a bloody slave from the first day I played with Sabbath." Ozzy paused to light a cigarette. "We went on the road for months playing all arenas and stadiums but by the time we got home we were broke. The roadies made more money than the band. So the next day I went to our bloody manager's office to find out what the fuck happened to our money. So the arrogant cunt gives me some bloody excuse that the profits got pissed away on tour expenses." Ozzy took another long swig. "I was so pissed, Rudes, I was ready to jump over his desk and kick the living shit out off him when he pulled out a set of keys from his pocket and threw them at me." Ozzy continued as he mocked his former manager. "Here are the keys to my Rolls Royce. That should even things out. I wanted to shove the fuckin' keys down his throat but I knew this was all I was gonna get out of the fuckin' bastard. So I just turned and walked away. A few months later when I got my next record royalty statement I found out that the crooked bastard had taken the cost of the Rolls out of my royalty check!" Ozzy was furious as he took another long swig.

"So you must feel better now that Sharon's managing you," I said as I tried to be positive.

"I'm not worried about Sharon. I trust her. I know she means well. It's her old man I'm worried about and at the end of the day he's the one who calls the shots."

"You must be looking forward to the end of the tour in a couple of weeks. Bet you can't wait to get back home and spend time with the family," I said.

"Let me tell you what it's gonna be like, man," he said. "As soon as I walk in through the door my wife is going to yell at me." Ozzy gets up, puts his hands on his hips and mocks his wife. 'John, you'd better leave Ozzy at the door before you come in.' Ozzy laughs as the bus hits a bump on the road and he falls back on the couch. "When I'm home all I want to do is spend time with my missus, Thelma, and my kids, Elliot, Jessica and Louis. Then during pub hours I'll go and hang at our pub. You know I got my own pub, problem is that I drink more than I sell!"

Ozzy joked. "You've got to come down to the pub one of these days. You'll have a blast. We'll hang out with old farmers from my village in Staffordshire and get pissed." You've got to meet my best friend. A while ago he got caught stealing cats for lab animal testing. Now he sells vegetables on the side of the road." Through all my years of touring I've come to realize that you don't really know your band mates until you've spent at least one tour with them on a tour bus. I walked away from that candid conversation with a whole different perspective on him. I finally got a glimpse of the real John Osbourne.

The following morning, August 31st, we checked into the Hilton in Clarkston, Michigan. That evening's performance was at the Pine Knob Music Theater in front of a sold-out crowd. It's always a magical feeling when you perform outdoors in front of a great crowd and the summer breeze rolls through the amphitheatre onto the stage to cool you down.

A reviewer of that evening's performance went like this:

> **"The entire hour-long set resembled a crazed Satan cult-worshipping session. On top of its chairs from the outset, people literally were climbing over chairs and other to get a better view of almost demonic former black Sabbath front man. Musically, Osbourne's set was one miserable, deafening song after another with many guitar chords barely discernible. His shrieking voice was hardly audible above the noise, which almost made Van Halen sound tame by comparison."**

We spent our next day off in Troy, Michigan. By now we had performed a couple of very successful shows and the tension between Ozzy and Sharon seemed to be slowly dissipating, so before the mood changed I decided to ask Sharon for the raise she had promised when I first joined the band.

"Hi, Sharon, can I talk to you for a moment?" I asked as I entered her suite.

"What's up?"

"Well, do you remember the raise you promised me once the tour got going and —?"

She looked at me and smiled.

"I'm sorry Rudy. Things have just been so bloody

insane around here that I forgot all about it. Tell you what I'll do it. You'll get your raise effective immediately and to make it up to you we'll keep you on retainer during the upcoming break. How's that?" "Great! Thanks, I really appreciate it." I replied.

From that day on, I no longer needed to ask for raises. Sharon continued to give me unexpected raises throughout our subsequent tours.

The following shows—September 2nd, at the Prairie Capital Convention Center in Springfield, Illinois; September 3rd at the Orpheum in Memphis, Tennessee; September 4th at the Fox Theater in Atlanta, Georgia and September 5th at the Cumberland County Memorial Auditorium in Fayetteville, North Carolina—went smooth with no major incidents, since we were nearing the end of the tour and everyone was in their best behavior, just looking forward to going home.

The September 6th performance at the Park Center in Charlottesville, North Carolina was cancelled. So after our performance in Fayetteville we drove to Columbus to spend our next couple days at the local Holiday Inn.

The September 8th performance at the Columbus Municipal Auditorium was in front of another near sell-out crowd of 4,500. Even though we had been playing the same Midwestern markets for nearly six months it was evident by the solid attendance that the band was finally gaining a strong following.

On the morning of September 9th we arrived at the Hilton in Tampa, Florida. After the sound check for that evening's show at the Curtis-Hixton Hall, Sharon asked Randy, Tommy and me to meet her in our dressing room.

"Now boys, there's a British DJ named Jonathan King that's coming to the show tonight. He's going to interview Ozzy before the show and then he's going to review the show.

Tonight looks like it's going to be a fairly light house

and Ozzy's really nervous that Jonathan's going to see him perform in front of a such small crowd after years of seeing him perform sold-out shows with Sabbath. So please try to put on the best show you can. If Ozzy sees you boys trying extra hard then he'll get into it too and forget that Jonathan's watching." We all reassured Sharon and promised to do our best.

As it turned out, Ozzy's pre-show interview with the DJ turned into a pub crawl and by the time we were on the DJ had passed out backstage, another unwitting victim of Ozzy's boozing.

On the afternoon of September 10th we arrived at the Holiday Inn Sunshine Parkway Hotel in Fort Pierce, Florida. That evening's show was at the St. Lucie County Civic Center in front of 1,533 fans in a venue that held 5,200. This type of low attendance was not unusual in South Florida, were most arena rock bands came to begin or end their tour since the nearby shipping docks provided a cost effective mode of transporting the equipment to Europe. Also, local arenas such as the Hollywood Sporatorium offered tantalizing deals for headlining acts that wished to combine their pre-production rehearsals with some fun in the sun.

After the show we drove for a couple of hours across South Florida's Alligator Alley and arrived at Fort Lauderdale's Marriot Hotel in time for Randy and I to hit the late-night club scene. Randy had never been to Florida before and by the time we got to Fort Lauderdale he was smitten by the Sunshine State's lifestyle.

"Rand, welcome to my country!" I joked as our cab dropped us in front of a club lined with beautiful girls waiting to get in. The bouncer immediately recognized me and let us in. "I used to play in the house band here before I moved to LA."

"Wow, she's a looker!" I said to Randy as we approached the prettiest girl in the room. Let's see if she's got some friends." I introduced us. "Hi, I'm Rudy and this is Randy "Aren't you that guitar playing fellow from the old Black Sabbath singer's band?" she asked Randy with a sweet southern accent.

"Yeah, that would be me," Randy answered while I pondered the possibilities our celebrity status brought with it.

"My boyfriend loves your record! He's a guitarist and that's all he listens to," she said, as my anticipations quickly deflated. "How would you like to come over to our place? He's been having a tough time trying to find a band to play with. Meeting you would really cheer him up," she explained.

"Sure, I'll come over," Randy answered as he looked at me too embarrassed to decline.

"Rand, you just can't go to some stranger's house in the middle of the night," I warned him, pulling him aside. "This is Florida. People disappear from here all the time."

"Well, why don't you come with me then? After all, this place's not really my scene. I'd just rather spend a few quiet hours at someone's house."

When we pull into the driveway of the young couple's home we could hear Blizzard of Ozz blasting from inside the house. As you'd expect, the struggling young local guitarist almost passed out when Randy entered the modest living room. I could see in Randy's face how comfortable he felt in the relaxed surroundings as he talked about music and showed the young guitarist a few of his techniques until dawn.

Personally, the September 11th performance at the Sunrise Theater was a special occasion. This was the first of two near sell-out nights in the place where I grew up dreaming of someday playing in a band like this. But most important, it was the first time my parents saw me perform with the band.

Upon arriving at the backstage area with my parents I ran into the members of Def Leppard, their painfully sun burnt torsos smeared with aloe vera.

"Don't say a word!" Joe cracked before I could ask what happened. "We went on a fishing trip early this morning and our boat's engine broke down. It took hours before the Coast Guard came and towed us in."

"Is it as painful as it looks?" I asked.

"Bloody worse, mate, bloody worse!"

Right before show time I escorted my parents to the safest place I could find in the venue, right next to the monitor board. As I watched their faces I was convinced that our spectacular light show and the great musicianship of my band mates had surely impressed them.

"So what did you both think of the show?" I asked them later in the catering room.

"Well, I really liked the guitar player," my mother said in Spanish, amazing me with her keen observation. "He had a good tone. I could hear everything he played perfectly. He did a well-structured solo and moved very well onstage. The drummer was very animated during the show and I especially liked the part in the drum solo where he played with his hands. You played and moved well. But the singer, I'm not sure." She shook her head. "He was out of tune all night and didn't have any moves. He just looked lost on stage."

"Well, Mom, that's part of Ozzy's charm," I said, as she shrugged her shoulders and glanced over at my dad who was busy eating a snack from the dessert bar."

The following day, September 12th, my folks and I spent most of the time hanging out by the Marriot Hotel pool along with Randy and Tommy. Much to my surprise Randy felt at home in Florida and told to me that of all the places he had visited in the U.S., south Florida was his favorite.

That evening we did our second consecutive

161

performance at the Sunrise Theater. Besides the May 2nd performance at the Palladium in New York, these south Florida performances were the only other multiple show dates. Though the show was not a near sell-out like the previous night, the 2,700 fans in attendance turned out to be one of the most frantic crowds of the tour. I had the extra-added fulfillment of having my best friends from Miami, Abbey and Sergio, watch the show from behind my amp line as they made funny faces and tried their best to distract me.

The following morning, we arrived at the Hilton in Daytona, Florida. After a quick check-in we took a two-hour bus ride to Disneyworld to do a photo shoot with Ross Halfin, a jovial and talented British photographer that had been traveling during the tour so often with us that we considered him a member of the group. During the trip Ross took candid photos such as me giving Randy a hair trim and Ozzy fooling around while getting ready for the photo shoot.

When we got to Disneyworld on that Sunday afternoon the place was packed with tourists. Most of them didn't recognize us except for a few sailors on shore leave that happened to be fans of Ozzy from his Black Sabbath days. As we moved around the crowded amusement park I was not aware that the band photo on the inner sleeve of the Diary of a Madman record would come from this photo shoot. Through the years this inner sleeve photo has been the cause of much confusion among the fans since the album credits were written in an ancient Druid language. To set the record straight, even though Tommy and I are pictured on the inner sleeve, Bob and Lee made the record along with Randy and Ozzy before Tommy and I joined the band.

That evening's performance, the last show of the Blizzard of Ozz tour, was at the Peabody Auditorium in Daytona Beach in front of 2,560. The last show of any tour is always a bittersweet occasion. On one hand you're happy because you're going home, and if the tour is successful, you get to reap the rewards that performing in front of thousands of fans can bring. On the other hand, as this was my very first tour, added with all the great memories I got to share with Randy, Ozzy, Sharon, Tommy, Motorhead, Def Leppard and our crew, I just wished it would never end. But then, all good things must. I chose to look forward to the Diary of a Madman tour coming up in just a few weeks.

On the morning of September 14th the band and crew boarded our flights from Orlando bound for our respective destinations; mine was back to Los Angeles to spend four out of our six weeks off at the Oakwood Apartments in Studio City. Besides getting together with Randy on a couple of occasions I really didn't get to hang out with him that much during the break. I knew how important his private life was and after spending months on the road with him I wanted to respect his privacy.

Towards the end of the tour all I heard him say was how much he was looking forward to staying at home with Jody, playing with his Z trains and ordering Chinese takeout.

Upon arriving in Los Angeles, one of the first items on my agenda was to collect my paycheck from Jet Records, just as Sharon had promised.

"Good afternoon, Jet Records, may I help you?" The receptionist answered.

"Hi this is Rudy, Ozzy's bass player. I'm supposed to drop by and pick up a paycheck," I said.

"Hold on a moment, please." Muzak played over the phone. "Rudy, Don wants to talk to you. He's available this afternoon." "OK," I answered, "I'll be over." During my time with the band I had heard some horrific stories about Don's negotiating tactics so I knew this was not a good thing.

"Rudy have a seat," Don said, as he stood behind a massive desk in his plush office. The walls were covered with platinum records from his most successful bands, Electric Light Orchestra and Air Supply. "Now, what's this I hear that you're supposed to pick up a pay check?" I can't pay you while you're off the road. I've never paid any musician for not working."

"But Don, Sharon promised me I was going to get paid during the break." I cautiously stated my case.

Suddenly Don's eyes started blinking real fast, I thought they were going to pop out as he turned red and clenched his fist.

"Listen to me. I don't care about what my daughter has promised you. I call the shots around here and if you don't work, you don't get paid. Do I make myself clear?" Don pounded his desk for emphasis. I left before someone hung me over Benedict Canyon by my ankles.

One cool September evening I went over to the Florentine Gardens, a club in Hollywood, to see Kevin perform with his band DuBrow. After the show, Kevin invited me to a party in the Doheny Estates, an exclusive Hollywood Hills neighborhood. I couldn't believe my eyes when I walked in through the door and saw so many beautiful women. It seemed like every girl I saw was more beautiful than the previous.

I was standing in the garden having a casual conversation with one of the members of Kevin's band, when suddenly she walked by. There've been a few moments in my life that will be forever etched in my memory: leaving Cuba, my first onstage performance with Randy, Ozzy and Tommy, and the first time I saw the love of my life. She looked like she had stepped out of a Beach Boys' song with her surfer girl long blonde hair and tanned silky skin.

"Hi I'm Rudy, what's your name?"

"Rebecca," she said with an attitude that exuded fire

and ice. As I got lost in her green eyes during our conversation I failed to realize that the party was over, so I invited her to join me for breakfast.

"Can I borrow some change? I need to call my mom," she said as I quickly handed her all the coins in my pocket. I thought for sure that she was coming home with me. What other reason would she have to call her Mom at this late hour?

"Thanks for breakfast. I'd better get home," she said returning to our table.

"Is everything all right?"

"Everything's fine," she said. "It's just that I live with my mom
and I don't like to leave her alone."

Those words sealed it for me. Not only was she beautiful but she also had old-fashioned family values, truly a rare combination in such a hedonist town. I knew in my heart we'd be seeing a lot of each other soon.

A few days later I went to a music store and purchased an all maple Fretless Fender Precision bass guitar that I got to play on stage for the following tour. The honey blond finish of the bass reminded me of Rebecca's hair so I nicknamed it "Becky." Was I smitten or what?

One afternoon I got a call from Sharon telling me she had a surprise and to come by the office to pick it up. The first thing that came to my mind was that somehow she had talked Don into giving me the check she had promised.

"Hi, Rudy! Come in, come in. I've got a surprise for you."

Sharon said,

"Here it is. Isn't it amazing!" she handed me a hefty black leather bound book with the title Ozzy Osbourne, Blizzard of Ozz Tour, 1981 inscribed in red and my name under it in gold letters.

"What is it?" I asked as I held the book.

"It's your life for the past six months. Go ahead, open it up. It has all the itineraries, reviews and interviews from the whole tour. Our publicist Michael Jensen worked very hard putting it together." Sharon was beaming with pride.

And she had every reason to since she was the glue that kept the tour together. On the other hand, I stood there looking through the pages of the book, forcing a smile and filled with disappointment that I hadn't gotten the check I'd hoped for. Little did I realize that afternoon that the book she gave me would soon become one of my most prized possessions.

On October 11th I left Los Angeles to spend a week with my parents in Miami before heading out to England to commence the European leg of the Diary of a Madman Tour.

A few days before I left Miami I received a call from Sharon. "Rudy, there's a call from you," my mother said handing me the phone. "It sounds like a little girl." It was Sharon.

"Hi, it's me," she said. "I just want to make sure everything's all right and you're ready to go to England."

"Oh yeah, I can't wait to get back on the road. By the way, am I going to be able to travel through all of Europe with my re-entry permit?" I asked.

"Oh yeah, I asked legal and they said that if you didn't have problems getting into England then you should be all right elsewhere." As I hung up the phone little did I realize what troubles lay ahead.

13
I'm a Bloody Guest in Your Hotel!

On the morning of October 20th, I arrived at London's Heathrow Airport after a grueling ten-hour flight from Miami. When I reached customs I handed my travel document to the agent.

"May I see your passport, sir?" asked the stoic agent.

"That's the only travel document I have," I explained.

"Sir, this is a re-entry permit with the sole purpose of allowing you re-entry to the United States. You need a visa and a valid passport to enter the United Kingdom. Please come with me."

I followed him to a private room flanked by armed guards.

"You only get one phone call to sort out your situation." He handed me the phone.

I fumbled through my wallet looking for Sharon's contact phone numbers.

"Jet Records, how may I direct your call?" answered the operator.

"Oh, hi, this is Rudy, the bass player in Ozzy's band. Is Sharon in the office?" I asked.

"Please hold." The muzak played for a few moments.

"Rudy, where are you?" asked Sharon.

"I'm being detained at customs. The agent says I can't get into the country without a visa and a passport."

"Don't worry," she said. "Jake's at the airport right now with your work permits and visa. I'll page him and let him know that you're being detained at customs. He'll get it all sorted out for you. Just sit tight."

"Oh don't worry, I'm not going anywhere," I said as I watched the armed guard's silhouette through the glass door.

While I waited for a couple of hours in the detention room I couldn't help thinking about what happened to Randy when he first went through British customs a couple of years earlier. The dreadful thought of being deported or even worse, sent back to Cuba, rushed through my mind.

"Everything's in order, Mr. Sarzo," the agent announced. "You can go now."

After finally clearing customs I made my way to the main terminal where a pale, slender young man approached me.

"Mr. Sarzo, I presume?" He smiled and helped me with my luggage. "I'm Jake Duncan, your tour manager." He introduced himself with a thick Scottish accent. "Let me tell you. I had to pull some heavy strings to get you in. They rarely come across travel documents like yours. Fortunately, I know a few people at customs, otherwise you'd be on your way home right now."

"Home's not where I dread going back to, Jake," I said feeling relieved.

As Jake drove through the picturesque streets of London I was filled with the anticipation of finally spending a few weeks in England and experiencing the musically open-minded culture that spawned most of my rock heroes. Through the years I found it ironic that while British artists like Led Zeppelin, the Rolling Stones and Cream where influence by American blues artists, most rock musicians from my generation living in America got exposed to the blues by these and other hard-rocking, larger-than-life British bands that invaded our shores during the '60s and '70s. With time I came to realize that the American blues embraced by my rock heroes and the Afro-Cuban music that made up the soundtrack of my childhood came from the same musical cradle, Africa.

During the 1500's, the slaves in the Caribbean were allowed to play their native percussion instruments and perform their polyrhythmic music by their Spanish masters. On the other hand, the Anglo plantation owners in America did not allow the slaves to play anything for fear that they would use the African drums to communicate among the neighboring plantations and spark uprisings. Out of the need to express their misery, the slaves of the American South chanted their laments while working in the cotton fields, giving birth to the blues. In the early 1900's, the acoustic guitar became synonymous with the blues as it delivered eerie melodic counterpoints and syncopated rhythms while in the hands of the great blues pioneers.

In the late 1950s and the early 1960s, records by American blues artists such as Willie Dixon, Howlin' Wolf, Muddy Waters and the legendary Robert Johnson started making their way to the English shores as most young British rock musicians eagerly embraced their visceral sounds. Covers of these blues classics can be found on most of the British Invasion icons' early recordings.

It was with this kind of traditionally British musical open mindedness that Ozzy embraced Randy's genius and gave him the freedom to explore his musical prowess. Like Jimi Hendrix a decade before, it wasn't until Randy arrived in England and underwent a musical and image makeover, that he emerged as one of the most revered rock guitar heroes of his generation.

"Here we are laddie, your home away from home, at least for the next few days," Jake quipped as we arrived at the Shepperton Moat House Hotel situated on the banks of the River Thames.

While Jake checked me in I cruised over to the lounge looking for some familiar faces.

"Hey Rudes, you finally made it!" Randy greeted me as he sat alone at a table sipping an iced tea.

"Actually, I should've been here sooner but I was detained at customs for a couple of hours," I explained as we shook hands. "Yeah, I know the feeling! Just be glad they didn't send you back." He snickered as I joined him at the table.

"How's Ozzy?" I asked. "Well, it seems that during the break things didn't go well between him and Thelma. He's been on a major wobbler ever since he got here."

"Have you seen him today?" I asked.

"Wait." Randy checked his watch. "It's not pub hours yet so he must be passed out in his room."

The following afternoon, October 21st, we began a full week's rehearsal at nearby Shepperton studios in preparation for the European Diary of a Madman Tour.

I was familiar with the rich film history of the studio but I was most impressed with the fact that many of the British rock elite had taken advantage of the spacious facilities to rehearse their full-scale productions. As I walked into Stage D I could barely contain myself with the thought of the Who rehearsing and filming such legendary projects as "Quadrophenia" and the "The Kid's Are Alright" within the heavily soundproofed walls.

The overall atmosphere at rehearsals was laid back as the mostly English crew felt comfortable getting into the groove of being home. The rehearsal schedule was based on the "pub hours." While the pubs were open early in the afternoon, the band and crew would take a break and have a couple of pints of beer and the traditional cucumber sandwiches. Later in the afternoon when the pubs closed, we all went back to work. A few hours later when our roadies' wristwatch alarms went off and the pubs reopened, we would end our rehearsals and head back to the pub until closing time.

Another British tradition I quickly embraced was Indian cuisine. I'll never forget the sight of our road crew spreading on top of our road cases greasy brown paper bags containing the most delicious onion bhajis, samosas and other spicy delicacies.

Another of the aspects I enjoyed about being in Britain was the socializing. A major cultural difference between Britain and America, was that unlike the U.S., with it's numerous choices of radio and television programs reaching every household, England's early '80's radio stations were limited to the government-operated BBC1, BBC2 and Radio 1. Besides these three, there were a few pirate radio stations that broadcasted underground programming from motor vehicles and small ships off the coast while avoiding the authorities.

Television programming was also limited. As I spent more time in England it became clear to me why this environment, with its minimal diversions, had become a musically fertile breeding ground.

As we began rehearsing I also noticed that the higher voltage in the UK, 220 volts, made our gear sound heavier than in America with its 110-volt standard. Randy always managed to get an outstanding tone even back during the Quiet Riot days. But at 220v, the Marshall stacks were screaming as the preamp tubes growled with over saturation.

Even though our upcoming tour was considered to be the "European Diary of a Madman Tour," we were actually special guests on Saxon's headline tour. Since we were limited to performing a 45- minute set, we rehearsed a condensed version of the previous Blizzard of Ozz tour.

On October 27th, after we finished our week of rehearsals, the band moved to the Portobello Hotel in the quaint antique row of London's Portobello Road. While in London, Randy and I spent most of our time sightseeing, shopping for rock paraphernalia at the Kensington Market and hanging out at trendy nightspots like Stringfellows, Tramps, and Morton's.

On November 4th, the band and crew departed from Heathrow Airport bound for Hamburg, Germany to commence the tour. Upon landing, I watched everyone from our entourage clear German customs while I waited in back of the line.

"Your papers, please!" demanded the curt German customs agent.

"This is all I have," I explained.

"Where is your passport? Where is your visa?" the agent barked as he slammed my re-entry permit on his desk. Suddenly, soldiers armed with machine guns gathered behind the agent, aiming their guns at me, as he angrily shouted insults in his mother tongue. Relief came over me when I saw the German tour promoter, Ossi Hoppe, coming quickly to my rescue.

"The customs agent wants to know how you got here from Cuba," Ossi translated

"Actually, I flew in from England with the band," I explained nervously.

"Wait right here," Ossi said, as he and the agent went into an adjacent office while the soldiers held their aim.

"OK, let's go before they change their minds," Ossi said, returning. "You sure picked a fine time to land here without a passport. Are you aware that Hamburg Airport is the center of hijacking activity in Europe? You should consider yourself lucky that all the customs agent wanted was for someone to pay for your visa. I thought they were going to send you back to Cuba." If there ever was a decisive moment for me to get my U.S. citizenship and passport, this was certainly it.

As soon as we arrived at Hamburg's Eurocrest Hotel I joined Randy at the bar and threw back a couple of vodka tonics to take the edge off.

"Now boys, don't make any plans for tonight," Sharon said, handing out room keys. "We're all going out to the Star Club for a few drinks."

The legendary Star Club was situated in the heart of the Reeperbahn/St Pauli area, Hamburg's red-light district. The club was famous for being the early training ground for the Beatles prior to "Beatlemania."

As our taxi sped through the bustling streets of

Hamburg that crisp autumn evening I gazed at the majestic Baroque and Renaissance buildings bathed in neon light. "Reeperbahn!" shouted the German taxi driver as we came to a quick stop at the entrance of a narrow alley way dotted with flashing signs as far as the eye could see.

"I hope we're at the right place," Sharon said as we looked up at a sign that read "Salambo Club" with a bizarre cartoon depiction of a man bowing an upright bass with his humongous penis.

"Yeah, I remember this!" Ozzy said, excitedly. "I played here at the Star Club with Sabbath when we were still called Earth. Bloody hell! I guess they have new owners." We watched the sleazy clientele entering and exiting the club.

"This place was a rock club when Daddy owned it back in the '60s," said Sharon. "I'm not sure what it is now.

When we walked through the door Randy and I couldn't believe our eyes; beautiful topless showgirls paraded on stage in what appeared to be a Las Vegas-style spectacle. Randy and I grabbed a table in the back corner while Ozzy and Sharon ventured on to the second floor of the nightclub.

"Wow! Can you believe the bodies on those chicks?" I said as the waitress brought our drinks.

"Yeah, we lucked out!" Randy grinned as we toasted. The show continued as more beautiful women came on stage for the grand finale. Suddenly, the music stopped and the showgirls removed their bikini bottoms right on cue and revealed something that really surprised us: their male genitals!

"What? Hey, what the hell is going on?!" Randy yelled, spilling his drink.

"Holy shit! Those are dudes with tits!" I said, stunned.

"Let's get the hell out of here!" Randy said. We

bolted from our table and climbed the stairs to the top floor of the club looking for Ozzy and Sharon.

It got worse. We found Sharon and Ozzy cuddling while they watched a live sex act. When we sat down with them I noticed that the cocktail-filled table was actually shaped like a giant penis. Ozzy tapped my shoulder and pointed to the apathetic young couple dancing naked on a small stage close by. Ozzy grinned from ear to ear, bouncing to the beat of the robotic disco music. The stage lights dimmed as the pulsating song faded into a seductive ballad and the young couple proceeded to lie down on the small daybed and have intercourse right on stage.

"Sharon, I've got to get out of here," I said.

"Oh, don't be a wuss, have some fun, man!" Ozzy yelled as he applauded the bored love makers.

"Look, Ozzy. I rather be doing it than watching it.

"Well maybe if you shut the bloody fuck up and watch you

might learn something!" Ozzy yelled.

I looked over at Randy smoking quietly in a corner, shaking his head in disgust.

The following evening, November 5, we performed the first show of our European tour with Saxon. That night we rammed into our 45-minute set. All our pent up energy from being absent from the stage for almost two months culminated in one of the best sets the band had ever played. After the show, the members of Saxon came into our dressing room and kindly welcomed us to the tour. They seemed to be impressed with our performance and a bit concerned as to how they were going to follow us. But in reality they didn't have anything to worry about. Their combination of precision musicianship and elaborate stage production highlighted by a massive chromed "German Eagle" as their backdrop, truly defined heavy metal. Both bands presented their fans with a solid night of rock and roll.

Since the distances between shows were relatively short Sharon decided that the band would travel in two vehicles rather than a single tour bus. Jake drove a Ranger Rover over from England to Hamburg to transport Sharon and Ozzy while Tommy, Randy and I rode in a rented sporty BMW. Each night after the show, the three of us quickly changed into our street clothes and drove on the "Autobahn," Germany's high-speed expressway, with Tommy behind the wheel. His driving experience came in handy since our goal was to get to the next town as fast as possible and hit the local nightspots. Meanwhile, Ozzy and Sharon were usually a couple of hours behind us with Jake cautiously in the driver seat.

The November 6th performance in Wolfsburg was before another sold-out crowd. Immediately after the show Randy, Tommy and I blazed the Autobahn all the way to Koln in time to experience its exhilarating nightlife. The following day, November 8th was a scheduled day off so Randy, Jake and I spent the afternoon walking the gothic streets along the banks of the Rhine River before stepping out later that evening for another night of carousing. The next evening's sold-out concert was at the Koln, Sporthalle in front of an exuberant metal crowd.

The following evening, November 9th, we played at the Stadthalle in Offenbach in front of another rowdy sold-out crowd consisting mostly of military personnel from the nearby American Air Force base. The homesick servicemen gave us a rousing reception as we ripped into an emotionally charged set in appreciation of these courageous men and women.

After the show, Sharon and the band joined Heinz Kanibal, the president of CBS Records in Germany and his assistant Bettina, for dinner at a posh Italian restaurant. Also joining us in the private banquet room were Dave Arden, Sharon's brother and an executive at Jet Records, our promoter Ossi Hoppe, his wife Babs, and a couple of contest winners from the Los Angeles radio station KMET who had just flown in for the occasion. The two young men from L.A. were elated to be sitting at the same table with Ozzy who was more than willing to pose for pictures with them throughout the evening. And as most record executives had done before him, Mr. Kanibal chose the safest seat at the table, the one between Randy and me.

"Hey Ozzy! Can you tell us one of your wild road stories," one of the contest winners asked.

"Let's see," Ozzy mulled as he poured himself a large glass of white wine. "Ah, yes. There was this time that I was staying at this bloody swanky hotel in London where I had been knocking back a few pints at the bar when suddenly I had to take a shit. I was too pissed to make it to my room so I dropped down me pants and took a dump right in the lobby!"

The whole table erupted with laughter except Mr. Kanibal whose stern glance towards Bettina made her stop giggling.

"So the bloody hotel manager runs over yelling at me while I'm taking this huge dump. So I pulled out a room key out of me back pocket and shoved it his face and told him, It's all right, mate, I'm a bloody guest in your hotel!"

The table laughed again, except for Mr. Kanibal, who obviously had had enough of Ozzy's crude wit.

"Shit, Ozzy, that's the best story I ever heard!" shouted one of the contest winners.

"Here, I got another one for you," Ozzy finished up another glass of wine. "A few days ago me, Sharon, and the guys went to a live sex club in the Reeperbahn. In one of the private rooms upstairs there was this German couple shagging on stage right in front of us!" Ozzy had everyone's attention.

"No way!" marveled one of the contest winners.

"They started dancing to this bloody boring German

disco crap!" Suddenly, Ozzy climbed on top of the table and proceeded to strip off all his clothes to more vividly demonstrate what he'd seen that night. He humped the air buck-naked to the rhythm of the Italian music playing over the restaurant speakers. "Then they started shagging like two bloody mannequins. It was the most boring fuck I had ever seen!"

Ozzy re-enacted the live sex act. Watching him, Mr. Kanibal sat frozen with his mouth open. Meanwhile, the contest winners were having a blast snapping Polaroid photos of heavy metal's bad boy.

After Ozzy finished re-enacting his story he sat down and grabbed one of the large wine carafes from our table and proceeded to urinate in it under the table. When he was done, he placed the carafe back on the table as an unsuspecting waiter came by and moved it to another table. By the time dinner was over everyone in our party, with the exception of our hosts, were completely inebriated. As we staggered out, I grabbed a six-foot tall bottle of Chianti and somehow shoved it into the back seat of our car with half of the bottleneck sticking out the window.

Once I got back to my room I couldn't figure out how I was going to drink out of this absurdly large bottle of wine so I laid on the floor and let the Chianti flow into my gaping mouth. Not surprisingly, the next morning I woke up with a screaming headache and was stained with red wine from head to toe.

The next day Sharon faced the dilemma of Ozzy's extreme mood swings as he came to grips with the harsh reality that his marriage to Thelma was crumbling. Even though his depression worsened over the next few days, we still continued the tour with shows in Saarbruchen on November 10th, in Karlsrube on November 11th, and Bosenburf on November 12th.

The following day, we arrived in Stuttgart. While

Randy and I were at the hotel lounge we got a message from Jake to meet Sharon in her room immediately.

"Well, boys, this is it," she said. "We're pulling out of the Saxon tour. Ozzy just threw a major wobbler this morning and refuses to do the remaining dates." The stress of the last few days had taken a toll on her.

"So what are we gonna do next?" Randy asked with the tone of someone who had learned to expect the unexpected.

"Well, we can't go back to England right away," she said. "That won't look good. So we'll just go on ahead to Munich and wait it out. Maybe Ozzy will change his mind in the next couple of days."

On November 14th, while we waited for an evaluation of Ozzy's mental health and a decision regarding the remaining European dates, we cancelled that evening's Nuremberg and the following day's Orf shows and traveled to Munich. That afternoon we checked into the Munich Holiday Inn Hotel, famous for its nightclub the Yellow Submarine and its main attraction, a live shark that lurked through in the water tank surrounding the club.

Ozzy's depression worsened. He became a permanent fixture at the Yellow Submarine and quickly bonded with the lonely shark whose glazed eyes constantly glared at him. One evening the band and crew tried to cheer Ozzy up by treating him to a night on the town at Munich's hottest rock club.

"I must see your ID," a rude bouncer said, stopping Ozzy at the door.

"I'm Ozzy Osbourne," he stumbled.

"This man's drunk." The bouncer said, and he was right. Ozzy had been drinking non-stop since breakfast.

"Oh, he's all right," said a nearby crew member. "He's just
celebrating his new record. Don't worry, mate. We'll keep an eye

on him." The bouncer removed the velvet rope and let us in.

Unaware that Munich was a late-night city, the club was completely empty when we arrived. Bored and tired, Ozzy laid down on a sofa and passed out. Moments later, a couple of bouncers picked up Ozzy and carried him out the door. The DJ blasted "Crazy Train" over the deafening disco sound system.

In an attempt to keep Ozzy from drinking himself into oblivion, Sharon gave strict orders to the hotel staff not to serve him alcohol. But Ozzy figured a loophole by ordering heaping bowls of consommé with brandy at the bar. I watched him with pity as he was hunched over the bar, his trembling hands lifted the steaming bowl to his lips, slurping and spilling most of it down his stained buffalo coat.

One afternoon, out of complete boredom, Randy, Tommy and I crashed into one of the hotel's conference rooms where a chiropractor's convention was being held. On our way out we each grabbed plastic models of spinal cords as souvenirs and made our way to the bar to join Ozzy. We tried to strike up a conversation with him but he seemed to be in a catatonic state. He stared menacingly at two German businessmen and their female companion at an adjoining table.

Suddenly without any warning, Ozzy grabbed one of the spine model's plastics pieces shaped like a vertebrate and hurled it with all the strength he could muster in the direction of the adjoining table. The impact of the plastic projectile made a sharp cracking sound as the unsuspecting woman was abruptly smacked in the back of her head. The chatter in the lounge turned into eerie silence. After a few moments considering the possibility of landing in a German jail, the conversation at the adjoining table continued without any acknowledgement of Ozzy's assault, as if nothing had even happened.

Ozzy smiled wickedly and rubbed his hands.

"Bartender! Another bloody bowl of consommé!"

After a couple of days in Munich it was becoming clear that we had overstayed our welcome at the hotel. The staff was ignoring us.

"Rudy have you seen Sharon?" Jake walked up and asked as I was about to order dinner.

"No, I haven't seen her all day," I answered.

"No one can find her and she's not answering her phone," Jake said with concern.

"Hmm, that's strange."

"I'm going up to her room to see if she's there," said Jake.

"I'll go with you."

As we rushed through the lobby towards the elevators I spotted Ozzy wearing his buffalo coat. He was running like a stampeding bison ramming his head into a large potted tree. After the pain of the head butt wore off, he turned around and charged the tree at the opposite end of the lobby.

"Looks like Ozzy's finally lost it," I said to Jake.

"I know better than to get involve in that, only Sharon can deal with him." admitted Jake.

"Sharon! Are you in there?" Jake shouted as he pounded on her door. "Rudy, call the front desk and get someone with a pass key right away!" Jake said urgently.

A few minutes later the hotel manager arrived and opened the door as far as the security lock would allow.

"She's got it locked from the inside, we're going to have to bust the security lock!" the manager said as he kicked in the door. "She's not in her bed. Check the bathroom," Jake yelled as we searched the suite.

"She's in here! Come quick!" the manager shouted.

"Oh my God! Quick get a doctor!" Jake was in a panic. Sharon was unconscious in the bathtub.

A few moments later the paramedics arrived in time and were able to revive her. Another close call.

Later that evening Jake called Randy, Tommy and me to his room.

"OK, this is what's going on. I'm going to drive Ozzy and Sharon back to England while you lads drop the rented car in Paris at the airport and fly back to London. Once we're all back in England we'll start production rehearsals at Shepperton for the American tour before we begin the U.K. dates." Jake paused. "I don't know. Looks to me like Ozzy's finally snapped," Tommy said.

"We'll have to wait and see," said Jake. "Sharon's taking him to a shrink as soon as we get back to England."

The remaining European tour dates with Saxon were cancelled. The 17th in Heidelberg, 19th in Dortmund, 20th in Wurtenberg, 22nd in Geneva, 23rd in Streburg, 24th in Paris and 25th in Lille.

On the morning of November 17th we drove from Munich to Paris and checked into a posh hotel late that evening on the City of Light's grand boulevard, the Champs Elysees.

The following morning, November 18th, Randy and I celebrated my birthday by driving and sightseeing around Paris before heading to Charles DeGaulle Airport. Later that same evening, a limo was waiting for us upon our arrival at Heathrow.

Much to my surprise, Sharon had arranged for a birthday party in my honor at an upscale London restaurant called Rags. Ozzy, Sharon, Jake, Don Arden and members of Jet Records' staff were all gathered upstairs at a private room where I was greeted to a rousing chorus of "Happy Birthday." I was profoundly touched by this, especially amid all the insanity. It was a bittersweet occasion seeing Ozzy sitting at the head of the table with his head down, oblivious to the celebration around him. Nevertheless, it meant the world to me that he had made the effort to be there.

14
Come on Boys! Let's Go See Ozzy

The band once again stayed at London's Portobello Hotel from November 19th till the 22nd while Sharon had Ozzy institutionalized at Saint John's Woods Clinic for a psychiatric evaluation. While in London, Randy, Tommy and I visited the Jet office to go over last minute details for the upcoming Diary of a Madman U.S. tour. A shabby-chic young woman handed me a garment bag.

"You must be Rudy," she said. "Hi, I'm your stage clothes designer. I've got some outfits that I would like for you to try on and make sure they fit. I've got Randy in the other room trying on some stage clothes as well. So go in here, put these on and I'll be right back." She led me into to an empty office.

I was excited to see what my new stage look was going to be as I hastily unzipped the garment bag.

"What the hell is this?!" My bellow echoed off the walls as I held up a magenta chiffon puffy shirt.

It looked like lingerie for an overweight naughty housewife. I tried it on just for a laugh and went out in the hallway in search of a mirror. I bumped into Randy wearing a matching shirt. We pointed at each other and laughed hysterically.

"I think we better have a talk with Sharon!" Randy said as we walked past the snickering secretaries.

"What the fuck?!" Sharon cried as she got her first glimpse of us. "I can't wait to see what she's done for Ozzy," quipped Randy.

"I specifically told her that it's a medieval castle theme," said Sharon, "not a bloody transsexual bordello."

"Well, maybe we're supposed to be the fairies!" Randy laughed. "That's it! Take those bloody awful things off! That cunt's fired! Where is she?" Sharon stormed out of the office.

The following day she brought in another stage clothes designer with a clearer vision of medieval, heavy-metal fashion.

After changing back into my street clothes I ran into Tommy in the hallway. He was looking at a copy of the new Diary of a Madman record.

"Is that the new record? Wow, let me see!" I said. "That's a pretty scary cover." I remarked as I gazed at the artwork of a demoniacal Ozzy leering back at me from a satanic lair.

"Not as scary as what's on the inside," Tommy said. I pulled out the inner sleeve and saw a group picture taken during our September 13th Disney trip. Ross Halfin photographed the session, with us surrounded by undecipherable cryptic text.

"Do you have any idea it says?" I asked.

"I asked Sharon and she told that it's some kind of an ancient Druid lingo," Tommy said. "It's supposed to say 'The Ozzy Osbourne Band' on top and the rest is the album credits."

"I can't find any credits that say who's playing on the record," I said. "This is going to create a lot of confusion having our photo on the record without us having played on it."

"Yeah, we'll probably have to spend the rest of our lives explaining why our picture's on the record but Bob and Lee played on it." Tommy said as he walked away, clearly displeased. The following evening Randy and I went out for drinks at London's trendy Polynesian restaurant Trader Vic's. After a few rum- soaked cocktails Sharon came over and joined us.

"Hello boys, I'm so glad I found you here!" She cheerfully greeted us.

"Sharon," Randy spoke up, "we're all concerned about Ozzy's condition. We haven't heard from him. Is he all right?"

184

"Oh, he's doing just fine. I just spoke with his doctor and he's anticipating his release in time for the U.K. tour."

"Where is he?" I asked.

"Oh, he's at a clinic just up the road in St. John's Woods. And you know what?" she said with a gleam. "Ozzy would love to see you." Sharon signaled the waiter for our check. "Come on boys, let's go see Ozzy."

That rainy night as our cab sped through the bustling streets of London, feeling comfortably numb from the exotic libations, I was totally unprepared for the sobering scenario that awaited us.

When we got to the clinic, the somberness of the dimly lit hallway transported us into a black and white movie resembling the dreary Victorian atmosphere of the film The Elephant Man.

"Let me go in first," Sharon whispered. "I want to make sure we don't wake him from a deep sleep." She walked into the room. "Hello, Ozzy. It's Sharon." Her voice was soft and slow. "I've brought with me some friends who want to see you." She gestured to us. "Come on in boys, but be very quiet. He's under a lot of medication and any excitement might upset his condition."

I walked into the shadowy room I barely recognized Ozzy as he laid on a small, stark iron bed which only justifiable purpose seemed to be for the shackling of unruly patients. Next to his bed was a small table with lamp, a bowl and a water jug. A changing screen in a corner of the room completed the spartan furnishings.

"Hi Ozzy. It's Randy and Rudy," said Randy softly. "We've dropped by to see how you're doing."

Ozzy's slumped body gave the impression of a man in a state of psychotic depression. When Ozzy finally connected with reality he slowly raised his head to reveal the biggest smile I had ever seen and lifted up his arms to hug Randy. But as soon as Randy bent over to hug him, Ozzy dropped his head and started crying.

Randy was surprised. He stood up and looked at me with sadness. Ozzy once again raised his head and cheerfully smiled but immediately dropped his head and moaned. Sharon, Randy and I tearfully stood by as we watched Ozzy go through a succession of extreme mood swings.

"It's better if you leave now," the nurse ordered as she hurried into the room. "All this excitement is aggravating his condition." When we were halfway down the hall, I looked over my shoulder and watched the nurse administer a shot as Ozzy slowly sank back into a deep slumber.

The night before we departed from London to begin our preproduction rehearsals at Shepperton Studios, Rod McSween, the band's booking agent and close friend, met Randy and me for drinks at Morton's, one of London's trendiest night spots. Rod is one of the most thoughtful people I've ever met, although his omnipresent boyish grin often projects an aura of mischievousness.

"Do you boys fancy going next door to a private club?" He asked. "I think you will be more comfortable there."

"Yeah, why not?" Randy said. "I don't think we could be any more ignored there than we are here."

We walked around the corner for about half a block until we came to a nondescript door at the top of a short stairway. Rod gave what seemed to be a secret knock as a man in a tuxedo answered. "Good evening Mr. McSween," said the doorman. "I see you've brought some friends with you tonight. Welcome gentlemen." Upon entering the parlor I was impressed by the posh decor and the bevy of beautiful, elegantly clad women. Unlike the previous nightspot, the mix of distinguished looking Middle Eastern and British upper crust gentlemen mingling with the ladies didn't seem to mind our obvious heavy metal look.

"Now this is more like it," Randy said as he surveyed the scene and ordered a drink.

"Guys, I want this to be a night you'll never forget," Rod announced, holding up a glass. "Just relax and enjoy. Cheers."

It wasn't long before a statuesque young woman walked up to Rod and hugged him.

"I want you to meet my friends, Randy and Rudy," Rod said as he flashed that grin.

"You are both musicians, oui?" she asked with a seductive French accent.

"Yes, we play in Ozzy Osbourne's Blizzard of Oz," Randy replied

"Sorry, never heard of zee band. But, it doesn't matter, I think you're cute anyways." She flirted as Randy blushed. "So, why don't you tell me more about zee Ozzy Osbourne band, oui?" She led Randy by the hand to a nearby red velvet couch.

After a couple of drinks and few more visits by an array of beautiful women Rod walked over to the young woman sitting with Randy and whispered in her ear. He came back to the bar.

"So, Rudy, have you picked out one yet?"

"What do you mean pick out?"

"Have you picked out the hooker you want to go home with? "Hooker?"

"Why the bloody hell do you think they're all so friendly?" Rod laughed at my naiveté.

"Well, I've never had to pay for it so how the hell would I know?" I replied as I realized that Randy probably hadn't either. "We'd better let Randy know," I suggested.

"It's too late now! He just left with his new friend."

Returning to our hotel, I grabbed my room key from the retiring night clerk and went straight to bed. Moments later I was awakened by the tapping sound of someone throwing pebbles at my window. I got up to open the window and found Randy standing in the middle of the street wearing nothing but a lady's bathrobe.

"Holy shit, what happened to you?"

"Never mind what happened! Just let me in! I'm freezing!"

I quickly put some clothes on and ran down the staircase to let Randy in.

"Shit, there's no one behind the desk! I can't get the key to my room," Randy said, looking strange as he hugged the pink embroidered chenille bathrobe.

"I've got an extra bed in my room. You can crash in it for the night. So what the hell happened?" I asked.

"What a nightmare!" Randy said, his face barely peeping out from under the blankets. "She was really sweet back at the club. We were just talking about Paris and I don't know." Randy paused for a moment. "It just felt good to have a nice conversation with someone outside of our group. So she invites me back to her place and that's when things started getting weird. We were sitting, talking and having drinks when she grabbed my hands and insisted that I let her paint my fingernails. I thought it was a bit weird but I just went along with it." He revealed his ruby red fingernails. "After she was done, she excused herself and went into the bedroom. A couple of minutes later she came out wearing nothing but a skin tight black leather corset, stiletto heels and a riding crop. I started thinking, 'Hmm, this could be pretty interesting. She began dancing around the room. Then she came over and slowly started taking my clothes off and tossing them around the room. She grabbed my foot and started to paint my toenails. I'd had it with her nail-painting crap so I resisted and that's when she went totally nuts on me. She started whipping me with her riding crop and yelling at me in French! So I pushed her to the side and ran. She chased me around the room and that's when I grabbed my shoes and the first piece of clothing I saw and ran out the door." He paused. "You know, Rudes, all I wanted was someone to talk to. There's so much pressure all around us. Ozzy is in the loony bin. Meanwhile, we have a new record out and we're getting ready for the biggest tour we've ever done. There are so many uncertainties surrounding this band. I'm just not sure about our future anymore."

The following afternoon, November 22nd, we began a week's worth of rehearsals at Shepperton. The tight pre-production schedule was a welcome distraction. It was during these rehearsals that Randy, Tommy and I were joined by keyboardist Don Airey. Besides having previously recorded with Ozzy's band, Don was already a studio and touring veteran of such British rockers like Coliseum II, Black Sabbath and Rainbow. While on tour, Don's very British demeanor earned him the nickname of "The Vicar."

One of the tasks of the pre-production rehearsals was to learn all of the remaining songs from the new Diary of a Madman album, as we were already performing "Believer" and "Flying High Again" as well as "Goodbye to Romance," the Beatle-esque ballad from The Blizzard of Ozz album. Once we were joined by Ozzy at rehearsals, then he could pick and choose which of the new songs were suitable for his live vocals. Since there was nothing else we would rather do than play, we quickly learned all the new songs and spent countless hours polishing our set as Don's keyboard wizardry took our sound to a truly high level. Impressed by Randy's guitar prowess, Don took it upon himself to learn all of Randy's guitar solos and doubled them live adding a thick extra layer to Randy's already textured wall of sound.

Another objective was for the band to get accustomed to performing in the new massive Medieval Castle staging designed by one of Britain's top production designers,

Simon Woodruff. Since the staging was not yet fully completed all we had to work with were the spiraling frames that held the castle's facade.

"Rand, I'm a bit worried that we're going to be dwarfed by the size of this set," I said, standing down stage and gazing at the three towering frames that spread across the stage's background. "Yeah," agreed Randy. "I just hope the audience will still remember the band after they've seen the show!"

During pre-production we all took notes of the challenges we would be facing with this new live set. There would be the diminished power of our sound due to the distance from downstage to the backline, which was hidden behind the castle walls.

There was also the enormous height of Tommy's drum riser, which made it virtually impossible for him to hear the rest of the band as well as make eye contact with us during the show. After careful consideration, Sharon decided that we would make all the necessary adjustments for these conditions. We would re-enforce the monitor system and placement of support amplification for Randy from the pit on his side of the stage. This would happen once we began the final phase of the pre-productions rehearsals in the U.S. with the completed staging.

It became a custom after rehearsals for the band and crew to gather at the local pub on the village square.

"Wow, who's that chick?" Tommy asked the bartender as the raven-haired young woman played darts and flirted with some of the locals.

"That's Jo Jo Laine, Denny's missus," the bartender offered, referring to Denny Laine, Paul McCartney's Wings guitarist. "She's a looker, ain't she?"

"I sure would like to meet her," Tommy said, pointing her out to Randy.

"Here, I'll introduce ya." He waved at Jo Jo from across the room and she came right over.

"Hi, I'm Jo Jo," she said to Randy, ignoring Tommy.

"Guess I've been shot down!" Tommy said, joining our crew at an adjacent table. It was obvious that Randy and Jo Jo were hitting it off. They found they had many things in common and, as Americans in a foreign land, they shared a longing for a bit of company and conversation.

"Hey guys, Jo Jo wants us to come to her place for drinks," Randy said.

"It's Brian Jones' old house," Jo Jo added.

"Is that the place where he drowned?" I asked my curiosity for rock and roll history awakened.

"That's the place," she said. "It's only a few minutes up the road. I know you'll be comfortable there."

I was truly impressed when we arrived at the picture-perfect Tudor house with its lush fairy-tale setting. As the wife a touring guitarist, Jo Jo was familiar with the rigors of the road and did everything possible to make us feel at home. As I looked around the antique-filled house I came upon an opened book displayed on a lectern at the bottom of the staircase.

"That's the same staircase as in the drawing," Jo Jo explained. I stared at a picture of a cartoon Christopher Robbin descending a staircase.

"It's a first edition Winnie the Pooh," she said. "It came with the house. This was A. A. Milne's home and the surroundings were his inspirations for the stories. Here, let me show you." I followed her into the garden.

"It's dark now and you can't really see it very well but there's an entrance to a forest over there. That's where Winnie the Pooh and the rest of the characters came alive in Milne's imagination. And, oh yeah," Jo Jo paused for a moment. "That's the pool where Brian Jones drowned."

I pondered the irony of the House at Pooh Corner, and all its wonder for kids, being the same home where a founding member of the Rolling Stones met his untimely death.

Late in the afternoon of November 28th, our last day of preproduction, Ozzy was released from the clinic and joined us at rehearsals. Looking disheveled and confused, Ozzy wandered on stage and took a long look at the towering bare castle frames, wobbled off the stage and went to sleep on a couch.

"Sharon, is he going to be able to rehearse?" Randy asked.

"This is our last day and we need to decide what new songs we're adding to the set," Tommy added.

"Yes, I know," agreed Sharon, thinking. "I've got it! We'll make Ozzy cue cards with the lyrics so he can try the new songs." About an hour later, Ozzy staggered back up on stage and attempted to sing the new songs as one of the crew members held cue cards in front of him. Ozzy's attempt to reach the high notes was dreadful as the medication had taken a toll on his vocal chords. "Sharon, I can't sing these songs. My voice is fucked."

"Well, Ozzy, we can't go back to the States and do the same set list as the last tour," she explained. "We need to add at least one more song from the new record, so pick one."

"Ozzy," Randy offered, "how about 'Over the Mountain?' We could use another up-tempo song in the set."

"Oh, bloody hell, let's do 'Over the Mountain,' but it has to be the opening number. It's too fuckin' hard to sing later on in the set."

On November 29th we began the U.K. Diary of a Madman headline tour at the Bristol Colston Hall. These intimate theater dates were considered a warm-up for the more ambitious U.S. arena tour. The tour's opening act was a Jet Records band called Girl. These charismatic young glam rockers had an adoringly devoted female following but ended up being loathed by the working-class metal fans that found their lead singer's upper crust attitude unacceptable.

"Hey, welcome to the tour, guys. I'm Rudy, Ozzy's bass player." "Hello, mate. I'm Phil, the singer, and this is Phil, our lead guitarist," said the young man with jet-black spiky hair and classic pop star features next to a fair-haired guitarist that resembled a young Rod Stewart.

"Oh, that's easy, Phil and Phil."

"Listen, mate. Do you have an extra stage shirt that I can borrow just for tonight?" the singer asked politely. "You see, we've been busy traveling and I haven't had the chance to do my wash." "Not a problem, I got a brand new shirt that will suit you just fine." I ran out the door and brought a shirt back from our dressing room. "I just got it at Kensington market a few days ago. I think it will fit you." Phil grabbed the black shirt wrapped in multiple belts and chains.

"Thanks mate, this will do," he said, standing in front of a mirror sizing up my shirt.

That evening I stood on the side of the stage to catch a bit of their set. I was amazed when the mostly male metal audience began spitting at the singer from all directions. I was both impressed by the audiences spitting prowess and Phil's tenacity as he defiantly leered back at them while my shirt became the moving target of a heavy metal spitting contest.

"Here you go, mate!" Phil said after their show as he walked into our dressing room bare-chested, holding my spit-soaked shirt between his fingertips. "That's a bloody smashing crowd out there. I couldn't believe all the flying gobs. They sure are ready for ya now!" "Uh, well, that's all right, man. You can keep it."

"Well, cheers, mate! I quite fancy how the gobs stick to it!"

The following performances, November 30th, at the Sophia Gardens in Cardiff, Wales, and December 1st, at the Montfort Hall in Leicester, England were in front of sold out crowds. But even though the band was at the top of its game, Ozzy's constant state of depression took a toll on his performance and tested the limits of his relationship with Sharon.

On the morning of December 2nd we arrived in Liverpool, the birthplace of the Beatles. This rock and roll mecca has always held a special place in the hearts of virtually every musician of my generation, so it was mandatory that Randy and I made our pilgrimage to the Cavern Club, the musty cellar where the Beatles paid their dues as the house band.

That evening's performance at the Royal Court turned out to be the thrill of a lifetime for Randy and me as we treaded the same boards where the Beatles and numerous other British rock legends had performed. On our way to the stage as Randy and I passed by Girl's dressing room we heard Phil practicing his guitar.

"You know, Rudes, that guy's pretty good," Randy said as we stopped outside the door for a quick listen.

"Yeah," I agreed. "I can't believe he's still playing after their set."

"He's definitely got the right attitude," said Randy. "If he keeps it up I bet you someday he's gonna be huge."

Randy would've been pleased with his prediction. In less than a year, that guitarist, Phil Collen, replaced Pete Willis as the lead guitarist in Def Leppard, a move that propelled the band into superstardom. A few years later, the Girls' singer, Phil Lewis, went on to become an MTV favorite with the Los Angeles band LA Guns.

After the show, Randy, Tommy and I met at Sharon's hotel suite.

"I'm afraid I'm going to have to pull the rest of the UK dates and start the rehearsals in Los Angeles a few weeks early," Sharon announced. "As long as Ozzy remains here, he'll be reminded of his failed marriage and I fear that his depression will get worse."

"Didn't the doctors treat him for his depression?" Randy asked. "Oh, Randy, when the doctor released him they flat out told me, 'Madame, Mr. Osbourne's certifiable. There's nothing we can do for him.'"

The following day, December 3rd, we returned to London. The remaining UK dates—December 4th at the Edinburgh Playhouse in Edinburgh, December 5th at the Glasgow Apollo in Glasgow, December 6th and 7th at the Newcastle City Hall in Newcastle, December 18th at the Manchester Apollo in Manchester, December 19th at Leeds Queens Hall in Leeds, December 22nd at the New Bingley Hall in Stafford, and December 24th and 26th at the Hammersmith Odeon in London—were all cancelled.

On the afternoon of December 4th, Sharon threw a joint birthday party for Randy and Ozzy at Rag's, the same restaurant where they previously held my birthday party a couple of weeks earlier. Among the attendees were a few Jet Records staffers, rock journalists, and the members of Girl. Everyone at the party was getting plastered and having a great time except for Ozzy who was passed out at the head of the table. Most of the guests brought some very unique presents for Randy and Ozzy. One of the most memorable was from the guys in Girl who found it irresistible to present Ozzy with an antique stuffed dog in a glass case.

"Ozzy, look at what the boys from Girl brought you!" Sharon exclaimed as she displayed the present.

"What the fuck is it?" Ozzy asked, groggily lifting his head off the table.

"It's your new pet!" Sharon joked as Ozzy dropped his head on the table and closed his eyes. It wasn't until a generously proportioned belly dancer showed up that Ozzy finally came alive. She danced around him while he gladly placed his head between her ample breasts.

The celebration was now finally in full swing as the wine flowed and party favors flew about the room. The guys in Girl then decided to take revenge on a journalist who had previously given them a poor review. In the midst of all the chaos, Phil Lewis and Phil Collen picked up an oversized bucket of ice and poured it over the unsuspecting scribe. This triggered an all-out food fight that turned the private upscale room into a battle zone. When everyone ran out of food to throw, glasses, bottles and furniture started flying. This was the cue for Randy and me to take cover behind the bar.

When the skirmish subsided, Randy and I stood in the midst of what was—just moments before—an elegant dining room. The maitre d' stood in the midst of the debris tallying the damages.

15
Let's Knock It Out and See What Happens

On the morning of December 5th, we flew from London to Los Angeles to prepare for the upcoming Diary of the Madman US Tour. Sharon and Ozzy stayed at the Arden's estate while Randy got to spend some much needed time at home with his family and Jody. Meanwhile, Tommy, Don, the crew and I made the Beverly Hilton Hotel our home for the next few weeks.

A couple of days after our return we began our pre-production rehearsals at the legendary Renmar Studios in Hollywood, one of the very few facilities in town with enough ceiling height to accommodate our full production.

"Hey birthday boy!" I yelled at Randy while he sat outside the studio playing his Les Paul in the warm California sun.

"Oh, Rudes, it's so good to be back home!"

"Here, I got you a little something," I said, handing him a present.

"Oh, man, you didn't have to." He carefully unwrapped the box.

"Wow, how did you know I wanted these?" Randy wondered as he held up the Z scale train set pieces.

"A little bird named Jody told me."

"I should've known. Thanks, Rudes," he smiled as we shook hands.

"So is it all here yet?" I asked.

"Yep." Randy said, lighting up a cigarette.

"How does it look?"

"I think you'd better see for yourself!"

Though we had already spent time at Shepperton Studios rehearsing in the looming shadows of the staging's bare frames, I wasn't prepared for the overwhelming sight of the completed set.

"It's so much bigger than I thought it would be!" I said in awe as we gazed at the medieval castle replica that would be our backdrop during most of the tour.

"Yeah, it's so tall that they had to get rid of the stage in order to

hang the lighting rig."

We would be rehearsing on the ground rather than on our usual six-foot high stage. After my initial shock, I closely surveyed the details of the castle's fayade. The centerpiece of the set was a simulated stone arch with a stained glass window that measured over 20-feet high and served as the backdrop for the drums and a series of special effects during the show. The arch was embellished with iron crosses and flaming torches, accentuating the gothic motif. The center structure was flanked at each side by similar arches with exact reproductions of medieval balconies, gates and portcullises. These three arches were connected by two ivy covered faux stone castle walls measuring six feet wide by five feet tall. The showpiece of the set was an eight-step high staircase that doubled as a massive seven- foot drum riser as well as the platform in which various impressive special effects would emerge during the show.

"I just know this is going to suck. I can't fuckin' hear myself!" I heard Tommy yell from the towering drum riser at our monitor engineer as he tried to hear his drum kit through the standard floor monitor wedges placed behind him. "This drum riser's so high I'm gettin' a nose bleed!"

"Yeah T.A., we're gonna need binoculars just to see your cues!" said Randy.

"I don't know how in the hell I'm going to be able to hear you guys from up here, I can barely hear myself," Tommy complained.

"I can barely hear myself with all of the amps hidden by the stupid castle," Randy added.

"I don't know how we'll be able to play like this,"

said Tommy, throwing down his sticks. "Somebody get Sharon on the phone."

A couple of hours later Sharon showed up.

"OK, what's the problem?" She seemed more stressed than usual since she was dealing with every single detail of the most logistically ambitious arena tour to date, while keeping Ozzy's mood swings in check.

"Well, for starters," Tommy griped, "why are my drums sitting on top of this metal grid? I have no coupling with any solid structures, it's like I'm floating on air."

"That's because your drums are going to be raised by a forklift at the beginning of the show," Sharon explained. "It's all part of the intro we have prepared, you'll get the whole idea when we have our run-through during sound check."

"So then, I'm basically screwed since I'm relying on the usual monitor wedges and they're not loud enough to compensate for the lack of sound, right?"

"Don't worry," Sharon assured him. "We'll just have the sound company come up with a drum monitor system that will take care of your problems

"Sharon, that's fine for T.A.," said Randy, "but I hate the sound of my guitar through the monitors and my amps are so far behind and muffled by the castle walls. I was thinking of setting up my amps as usual in front of the walls."

"Sorry Randy," Sharon apologized. "I know how important it is for you to have the right sound but I'm afraid it would ruin the clean look of the stage."

"Then how about if I put a Marshall stack in front of me instead of the usual monitor wedges?" Randy asked.

"That's fine as long as you hide them in the pit where they can't be seen."

"How about you, Rudy? Are you having problems too?" She asked.

"Yeah, but I can always ask the sound company to beef up my two front wedges with 15-inch speakers and pump a bit of bass into my side-fill. It will probably sound better than my back line anyways."

"Donald? Can you hear the boys all right from up there?" Sharon yelled.

Don Airey's keyboards were set up 10' above the stage on the balcony behind me.

"If playing up here is the only way I can be on stage then I guess I can trust the sound company to make all the necessary adjustments to my monitors," he politely consented.

"Well, then I'll have a talk with TASCO as soon as possible and make sure you boys are taken care of," Sharon said, sounding in control. "I want to make sure everything's right before I bring Ozzy down to rehearsals. I just know he's going to take one look at the size of the set and throw a major wobbler."

The very next day, a truckload of reinforcement sound gear arrived. Tommy's standard monitor wedges were replaced by a couple of side-fill monitors that were rolled underneath the metal grid. Instead of the sound coming from behind him, Tommy sat above the monitor giving him the powerful drum sound he needed.

Randy surrounded himself with a Marshall stack by tilting one cabinet in front of him and another stage left next to the side-fills. As requested, my backline amps were reinforced with two floor monitor wedges containing a pair of 15" speakers and a midrange horn. The stage right side-fill pumped with an evenly balanced mix of all the instruments. Being a seasoned professional, Don rose above all the challenges that playing under such difficult circumstances presented while contributing his world-class musicianship. We were now finally ready for Ozzy to come down.

"Fuck me, Rache!" Ozzy muttered as he entered the

studio and set his eyes on the castle. He looked like a kid on Christmas morning that unexpectedly got the bicycle of his dreams.

"Come on guys, let's rock and roll!" Ozzy yelled into the microphone in an uncommonly upbeat fashion as we hurriedly joined him on stage. Ozzy's cheerfulness spread across the room as we started playing the show's opening number, "Over the Mountain." But the moment proved fleeting.

"Stop! Stop!" he yelled into the microphone waving his arms in the air. "I can't hear a bloody word I'm singing." The sound crew gathered around them offering a few solutions.

"Well, we've never had to deal with a situation like this before," the monitor engineer explained. The band is so far away from their back line that we had to compensate by having their monitors really loud. That forces the vocals to compete with the overall stage volume. What we can do," he suggested, "is to place floor wedges across the stage, adding volume to your vocal monitors."

"What about the side-fills?" Ozzy asked. "Add more side-fills and pump voice through them!"

"That's not a good idea," Sharon interrupted. "As it is, they already obstruct a good portion of the stage and I was hoping to sell those side seats."

"We can always fly the side-fills," the engineer suggested.

"Oh, I don't think so," Sharon said. "Having to pay for extra rigging every night might turn out to be too costly."

"I don't give a fuck how much it costs," Ozzy bellowed, walking out of the studio. "Just bloody do it!"

The Arden's were well known in the music industry for throwing lavish Christmas parties and 1981's was no exception. I asked Rebecca, whose afterglow had left a

201

lasting impression on me while we toured abroad, to be my date.

"Now remember," I warned her, "Sharon's going to test your character by offering you things. Don't get me wrong. She's really nice and I know you both will get along. It's just that she's very protective of our inner circle."

We entered the spectacularly decorated house filled with party guests. Sharon greeted us cheerfully, introduced herself to Rebecca and whisked her away to show her around.

I made my way to the game room where I saw Ozzy and Randy checking out a plush red velvet medieval throne.

"Hey, Rudes, check this out!" Ozzy said as he sat on the throne. "This is how I'm going to appear onstage."

He placed his arms on the armrests and his legs out front. Randy giggled as he pulled down red roller blinds over Ozzy's arms, body, lap and legs completely concealing him inside the throne. I noticed that Ozzy was holding a couple strings that kept the blinds in place.

"Here's Ozzy!" he grinned, mimicking Jack Nicholson's character in The Shining. As soon as he released the strings, the roller blinds quickly rolled back revealing him in a split second.

"Wow, that's really cool!" I said, impressed.

"Yeah, it was expensive as fuck, too. Sharon had this bloody magician design it. As soon as he finished building she had him snuffed." Ozzy joked.

"You're not gonna believe the other stuff he made for Ozzy," Randy said as he walked over to a big brown trunk and rummaged through the contents.

"I can't wear that on stage! I'll look like a total cunt!" Ozzy burst out laughing as Randy started chasing him around the room wearing a leopard print cape with big sharp claws and a football helmet covered with a leopard's head with red blinking eyes.

"If you think that's daft wait until see what you boys and the crew will be wearing on this tour," Sharon kidded as she and Rebecca entered the room.

"She's really nice," Rebecca whispered in my ear as she grabbed my hand.

"I told you," I answered and smiled.

After dinner we all gathered around the massive Christmas tree in the al fresco living room to open presents.

"Wait till you see what we got you! You're gonna flip!" Ozzy told me as he grinned and rubbed his hands. Not only did I not have a clue, I didn't expect a present from Ozzy and Sharon at all.

"And this one's for you," Sharon grabbed a beautifully wrapped box from under the tree and handed it to me. I slowly unwrapped the box as Ozzy waited for my reaction.

"Oh, my God, this is awesome!" I exclaimed as I held an incredible black lizard-skin belt bejeweled with five sterling silver shells, each about the size of a baseball.

"It's a Kieslestein-Cord," Sharon pointed out.

"Yeah, the bloody store clerk said that there are only two like it," Ozzy proudly explained. "One's in some bloody museum in New York City and the other one's yours."

"Ozzy got the smaller of version of your belt," Sharon said as Ozzy pulled up his jacket to reveal it.

"Wow, Oz, why didn't you get this one?" I asked.

"When I saw both belts I immediately thought the bigger one was more you," Ozzy answered.

I was overwhelmed by their kindness.

"This is the best present ever," I said while I hugged them both. Around Christmas time the red hot new television show, "Entertainment Tonight," came to our rehearsals at Renmar to tape a segment. We tried our best to capture the energy of our live shows for the cameras but found ourselves at a disadvantage without an audience and the concession of drastically lowering our stage volume in order to keep the video cameras from jittering. Though only a small portion of our show was taped, this turned out to be the only professionally shot footage from the Diary of a Madman era with Randy Rhoads.

I woke up that Christmas morning in my Beverly Hilton Hotel room as the bass player in the hottest new rock band in the world, with Rebecca, the sweetest and most beautiful girl I had ever met lying next to me. These circumstances came in stark contrast to my previous Christmas, when I woke up alone and destitute on a bedroom floor at Kevin DuBrow's Sherman Oaks apartment. Nevertheless, that lonely morning I received the most unforgettable gift ever, understanding the true meaning of Christmas. Instead of concerning myself with the usual distractions like exchanging gifts and holiday reveling, I spent the day in my room quietly meditating and observing the Lord's birthday. Truly, it was my most meaningful Christmas ever.

Shortly after the holidays we resumed our pre-production rehearsals.

"Sharon, we need to talk," the production manager said while she and Ozzy discussed the set list.

"What is it?" she asked. "The crew's refusing to wear the robes." "They can't bloody refuse to wear them. It's all part of the medieval theme of the show."

"Sharon, they're threatening to quit."

"Fuck 'em. Let them quit! We've spent a fortune on these robes and they're going to wear them or we'll find another crew that will."

"I'm afraid we don't have enough time to pull a new crew together with only a few days till opening night."

"Oh, bloody hell!" Sharon was exasperated. "All right then, tell them they don't have to wear the bloody robes ... On second thought, I need to have a word with the Ox. He's going to be standing behind Tommy on top of the drum riser during the show in plain sight of the audience. It's a must that he wears the executioner's outfit," she insisted. "It's hooded, so he doesn't have to be concerned about anyone recognizing him."

The morning of December 30th we flew from Los Angeles to San Francisco to begin a day-long marathon at the Northern California rock landmark, the Cow Palace, which included last- minute pre-production adjustments, a nearly endless sound check, interviews, and award presentations, all culminating with the opening night of the tour.

With the full production set up on our own stage we were then able to rehearse the last remaining special effects of the show.

"You want me to do what?" Ozzy yelled at Sharon as he stood trembling on top of a faux metal 10' replica of a gauntlet.

"Ozzy, just listen to me," she said, trying to calm him down. "At the end of the show, the stage's going to be filled with smoke and the hand's going to come out from underneath the drum riser. All you have to do is to climb on top of the hand and hold on to the hand-rails as the hand goes up in the air. When the hand extends over the first few rows out into the audience, sparklers will be set off from each of the gauntlets four fingers. The only thing you have to do is to step on the lever behind you that will release the catapult and hurl the raw meat into the audience."

"I ain't bloody doing it! I'm afraid of heights!" Ozzy whined. "Oh, here you pussy. Let me show you!" Sharon said as she shoved Ozzy off the massive prop and rocketed 10' into the air. "See how easy it is?!" She shouted from above.

"Well, why don't you bloody do it?!"

"Ozzy, we've spent way too much money building

this bloody thing for you to resist getting on it. You're going to climb up on this thing at the end of the show even if I have to drag you up here myself."

"Oh, bloody well," he muttered, wobbling towards the dressing room.

On our way to the stage to begin our sound check, Randy stopped for a few moments to do an interview. One of the questions was regarding opening-night jitters.

"I'm not so nervous," he said, casually. "It's just that there's so much going on and there's not enough time to do anything. I'm not confident about everything yet. I haven't had time to sort everything out."

When asked about how he's handling all the success, he humbly replied,

"Since I started this, great things haven't stopped happening. It gets to the point where you don't know how to handle all the good news. Everything is great. You just dream of being in a band and getting the chance to do it."

The interviewer asked if being with Ozzy was close to his dreams.

"Well, I think this is beyond it, 'cause I'm really lucky to jump from a local band to headlining like this. When we got together it was like, 'Let's knock it out and see what happens.'"

When Randy wrapped up the interview, we continued towards the stage to get on with sound check. After sound check Randy and I were approached backstage by a dwarf.

"Hey, you guys look like you're in the band. I'm John Allen," the friendly little person introduced himself. "I've been hired to be part of your show. Do you know where I can find Sharon Arden?"

"She's probably in the production office down the hall," Randy said, as he pointed our new member in the right direction. "I can't believe we're gonna have a dwarf on stage with us. This band is turning more into a circus every day."

That evening before the show Randy was presented with the "New Best Guitarist" award by Guitar Player and Sounds magazines. It was a dream come true for Randy as he cradled his trophies and smiled for the cameras alongside Ozzy. It was during this presentation that Randy came to realize that his talents were being appreciated by both his peers and the public. These accolades proved to be the defining moment that inspired Randy to make a commitment to raise his musicianship to the next level.

As we drew closer to show time, the intensity backstage built to a fever pitch. Last-minute changes to our production were made with the inclusion of Little John into our show, adding extra duties to our already strained road crew.

Finally, it was show time. The deafening roar of the sold-out crowd sent a chill through every nerve in my body as we took our places behind the curtained stage. From my vantage point, inside the portcullis on stage right, the only band member I could was Ozzy jittering inside the red velvet throne perched high on top of the massive drum riser. An edited version of the Diary of a Madman acoustic guitar intro came blaring through the PA as we all awaited our musical cues to appear onstage. The heavy guitar riff cue signaling for the Kabuki curtain to drop blared through the speakers but the curtain remained in place. I could see that Ozzy didn't realize the curtain was still up.

Upon hearing his choral cue, Ozzy materialized onstage as he released the cords that held the roller blinds in place. Totally confused by the curtain still being up, he wobbled off the throne and grabbed the four-foot, black plastic cross that lay at the foot of the drum riser and began to shake it at the curtain as if summoning it to come down. Suddenly chaos ensued backstage as Sharon started yelling at Simon Woodruff, the production designer, while the crew tried to bring the curtain down before the intro music ended. When the intro music finally stopped, the curtain was still up, turning the audience from cheers of anticipation to thunderous hostility.

While the crew desperately ran in all directions I watched Sharon exasperatedly tugging at the curtain, attempting to bring it down on her own as the boos of the crowd grew to a deafening pitch. Finally, a crew member climbed to the top of the lighting rig and dropped the curtain one eyelet at a time thus slowly revealing the stage to the agitated crowd and ruining our "coup de theatre."

Onstage, I feared that it would be difficult to recover from such a debacle. But as soon as Tommy ripped into the drum intro of "Over the Mountain" and the flash of the white sparklers flew across the stage we left it all behind and got on with the show. While I played my fretless maple Fender Precision in front of the jam-packed 10,000-seat arena, I was still conscious of my given perimeter and did the best I could within the boundaries to project to the back of the venue.

I was also impressed by how great the stage production and the band looked. Ozzy wore a red chain mail mediaeval jumpsuit and jacket, accentuated by a studded leather belt and codpiece. Randy was the textbook book rock guitar god dressed in black leather and studs. He was Sir Lancelot strapped with a Les Paul. Tommy, a total creature of comfort on stage, wore a matching white tank top and tights. During the show his drum tech stood behind him in plain sight of the crowd dressed in an authentic, black, hooded executioner's outfit. Don, playing from the castle balcony behind me, got into the full spirit of the Gothic theme and wore one of the hooded monk's robes that the crew had refused to wear. I wore black leather pants and a suede top with a studded belt and knee-high red leather boots.

208

The next song, "Mr. Crowley," had a more dramatic impact during the eerie keyboard intro as the stage went dark and Don's back-lit silhouette spread across the stage while Ozzy stood center stage inside a cone of overhead lights. Other dramatic effects were added to our production of the song, such as pillars of smoke rising from underneath the monolithic drum riser, climaxing with spectacular pyrotechnics.

During "Crazy Train" the castle was bathed in white lights as we pounded out the intro. The stage was brightly lit to compensate for the mood of the up-tempo feel of the song giving the audience a first glimpse at the intricate details of the impressive stage.

For the moody "Revelation (Mother Earth)," the lights were brought down once again during the soft intro until we segued into "Steal Away," with the bright overhead lights accentuating the intro riff. Immediately after the song ended, Little John appeared on stage from a tiny trap door in front of the drum riser dressed in a brown, hooded monk's robe. He offered Ozzy a drink from a goblet. Ozzy then introduced him to the crowd and proceeded to playfully kick him off the stage back in the trap door. Some of Little John's other comic relief antics included going on stage to wipe the floor and pick up debris while Ozzy chased after him.

During the "Suicide Solution" guitar solo, Ozzy exaggerated his visual antics in front of the arena audience as he grabbed Randy by the hair and pretended to lift him off the ground. Meanwhile, I played my Music Man Sabre bass upside down while I banged my head in a trance.

From "Suicide Solution" we segued into Randy's guitar solo as all spotlights bathed him, while the castle was softly lit in the background. As we exited the stage, all eyes fell on him during his spectacular solo. From his solo the band came back onstage and we segued into an instrumental passage that linked Randy's and Tommy's

209

solos. The melodic riff of the instrumental was played in unison by Randy and Don, which added a rich texture to the sound.

From the instrumental number we segued into Tommy's drum solo that included all of his signature techniques, including his crowd-pleasing bare-handed drum solo finale accentuated with pyro explosions. Immediately after Tommy finished taking his bow, we reprised the instrumental passage once more as Ozzy returned to the stage.

While we sustained our final chord, Ozzy introduced the soloists, Randy and Tommy, as we gently segued into the soft intro of "Goodbye to Romance." Suddenly, Little John, wearing a safety harness under his robe, was hoisted up in the air 20 feet above Tommy with a noose around his neck. As we performed the melodic ballad, Little John's body twitched and writhed much to the crowd's amusement as he acted out his execution. During "Flying High Again" the castle walls were bathed with bright colors to accentuate the bright tempo of the song.

For the Black Sabbath portion of our show, the castle was lit up to look like a cathedral. The center arch framed a luminous screen with the image of a colorful stained glass window projected on it. As Tommy began pounding the ominous bass drum intro of "Iron Man," a rotating black cross was projected on screen over his head. Ozzy yelled for all the lights in the house to come up so he could see the faces in the crowd as the band thrust into the lumbering classic.

From "Iron Man" we lurched into "Children of the Grave." A menacing skull appeared on the screen as the spotlights swept over the audience like searchlights looking for escaped convicts.

Much to Ozzy's disapproval, one major change in our live set that night was the elimination of our encore. So instead of getting off the stage after "Children of the Grave" and waiting for the audience's call for more we went straight into the metal anthem, "Paranoid". We ended the set with a climactic display of pyrotechnics as we hit the last chord and quickly exited the stage.

As the audience started yelling for more the stage was filled with smoke.

"Go on, Ozzy! Just remember all you have to do is get on the hand and kick the lever on the floor after the pyro on the fingers go off." I heard Sharon give Ozzy last-minute instructions as she sent him back on stage.

The front steps of the drum riser raised slowly as the gauntlet crept onto the stage from below. Unfortunately, there was so much smoke on stage that Ozzy couldn't locate the "Hummer" sized gauntlet as he wobbled across the stage waving his hands through the smoke hoping to find it.

Frustrated with the whole fiasco Ozzy got off the stage in the midst of boos from the crowd.

"Sharon, I can't find the bloody hand! There's too much fuckin' smoke!"

"You get back out there and get on it!" Sharon insisted.

"Fuck off! You do it," Ozzy said, heading back to the dressing room.

Boos from the crowd reverberated through the arena.

16
Are You Calling My Husband a Drunk?

The following morning, December 31st, we boarded an early flight back to Los Angeles. The trip back home was quieter than usual with everyone still reeling from the aftershock of the previous night's fiasco. Sharon was determined not to repeat the same mistakes during the sold-out New Year's Eve concert at the Los Angeles Sports Arena that evening.

Our equipment trucks caravanned through the night, arriving at daybreak for an early morning load-in. As the production was being set up, every single item was double-checked, especially the motor that turned the Kabuki curtain rod allowing it to fall on cue. In the midst of all the opening night pandemonium the staffer in charge had forgotten to plug in the motor. An overlooked detail like that can ruin a whole show. Not taking chances, Sharon decided to drop the opening act for that evening and push our show time a couple of hours later than scheduled in order to give our crew sufficient time to set up the elaborate production.

Much to Sharon's chagrin, the traditional encore was back in our set. Overnight she had come to the conclusion that you cannot do away with one of the "10 Commandments of Heavy Metal": "Thou shall get off the stage, wait for the crowd to chant your name, return to the stage, and play some more."

From that night on "Paranoid" was back where it belonged. Adding to the extra tension of the evening, Don Arden made his presence known backstage and made it ever so eloquently clear to everyone "that heads were going to roll if there were any fuck-ups." Adding to our stress was the fact that we were playing at home. Not only were we aiming for a flawless production but also for flawless performances. So when the lights finally came down, the deafening roar of the crowd sent a lump down my throat the size of a golf ball as we took our places onstage.

Once again I could see Ozzy sitting nervously inside the throne as the Diary of a Madman acoustic guitar intro came blaring through the PA. But this time when the cue for the Kabuki curtains to drop blared, the three curtains plummeted to the ground as crew members pulled them off the stage. The thunderous roar from the audience nearly drowned the musical intro as the medieval castle and the red velvet throne perched at the top of steps were suddenly revealed.

Right on cue, Ozzy materialized onstage amid a puff of smoke surrounding the throne. He then quickly stood up, walked down the steps, grabbed the cross and ran across the stage. Simultaneously, Randy's and my portcullis gates were slowly raised while Ozzy's throne was pulled back off the raiser and Tommy's drums slowly elevated.

Much to everyone's relief, the intro was perfectly executed, culminating with the pyrotechnic explosions and Tommy's "Over the Mountain" drum fill. With the production uncertainties behind us we were able to focus on the music. After we finished our encore, Ozzy came back onstage and reluctantly climbed on the hand. I could see the fear on his face as he rode the gauntlet high above the first couple of rows. As he settled down, Ozzy waived at the cheering crowd while sparklers flew from the fingers directly in front of him. He then took one step back and released the catapult, launching raw meat into the audience with most of it landing on the back of his head.

"Sharon, the whole thing's daft," Ozzy complained as he got off the stage. "You're making me look like a total cunt!"

"Don't worry, Ozzy. I've got an idea," Sharon assured him, as she put a bathrobe over his shoulders.

After a successful concert, the evening was capped with a New Year's Eve celebration at the Omni Hotel in downtown Los Angeles. The private party was attended by the band, family and close friends. As everyone in the room counted down the seconds ushering in 1982, I looked into Rebecca's eyes and kissed her. We didn't know it yet, but this would the first of many magic moments we'd share together.

The following day, January 1st, we traveled to Phoenix, Arizona to perform that evening at the Veteran's Memorial Coliseum. After our sound check Sharon was on a mission to carry out her new plan. "Jake, bring the caterer and Little John to the dressing room," Sharon requested. "I need for you to put any leftover meat from the deli trays in this bucket and bring it to me before the show."

The catering lady looked puzzled. "Don't worry. We're not going to eat it. We've got better use for it," she explained. "Now John, instead of having Ozzy release the meat into the crowd from the gauntlet, I want you to go across the stage during 'Paranoid' and throw the meat out into the audience while the boys are playing. Do you think you can handle that?"

Little John strained to lift the heavy bucket.

"Oh, I think I can handle it," he assured her, as he dragged the bucket out of the dressing room.

That night Little John appeared onstage during our encore looking like a young "Trick or Treater" after adding white face paint, penciled-in scars, and smeared fake blood to his already Goth costume. He dragged the bucket of meat, to the amusement of the crowd. Amusing, that is, until he started throwing the congealed cold cuts at them!

He slowly made his way across the stage, stirring up a ripple in the audience as the first 20 rows simultaneously ducked trying to avoid being hit. It was an amazing site. Suddenly, the tables turned as the audience retaliated by throwing the meat at Little John who after getting pelted a few times saw this as his cue to run off the stage. So without any hesitation the audience then proceeded to target Ozzy, Randy and me. The meat flew in our direction as we played, ducked and sidestepped around the stage.

"Now, that's a bloody great heavy metal show!" Sharon hugged Ozzy as we exited the meat-littered stage.

On the morning of January 4th we arrived at the posh Grant Hotel in downtown San Diego for that evening's performance at the Sports Arena. After a solid show in front of a huge crowd, there was a rare after-show party in Ozzy's suite attended by the band, groupies and hangers-on who had driven down from nearby Los Angeles.

Without Sharon in attendance, Ozzy was in rare form as he complied with a drunken groupie to sing a tune she had written in exchange for a lap dance. As the young lady was ready to remove her undies Sharon burst into the room.

"What the fuck's going on! Ozzy get that whore out of my sight!" Sharon yelled as the party guests stampeded out the door. "I can't leave you alone for one bloody minute."

"For fuck's sake, Sharon, I was just a having some fun."

"Well, if this is the way it's going to be on this tour then fuck you!" She stormed out of the room and slammed the door. "Ahhhhhggg!!" Ozzy let out a primal scream, pulled the mattress off his bed and tossed it out the sliding door into the swimming pool below. Randy joined in by chucking a chair out the window while Ozzy grabbed anything that wasn't nailed down. They emptied out the room. Even in my drunken stupor, I could see this was a cue to exit until I got the inevitable hotel eviction call from Jake. I laid in my bed fully clothed with my bags packed.

The next morning, I was surprised to wake up in the

same room, in the same hotel. We had finally found an Ozzy resistant hotel! Early that afternoon I passed by Ozzy and Sharon while they sat in the elegant lobby lounge having a cocktail. A couple of hours later I walked by the same spot and noticed that they hadn't moved an inch except for Ozzy who was beginning to slide under the table. Around dinner I walked by the lobby lounge again as Sharon waved me over.

"Rudy," said Sharon, "come and join us for a drink." Ozzy was slumped over the table.

"Thanks, but I'm on my way to get some dinner."

"Oh that's perfect we'll have one more drink and then we'll go to dinner together. Waitress, I'd like to order one more round." "Sorry, ma'am," the waitress said, "but I've been asked by the manager not to serve any more alcohol to Mr. Osbourne." "Excuse me, but are you calling my husband a drunk?" Sharon yelled, filled with indignation as she lifted Ozzy's head off the table.

"Sorry, ma'am but I have strict orders." She politely excused herself as Ozzy drooled with his eyes closed

"That's it!" she said. "Nobody calls my husband a drunk and gets away with it! We're checking out of this shithole immediately!" Sharon yelled as she dragged Ozzy into the elevator.

Within a few minutes I got the call from Jake.

"There's a hotel shuttle van waiting downstairs. Come down with your luggage as soon as possible."

While we sat waiting for Sharon in the van, she came running out the door like a bat out of hell

"Go! Go! Go! Go!" she screamed at the driver as she jumped in the van.

"What the fuck just happened?" Tommy asked.

"Wait. Let me catch my breath," Sharon said while taking her seat next to a nodding Ozzy. "I went to the Ladies Room and pissed in a glass. Then I walked up to the waitress and asked,

'Did I forget to give you a tip?' She smiled and said,

'Yes.' So I said, 'Here's your tip you cunt!' and threw the piss at her and ran!" She looked pleased. "Nobody fucks with my Ozzy. No one!" She kissed his forehead while he drooled.

The next morning January 6th, we traveled from San Diego to Tucson, Arizona to perform that evening at the Community Center Arena.

"Boys, how do you like it?" Sharon excitedly asked as we boarded our new tour bus.

"Ooh, it's got a kitchen," Rachel said. "I can't wait to cook you boys a great big pot of chili."

"The Jacksons used it on their last tour and Kenny Rogers before them," Sharon said proudly.

"Well, that explains the tacky western wagon painted on the side," Tommy comment as I bolted to claim the bunk furthest from the toilet: top bunk driver's side next to the back lounge.

"Ozzy and I are taking the back lounge. You all can have the rest of the bunks," said Sharon.

"Hi, I'm Andrew, your new driver." A bespectacled Southerner introduced himself from behind the wheel.

Later that evening Randy and I sat in the front lounge watching a movie during the after show drive.

"Rand, I haven't seen that look on your face in a while. Is everything all right?" I asked.

"Oh Rudes, I don't even know where to begin," Randy said as he lit up a cigarette. "I've been doing a lot of thinking. I don't feel like I'm myself anymore. Maybe it's because we've been spending so much time in L.A. It seems that now everyone wants to hang out with me. Like the other night in San Diego when everyone came down from L.A., I got drunk and started throwing furniture out the window with Ozzy. That's not really me. That's not the reason why I started playing the guitar."

Randy paused and took a drag of his cigarette. "I don't know. Maybe it's because since we started this

217

tour I feel like I have to compete with the stage. I look behind me and I see this great big castle, the enormous drum riser, Little John running around the stage. I just feel like I'm in a circus."

"Wow, I'm surprised," I replied. "I thought that after you got those Best New Guitarist awards you'd be feeling on top of the world."

"On the contrary Rudes. It's motivated me to get back to where I was before we started touring. You know, putting all my spare time into writing and learning classical guitar."

"So how are you gonna pull it off with our schedule?"

"Oh, I've got some ideas."

The next morning, January 7th, we arrived in Albuquerque, New Mexico for that evening's performance at the Tingley Coliseum. After an early check-in I met Randy for breakfast.

"What are you looking for?" I asked as he browsed through the local phone book.

"I'm looking for a classical guitar teacher. Wait, here's one," he said as he examined a local music store's half page ad. "Looks good. I'll call them after breakfast and book an afternoon lesson."

That afternoon I approached Randy during sound check.

"So, how was your lesson?" I asked.

"Well, when I got to the music store the teacher turned out to be a fan. All she did was ask me how I played the songs."

"Oh, that's hilarious! So you wound up giving her the lesson instead?" I asked.

"Yeah, not only that, but I paid for it, too," Randy said, and we both laughed.

The following morning, January 8th, we checked into the Little America Hotel in Salt Lake City, Utah, to spend a day off in this mellow Mormon city. As I lay in bed after dinner quietly watching TV, I could hear the usual racket coming from Ozzy and Sharon's room across the hall

Suddenly, I saw red flashing lights reflecting on my window. When I peered through the curtains I watched half a dozen riot squad cars hastily pulling into the snow-covered hotel parking lot. I heard the S.W.A.T. team stomping down the hallway until they stopped outside Ozzy and Sharon's door.

"Open up!"

I watched as the captain rapped on the couple's door.

"What's the problem, officer?" Sharon asked as she opened her door.

"Ma'am, we've received complaints from the hotel management that there's been some sort of domestic violence occurring in this room."

"Oh, there has to be a mistake, officer. As you can see, my husband and I are spending a quiet evening together." Ozzy poked his head from underneath the covers, waved and smiled. The officer surveyed the room for a moment.

"Sorry for any inconvenience, ma'am."

"Not at all officer, good night." Sharon smiled and waved at the officers as they marched down the hallway.

As soon as the last squad car left the parking lot, Sharon and Ozzy were brawling again.

The following evening, January 9th, we performed at the Salt Palace in front of a packed house. During our after-show drive we ran into a blinding winter storm as we reached the Rocky Mountains. We finally arrived the next afternoon, January 10th, in Boulder, Colorado to perform that evening at the C.U. Event Center. During the storm one of our semi-trucks broke down, subsequently delaying our load-in and show time by a couple of hours. In order to meet the evening's curfew, Sharon was left with no other choice but to drop the first opening band.

From the audience point of view it might seem unfair to cut the show short in order not to go over the curfew set by the venue. But the reason for such a curfew is simple: if you perform beyond it the promoter has to pay overtime to the stage hands, security, caterers, and others employed by the venue. This can run into the thousands of dollars. So that's why if a headliner goes over the curfew, the promoter can, according to their contract, fine the headliner for every minute they remain onstage over the set curfew.

The next morning, January 11th, we arrived in Omaha, Nebraska. In a singular act of harmonic convergence that not even Sharon could prevent, our band, crew and UFO, the special guest performers on the tour, spent a night off in the same hotel. This infamous British rock band had gained a bad reputation during the mid-'70s for their sex, drugs and alcohol lifestyle and their explosive onstage brawls.

That evening I made my way down to the rowdy hotel lounge for a nightcap.

"So tell me, Little John, how did you wind up on this tour?" I asked as we sat together at the hotel bar.

"My agent got me this job. I'm really an actor," he slurred and almost slid off the barstool. "I'm just doing this between acting jobs. As a matter of fact, I just finished a movie with Harrison Ford, it's called Blade Runner."

"No shit. What did you play in the movie?" I asked.

"I'm one of the toy soldiers. Harrison and I really hit it off," he boasted. "Bartender, all drinks on me!" Little John yelled as he stood on the barstool.

He downed his drink, lost his balance, and slipped off the stool as one of our crew members, Brooksie, caught him in mid-air.

"I've warned you already, little guy. You just can't keep up with the big dogs," said the brawny Brooksie, as he heaved Little John over his shoulder and carried him up to his room.

"Hey, Rudy, why don't you come over and join us?" Ross Halfin, our tour photographer, yelled from across the room.

"Wow, it's pretty crazy in here tonight with everyone staying in the same hotel," I said as I sat with Ross and some of the UFO guys. "I don't know if you've already met Pete Way and Paul Chapman," Ross introduced me to UFO's bassist and guitarist. "Well, not officially," I said, "since you guys joined the tour. But I must admit I'm a fan your band."

"Rudy," said Pete, "I didn't know what to expect from you when Ross told me you where into jazz and funk. I thought you'd be standing still up there onstage like some boring fart.

But I'm impressed by your stage presence."

"Well, Pete, coming from you that's quite a compliment!"

Paul chimed in.

"I haven't seen Randy all day. Do you know where he is?"

"He went out for a classical lesson this afternoon and he's probably up in his room practicing," I said.

"Wow, that's dedication," Paul said as he stared at his glass.

"By the way," I asked, "what's that you guys are drinking?"

Pete and Paul looked at each other. "It's a Nyquil cocktail."

"Oh, you guys have colds?" I asked naively. "Not exactly. You see, in case we can't score we send our crew to the drugstore to get us some Nyquil. After a few bottles it's pretty much the same buzz. Cheers." Pete took a swig and poured another bottle.

The following shows: January 12th at the Civic Auditorium in Omaha, Nebraska, January 13th, at the Municipal Auditorium in Kansas City, Missouri, January 15th at the Met Center in Minneapolis, Minnesota,

January 17th, at the Duluth Arena in Duluth, Minnesota and January 19th in LaCrosse, Wisconsin, all went rather smooth.

Around this time our opening act, Starfighters, was replaced by the British progressive rock band, Magnum. With over three weeks under our belt, the show was running like a well-oiled machine with no mishaps, mistakes, or major incidents as we made our way across the frosty Midwestern landscape.

On the morning of January 20th, we arrived in Des Moines, Iowa. That evening's performance at the Veteran's Auditorium would go on to become a defining moment in Ozzy folklore. That night there was an unusually uplifting mood. Ozzy was in fine form as he donned just about anything that was thrown on stage during the show, from baseball caps to flannel shirts. Halfway through the show, as I was doing my usual onstage head banging, I noticed a peculiar looking fuzzy crumpled black object right in front of me. I looked up and pointed it out to Ozzy and continued playing. Next thing I see is Ozzy picking this thing up, putting it in his mouth, and biting into it like some rabid dog. He wrestled it with his teeth, then spit something out into the audience.

"What's going on?" I asked as Ozzy was rushed off the stage after our final bow.

"Someone threw a dead bat on stage and Ozzy bit into it. Sharon's taking him to the emergency room," Jake explained

After the show our bus waited outside the hospital while Ozzy was being examined.

"Rudy, do you have any film in your camera?" Jake asked. "Sharon wants to take a picture of Ozzy getting a rabies shot." "Yeah, here," I said as I grabbed my camera from my bunk and handed it to Jake. About half an hour later Sharon and Ozzy returned to the bus.

"I'm fucked, man," Ozzy worried. "They can't find the bloody bat back at the gig to test it for rabies. The doctor insisted I get a rabies shot as a precaution."

"You should've seen Ozzy and this great big nurse with her big old nasty syringe giving him a shot on his thigh," laughed Sharon. "It was hysterical! I'm glad we took pictures of it. Can't wait to send them to the publicist!"

"Sharon, where do you want the rest of the rabies shots?" Jake asked.

"Just put the box in the fridge on the top shelf."

"More bloody shots? Sharon, my leg's fuckin' killing me already!" Ozzy complained.

"Oh, don't be a baby, Ozzy. It's for your own good."

We headed to our next destination with vials of monkey serum onboard.

On January 22nd we performed at the Mecca Auditorium in Milwaukee, Wisconsin. By the third day of painful injections Ozzy was beginning to feel the side effects of the treatment.

"Sharon, I'm sick," he whined. "My whole body's aching and I feel like I'm going to puke." Ozzy shivered backstage before the show.

"Oh, you'll be fine soon as you get up onstage. You'll be done with the treatment before you know it. Go on and have a great show, booby." Sharon kissed and hugged Ozzy as she helped him climb on stage.

A local rock journalist wrote of the evening's performance:

"Six thousand fans, most of them very young, crowded into the Auditorium Friday night and seemed to be seeking the same thrills that once were found at freak shows. Ozzy's stage set up, which looked as thought it had been appropriated from a Vincent Price movie, deserved grudging admiration for its economy of design. Though Osbourne

now emphasizes poor mental hygiene over demonology, the sole musical improvement since his Black Sabbath days was his new drummer, who proved his expertise throughout the performance. As a sort of gesture to his old fans, Osbourne, whose new veneer of professionalism forced him to start the concert on time, did a brief medley of Sabbath dirges, including "Iron Man" and his only classic, "Paranoid," a disquieting song that reduces everything he's done since 1970 to redundancy."

On the morning of January 23rd, we arrived in Madison, Wisconsin for that evening's performance at the Dane County Memorial Coliseum. In spite of Ozzy's continuous pleas to cancel the show due to the side effects from the monkey serum, the show went on as scheduled in front of a packed house.

On January 24th we performed at the Rosemont Horizon in the outskirts of Chicago, Illinois. By now the press was having a field day with the story of Ozzy and the bat. So it was no surprise to see the backstage area before the show filled with numerous celebrities intrigued by "the madman who bit the head off a bat onstage."

One celebrity that stood out was former Rolling Stones manager and producer Andrew Loog Oldham.

"Mr. Oldham, I'm Rudy, Ozzy's bass player. I'm a big fan of your work with the Stones."

"Well, thank you very much. I detect a Latin accent. Where are you from?" he asked.

"I'm Cuban."

"Really! My wife's from South America," he told me as our conversation shifted from English to Spanish. During our chat he told me he was there to meet with Ozzy and Sharon regarding screenplay he had written with Ozzy in mind, and that the timing to make the movie

224

couldn't be better with all of the current media attention.

With so much excitement going on before the show, Ozzy was in his best mood and physical condition since he started taking the daily rabies injections. That evening was marked by yet another magic moment in Ozzy lore as local Chicago photographer, Paul Natkin, captured the iconic onstage image of Ozzy lifting Randy by his arm during a guitar solo. The photo later graced the cover of the Randy Rhoads Tribute album.

A local rock reviewer wrote this about the evening's performance:

> **"Ozzy styles himself as a 'madman,' and that is somewhat puzzling given that he neither looks nor acts like one. 'I thought he was supposed to be crazy or something,' complained a former Black Sabbath fan, watching Ozzy walk around the stage in a pair of droopy jogging pants. 'He doesn't look crazy, he looks enfeebled. Like they let him out of the home for the night.' Indeed, instead of doing wild and crazy things himself, Ozzy spent most of his time exhorting the audience ('This is my kind of crowd, wild and reckless') to 'go f crazy' and urging them to cheer louder. The only offbeat touch to the whole proceedings was that Ozzy had a midget in a black robe scurry out on stage from time to time and hand him a towel or a drink of water. Really outrageous Ozzy!"**

The following day, January 25th, we stayed over at the Whitehall Hotel to spend our day off in Chicago. Mr. Oldham continued his script meetings with Ozzy with an in-room dinner that lasted until the light of day.

The following afternoon, January 26th, we boarded our tour bus to take a short drive to Champaign, Illinois for that evening's performance.

"How's Ozzy?" Randy asked as we rode through the bustling streets of downtown Chicago.

"He's passed out in the back lounge," Sharon answered.

"Is he feeling any better from the shots?"

"Well it's bloody hard to tell after he spent the whole night with Andrew drinking and God knows what else," Sharon complained.

That evening it was back to business as usual backstage with Ozzy's pre-show grumblings.

"Sharon, I don't feel good." Ozzy moaned while he hunched over.

"Well, you should've stayed in your room resting on your day off like you were supposed to."

"Sharon, I swear, it's the bloody rabies shots. They are killing me! I can't go onstage like this!" he groaned.

"Fine, do whatever the fuck you want. I've had it!" she said firmly as we all headed for the stage.

We began our show with the usual spectacular stage production and after a restful day off the band's energy was at full tilt as Tommy rammed into the drum fill intro of "Over the Mountain." The band's powerful sound was in direct contrast with Ozzy's feeble presence as he grabbed the mike stand and barely croaked the first words of the song, "Over the moun'—"

Suddenly, his body slammed on the stage and laid motionless on his side as the band continued playing. Sharon and Bugzee, our stage manager, ran to Ozzy and dragged him off by his arms and ankles while we continued playing. As the band had come to expect the unexpected, we kept playing without Ozzy until we finished the song and then walked off stage to await further developments.

"Ladies and gentlemen, the show's been cancelled." Bugzee addressed the bewildered audience. "Ozzy's had a bad reaction to the rabies shots and is being transported to a nearby hospital."

When we returned to our dressing room the backstage area was buzzing with commotion as paramedics rolled Ozzy's gurney into the awaiting ambulance. Sharon quickly hopped on board and held Ozzy's hand as the doors where shut. The wailing siren and the flashing red lights cleared the way for the vehicle as it sped into the night.

17
Sorry Mate, I Thought It Was a Bloody Taco Bell

After the onstage incident in Champagne, Ozzy refused to continue his rabies treatment. On January 29th, after taking a couple of days off to allow Ozzy time to recuperate from his reaction to the serum, we arrived in Terre Haute, Indiana to perform that evening at the Indiana Hulman Center.

By now the fans were expecting each night to see Ozzy bite the head off or blow up some unsuspecting creature onstage. Every promoter was warned by the local authorities that if Mr. Osbourne engaged in any act of animal cruelty onstage he, along with the promoters, would be arrested on the spot. But somehow this worked to Ozzy's benefit, since besides biting the head off the dove at the record company party and the bat incident, Ozzy's consumption of animals was pretty much limited to the fast food chain kind.

Nevertheless, once the show was over and Ozzy refrained from any animal cruelty onstage, the fans blamed it on the presence of the local authorities who most nights could be clearly seen by the crowd standing on the side of the stage keeping a watchful eye. With all the hoopla surrounding our supposedly gory show Sharon felt the pressure to make the performances more controversial. So each night before the show, Sharon had the promoter bring tripe, liver, tongue, giblets, liver, kidney, and other frozen variety meats backstage and add them to Little John's bucket.

That night during our manic encore of "Paranoid," Little John came onstage as usual dragging his bucket. He casually pulled out a long piece of tripe, whirled it over his head like a lasso and flung it into the crowd. The spinning meat flew right in the direction of the only

228

person standing in the sea of cowering fans, a panic-stricken girl who let out a blood curling scream as the tripe wrapped around her neck like an octopus. She then ran and disappeared into the crowd as she tried to rip the piece of meat off her neck. In retaliation, her boyfriend picked up a still frozen piece of liver and hurled it back at Little John striking him on his forehead and knocking him flat out on the stage. One of our crew guys came and picked up Little John and brought him backstage as we carried on with our encore. After the show Little John was taken to the emergency room where he was treated for a concussion and received 12 stitches.

The following shows, January 30th, at the Sports Arena in Toledo, Ohio and January 31st, at Richfield Coliseum in Richfield, Ohio were performed in front of packed houses. I couldn't believe my eyes when one of our crew guys showed me a Polaroid of the head of a freshly slaughtered cow lying in the snow covered ground outside the Sports Arena. Without a doubt, it was a gift for Ozzy from a devoted fan.

On the morning of February 1st we arrived in Pittsburgh, Pennsylvania, to spend our next day off. The following afternoon, February 2nd, Randy conducted a couple of guitar clinics before our sound check for that night's show at the Civic Arena.

"Hey Rand, how did it go?" I asked as we boarded the tour bus. "Well, I was a bit nervous at first," he said. "It's so different doing a guitar clinic in a room full of people than teaching one on one. I just feel like I'm on the spot and have to perform for them."

"Any questions about the bat?" I quipped.

"Yeah, and about the castle and Little John, but for the most part they wanted to know how I played the solos so I showed them a bit of 'Crazy Train' and 'Revelation.' Once I started teaching them I felt really comfortable. Just like the old days at Musonia but without having to show them Van Halen solos for eight hours a day. This time I was teaching them my music."

A local rock scribe wrote about the performance.

"The ads for last night's Civic Arena concert hailed Ozzy Osbourne as the "Metal Maniac," but a sell-out crowd - largely in their mid-teens - filled the Civic Arena last night to enthusiastically cheer Ozzy and his band. Some probably came to see if he'd do anything outrageous, say bite the tail off a cat. Others came for the music. The band, Randy Rhoads on guitar, Rudy Sarzo on bass and Tommy Aldridge on drums produces a loud, growling, thudding sound not unlike Black Sabbath's. Rhoads had an occasional good solo, but the most impressive performance of the night was a Civic Arena usher who did her biology homework while the concert roared. Some of the songs were easy to get caught up in. "Crazy Train," "Suicide Solution," "I Don't Know" stood out. "Goodbye to Romance," an attempt at a ballad, didn't come off. Even though Osbourne relies so heavily on showmanship, he's oddly uncharismatic onstage. He tends to stay put at center stage, his exhorting of the crowd is forced and cliche and for all the partying going on, his presentation seems as sullen as some of the music. But there's something about this crazy image he's perpetrated that appeals to young hard rock fans, and they did fill every seat in the theater-style arrangement at the Arena. The question nags at the back of the mind: Would he be as popular A.) Without his Black Sabbath lineage; B.) Without the ridiculous publicity stunts? The answer that keeps coming back: Doubt it."

The following shows February 5th, at the Civic Center in Lansing, Michigan, and February 6th at Keil Auditorium in St. Louis, Missouri benefited from the circus-like atmosphere surrounding our tour as we performed in front of near sell-out crowds.

Around this time Sharon made a couple of additions to our entourage. Rachel was exhausted due to having to take care of our high maintenance stage outfits and doing what she loved best, cooking for us in the bus. So Sharon hired a light-haired young lady named Lisa to relieve some of Rachel's workload. Another addition was that of a puppy named "Bonehead." Unlike the veteran touring Yorkie, Mr. Pook, the paper-trained pup would go in Randy's bunk and relief itself on his classical sheet music.

With the tour running smoothly Randy and I devoted our preshow time backstage to our own personal interest, his classical guitar studies and my newly acquired Roland bass synthesizer—much to Ozzy's annoyance.

"For fuck's sake Rand, stop that classical shit and let me hear you play some rock and roll, man!" Ozzy yelled as Randy continued playing his acoustic nylon string guitar. "And what the fuck is that noise coming from the other room?" Ozzy asked.

"That's Rudy messing with his bass synth," Randy explained as he paused to light up a cigarette.

"Bloody hell, it sounds like a slaughterhouse in there!" Regardless of Ozzy's concerns that Randy might lose his rock edge, it was evident that his dedication was raising his musicianship to the next level. With his constant studies and practice sessions, Randy's onstage chops gained better articulation and clarity as he sharpened his sound beyond his peers. Unfortunately, his masterful playing would only be experienced by those who could see him live.

As our tour steamrolled through the snow blanketed Midwest, the next shows, February 8th at Cobo Hall in

Detroit, Michigan, February 9th at Wings Auditorium in Kalamazoo, Michigan and February 11th at the Market Square Arena, were packed with cabin- feverish fans hankering for a night filled with Ozzy's unpredictable stage antics and Randy's molten metal histrionics.

After having performed at the Circle Theater across the road six months earlier, headlining the Market Square Arena was not only a triumph for the band but also for Sharon, who after seeing the Jacksons performance there, set their standards of professionalism as the watermark by which Ozzy and the band would be measured.

Unfortunately, our moment of glory would soon fade as events began to unfold, dragging us all into an irreversible downward spiral. In an attempt to beat out Black Sabbath to the release of their own live album, Jet Records forged ahead with a plan of their own.

"Hey guys, what's going on?" I asked Randy and Tommy as I boarded the bus.

"I just spoke with Sharon and she told me that the label wants us to record a live album of all Sabbath songs,"

Randy said as he sat smoking in the front lounge. "You're kidding!"

After coming to expect the unexpected, this news came in from out of nowhere.

"When is this supposed to happen?" I asked.

"They want it as soon as possible, probably in the next few weeks," Randy said.

"Well, what do you think, Rand?" I knew what a peeve it was for him to perform the three Sabbath songs in our set.

"Well, that's what Tommy and I want to talk to you about," Randy said. "After recording two studio albums of original music with Ozzy and all the touring I've done I feel that it would be a giant step backwards for me to record an album of all Sabbath material."

"I can definitely see your point," I agreed.

"We feel that the best way to approach the situation," added Tommy, "is for the three of us to go in and tell Ozzy and Sharon that we don't want to do the record."

"Well, guys, I can definitely see where you both are coming from." I said. "It's just that I don't feel that I'm in any position to refuse recording this album. Let's face it. I have no previous track record like the both of you, so what difference would it make at this point in my career to record an album of Sabbath songs? But nevertheless, Rand, I'll do it for you. You know I owe you this gig. If it wasn't for you I wouldn't be here." Without wasting any time, Randy confronted Ozzy and Sharon with his feelings on the matter. Though it was clear to them the repercussions that such a record release would have on Randy's career, Ozzy and Sharon were faced with an irreversible business agreement that stretched far beyond their control. They had to make this record one way or another.

Though I wasn't privy to any of the recording contract details regarding our Black Sabbath live re-recordings, it was easy to speculate from all the bits and pieces of information floating around within our circle.

Besides the obvious ego-driven attempt for Ozzy to beat out Black Sabbath to their own release, there was a rumor that Don Arden's Jet label had already cut the deal with CBS Records as the distributor and had already received an advance making it impossible for Ozzy and Sharon to decline the offer. Another popular theory was that Black Sabbath's original publishing deal with their previous manager had expired and that by re-recording these songs all the songwriters, including Ozzy, would see a hefty profit from their publishing royalties for the first time. That would also give Don, as Jet's label owner and artist's manager, an additional thick slice of the Ozzy pie.

To say that Randy's refusal to record the live album was a major disappointment to Ozzy would be an understatement. It created a rift in their relationship for the first time that only widened with each passing day. Ozzy resorted to his worst drinking binges I had ever witnessed. Each day he pushed Randy's buttons as we traveled within a suffocating, tension filled tour bus.

"I spoke to Frank Zappa and Gary Moore today and they're both willing to play on the record," Ozzy slurred, confronting Randy in the front lounge.

"Great. That's fine with me," Randy replied as he sidestepped Ozzy on the way to his bunk.

On the other hand, Sharon didn't seem to be too affected by Randy's unwillingness to participate on the record as she carried on making plans for the recordings.

"It's going to be the greatest rock spectacle ever," she announced as we rode in the front lounge. "The show will be at the Maple Leaf Gardens in Toronto. And not only is it going to be for a live album but we'll also be videotaping it. For the intro there'll be half-naked girls coming down from the ceiling at each side of the stage and all sorts of lasers and special effects." Sharon felt she could somehow persuade Randy to perform on the live album as we neared the recording date. Unfortunately, Ozzy didn't seem to see things the same way. Randy hid in his bunk, while Ozzy hid in his bottle.

In spite of the tension, the following shows— February 12th, show at the Riverfront Coliseum in Cincinnati, Ohio, February 13th, at the Rupp Arena in Lexington, Kentucky and February 15th, in Beaumont, Texas—were some of the best performances the band ever gave. No matter what the mood was backstage, the onstage chemistry between Ozzy and Randy conquered all.

The Beaumont show at the local wall-less rodeo arena was a special treat for the band for a couple of reasons. We had been trekking through the frozen

Midwest for nearly six weeks and it was nice for a change to breathe the balmy Texas air from the stage. Also, as in most of the "B" markets we visited, we performed that evening sans the castle production due to the limited dimensions of the venue. This gave the crew the opportunity to place our drums and backline in the traditional heavy rock set up. Randy was at his best in this surroundings—with his three white Marshall stacks almost directly over his shoulder and no castle to compete with.

Between songs during the Beaumont show, I saw what looked like a newborn baby land right at my feet. I quickly got on my knees horrified and realized that it was the biggest bullfrog I had ever seen, flat on its back and very dead. I could just read the next morning headlines, "Ozzy bites the head off a bullfrog!" So to avoid any further controversy or rabies shots I grabbed the bullfrog before Ozzy could see it and tossed over my bass amp barely missing Don Airey's head.

If the Beaumont show was to be considered one of the musical highlights of the tour, then the following performance, February 17th, at the Sam Houston Coliseum in Houston Texas, was without a doubt a dismal one as Ozzy performed on binge begun the previous night.

A local rock journalist wrote of that evening's performance,

> **"If Ozzy Osbourne is the demon king of heavy-metal then he was bent on taking his Coliseum audience with him into the depths of rock 'n roll hell. From the moment Osbourne sang, he hypnotized his fans with rock music as hard and driving as it can get. The sinister overtones of his earlier days were still alive in songs like 'Suicide Solution' and 'Goodbye to Romance' both from his first**

solo album, Blizzard of Ozz. And what Osbourne may lack in originality of theme, he and lead guitarist Randy Rhoads made up for in the energy and stamina needed to take the band from one blasting song to the next. As of 10:45 p.m., there was no dead bat incident, for which Osbourne made headlines in a concert last month, but his Houston fans didn't seem to mind."

Early the next morning, February 18th, Randy and I sat at the hotel's sky bar overlooking Houston, quietly drinking coffee before we boarded the tour bus.

"Oh, God, here he comes," Randy said. Looks like he's been up all night drinking. Just don't say anything and maybe he won't see us." We looked straight ahead and sipped our coffees. Suddenly all hell broke loose as Ozzy unleashed the biggest tirade I had ever witness.

"All you guys are fired! I want you the fuck off my bus right now!" Ozzy screamed as a barrage of insults and barstools flew while Randy and I ran for cover in a waiting elevator.

As we waited out the storm in our rooms, Randy was terribly upset, since he felt totally responsible for Ozzy firing the whole band. Later that morning Jake gathered Randy, Tommy, Don and me and brought us to Sharon's room.

"I'm afraid Ozzy's finally snapped," said Sharon. "I think it's best for everyone if you boys travel to San Antonio by plane." "But, Sharon," Tommy said, "that's only about a couple of hours drive on the bus. It's going to take us twice that long to get there by the time we drive to the airport and get on a flight." "I just don't trust Ozzy in the shape he's in," she said. "As a matter of fact, I think it's best if you boys get all your guitars and other belongings off the bus. You'll never know what he'll do next when he gets like this. But don't worry. I'll have

Jake travel with you. He'll take care of everything. Randy, are you all right? You look distressed." She gently grabbed him by the shoulders and looked him in the eyes.

"I have a lot on my mind. I'll be fine."

"I'll have a word with Ozzy after he gets some rest in the bus. Hopefully we can clear up this whole mess," Sharon said, as she hugged Randy.

Five hours later we arrived at our hotel in San Antonio to perform that evening at the Convention Center. As I walked through the lobby I saw Ozzy sitting at the hotel bar with our publicist Michael Jensen along with a journalist and a photographer from one of London's major rock publications, Melody Maker. I was amazed to see Ozzy in such a cheerful mood, but most of all, dressed in drag. In the midst of his drunken stupor, Ozzy had borrowed a hodgepodge of Sharon's and Lisa's clothes as he concocted a crossdresser pictorial with the historic city of San Antonio as the background for this most outrageous photo session.

The phone rang as I was walking out the door to meet the guys at the lobby for sound check.

"Rudy, this is Jake. Listen, whatever you do, don't leave your room until you hear back from me."

"Oh, no! What's going on?" I asked always expecting the unexpected but never this.

"Ozzy's been arrested for pissing on the Alamo. Sharon's afraid that if he's not released in time for the show there will be a riot at the venue."

"Well, I guess its room service for me tonight then," I replied as I hung up the phone and plopped into bed, completely exhausted from an emotionally draining day.

Ozzy was finally released later that afternoon and rushed back to the hotel for a much needed pre-show scrub down. In complete contrast to his fit of rage earlier that morning, Ozzy was in a cheerful mood joking in our dressing room backstage.

"You should've seen me. There I was running all

over this bloody town posing for pictures, wearing Lisa's big old floppy hat and Sharon's pants suit when I just had to take a piss. So I went behind this bush and started pissing on this wall when a bloody Texas Ranger taps me on my shoulder and says, (Ozzy imitates a macho Texan accent) 'Hey boy, what do you think you're doing?' So I answered, 'I'm just taking a piss, man.' So then the Ranger yelled at me, 'Hey boy, don't you know this is a National Monument?!' So I told him, 'Sorry mate, I thought it was a bloody Taco Bell! I saw a vein pop out of his bloody forehead and then he grabbed my arm and shouted, 'That's it boy! You're coming with me!' And he dragged my ass to bloody jail!"
Sharon continued.
"The bloody Rangers wanted to keep Ozzy overnight just to fuck with him. It wasn't until I told them that if he didn't make the sold-out show tonight they would have a riot on their hands. And that's when they reluctantly let him go." Sharon explained as we readied up for the show.

Though Ozzy and Sharon tried to make light of the circumstances, Randy just kept to himself, quietly playing his acoustic guitar in a corner of the dressing room.

A local journalist wrote of that day's events:

"Thousands of fanatical followers of rock star Ozzy Osbourne, whose bizarre stage antics include biting the heads off bats and other small animals, staged a mini-riot at the Convention Center last night. Eleven full-length, plate glass windows outside the arena were broken by the pulsating crowd of more than 13,900 as it entered for the rock concert. At least four paddy-wagon loads of more than 20 youths were hauled to Bexar County Jail and the Juvenile detention center last

night. Unofficial damage estimates to the windows was about $5,000, police said, to be paid by the promoters. Earlier in the day, Osbourne was arrested on charges of public drunkenness after he relieved himself on a column outside the Alamo. In doing that, Osbourne said he accomplished one of his lifetime goals. But he said his main goal in life is to use the White House steps as a public bathroom, too. Arrested about 3 p.m., Osbourne was released from jail about 4:30 p.m. after Jack Orbin, a producer of Stone City Attractions, cosponsor of the concert, posted a $40 bond. Osbourne, who underwent a series of rabies shots after biting the head off a bat earlier in his U.S. tour, said he stopped treatment because he "would rather have rabies" than take the shots." Police officers on duty at the concert were ordered not to allow any live animals into the Arena. Perhaps the most outrageous thing Osbourne did was grab a Dolly Parton-sized white bra that was tossed up from the crowd and twirl it around his arm while singing, then put it on and prance around the stage."

As the news of Ozzy's desecration of the Alamo spread like wildfire through Texas he topped the Daughters of the Republic of Texas "persona non grata" list and became the target of numerous death threats from regional vigilante groups.

In an ironic twist of fate, Ozzy and Sharon attended the White House Correspondents Association Ball on Saturday, May 4, 2002, 20 years after the Alamo incident. They were introduced at the event by the former governor of Texas, President George W. Bush.

18
Guys, We Need to Talk

The bus ride after the San Antonio show was an uncomfortably quiet one with all the band members retiring to bunks as soon as the bus pulled out of the Convention Center's parking lot. Though Ozzy had made a remarkable attitude adjustment by show time, it had been an emotionally draining day and we needed to let the dust settle overnight.

The following morning, February 20th, we arrived in Dallas, Texas, to perform that evening at the Reunion Arena. Later that afternoon we boarded the bus for sound check as usual. A sharp pain hit me in the pit of my stomach as soon as I saw Randy's somber expression.

"Rand, Is everything all right?" I asked.

"Guys, we need to talk," Randy said as Tommy, Don and I gathered around him. "I had a meeting with Ozzy and I've agreed to play on the record."

Relieved, I was ready to put the conflict behind us when Randy continued. "But with one condition: that after I've fulfilled my commitments to the live album I would record one more studio album and one more tour. That's it. After that, I'm going back to school to get my master's degree in music."

My jaw dropped to the ground. We were devastated. Though none of us could blame him for wanting to leave after the ruckus in Houston, the thought of us carrying on without our driving force was unimaginable. After hearing Randy's uncharacteristically resolute words, all we could do was hope that ultimately he would have a change of heart and stay.

The pre-show mood backstage that night was filled with mixed emotions as Ozzy felt victorious about winning the battle with Randy over the live album. But obviously Ozzy was also concerned that in the long run, with Randy's departure, he would lose the war. That evening I started my own personal count down as each performance took on a special meaning with Randy's departure looming in the not too distant future.

A local rock reviewer wrote these words about that evening's performance,

> **"An Ozzy Osbourne concert is the pin that bursts the balloon of Ozzy Osbourne hype. The man is a pussycat. And not a very well-trained one either.**
> **While an enthusiastic and comparatively well- behaved crowd waited 73 minutes for something to happen—for him to eat, or at least bite something— Osbourne waddled through a dismal set of irrelevant rock 'n' roll Saturday night at Reunion Arena.**
> **Besides, the dwarf came back from the dead at the end of the show and threw raw meat over a bunch of people in the first couple of rows. Of course, anyone buying tickets in the front row of an Ozzy Osbourne concert gets just what they deserve, too. The Reunion Arena manager was quoted earlier in the week as saying he would stop the show if Osbourne killed any animals on stage."**

The following day we arrived in Corpus Christi, Texas for that evening's performance at the Memorial Coliseum. By now, news about Ozzy's Alamo antics were spreading throughout this conservative state. The combination of multiple death threats from local vigilante groups and Ozzy's own threat to critters prompted the authorities to summon backups to reinforce the local police force. The authorities made their presence known to the crowd and the band as they sat through the whole show watching from the wings on my side of the stage.

Adding to the night's chaos was UFO's volatile behavior. While the band waited for their encore behind Paul Chapman's wall of Marshall stacks, Pete Way and Phil Moog got into a scuffle. The wall of amps came tumbling down as they slugged it out in plain sight of the cheering crowd before returning to the stage to play their encore. After the set ended, the fight carried on into their dressing room where Phil, a former British Golden Gloves boxer, single-handedly did an estimated $10,000 worth of damage.

A local reviewer wrote about that ruffled evening:

"Animal-lovers, take heart. Rock singer Ozzy Osbourne blasted through Corpus Christi last night and didn't bite a thing. For the past few weeks, humane society and city officials had expressed concern that Osbourne would repeat a bat-biting incident that occurred earlier this year at a rock concert. Spurred on by media publicity, more than 6,0 Osbourne fans jammed a sold-out Memorial Coliseum last night to hear Osbourne. Adding to the giant throng were nearly 50 off-duty and on-duty police officers. Earlier this week, city officials urged that ordinances regarding cruelty to animals be enforced during the concert. Humane society representatives had asked the City Council to look into the Osbourne concert because of previous incidents and rumors of repeat performances. Asked what would have been done if Osbourne had brought an animal on stage, Sullivan said, 'The officers are instructed to call me. What's next? We'll see when it gets to that."

During our long after-show bus ride across Texas, Randy sat alone in the back lounge listening to a cassette of one of his favorite jazz guitarists, Lee Ritenour.

"Hey Rand, got a minute?" I asked. "Man, I feel so bad. I hope you're not agreeing to play on the live record just to prevent Ozzy from firing us."

"Hey Rudes, don't worry. You know, when I talked to Ozzy he didn't remember anything about what went down that morning in Houston." He shook his head in disbelief. "I just figured that if I played on the live record that would bring me one album closer to fulfilling my contractual obligations and then I can go back to school and maybe do some studio work."

"It's sound like you're pretty determined."

"Well, yeah, I've already asked my Mom to look into music schools I can attend after this tour. And there's this editor for Guitar World, John Stix, who's offered to help me out with the New York studio scene. I've asked him to introduce me to Steve Gadd, John Luc-Ponty or Earl Klugh next time we play New York and he thinks it shouldn't be a problem." He was obviously excited about the prospects.

"Well, I know we still got some more time left to play together, but I want you to know that I'm really going to miss you."

"Hey, Rudes," Randy laughed. "You don't have to get so dramatic. We still have a least couple more years before I go." "Look," I said, "all I want to say is that I know how stifled you feel playing the same thing over and over again every night and..." I paused. "Well, whatever you decide to do in the end, you got my support." I shook his hand as I tried to compose myself.

On February 23rd we performed at the County Coliseum in El Paso, Texas. That afternoon during sound check we were visited by the Ozzy Osbourne Band Japanese fan club. The shy and courteous entourage kindly conducted back stage interviews and photo sessions with all the band members. Though they gave each of us their undivided attention it was easy to tell they were mostly impressed with Randy.

He had already built a strong legion of fans dating back to the Quiet Riot I and II Sony releases and by then had reached a guitar hero status in Japan even though he never got to perform there.

By then Ozzy had become Texas' most undesirable rocker and death threats followed us where ever we played. On the other hand, to the Mexican fans from El Paso and the neighboring south of the border town of Juarez, Ozzy had become a national hero as he unwittingly expressed their own feelings about the venerable Texas shrine, a landmark on the former Mexican territory that had taunted them for nearly 150 years.

That evening we watched from the stage in awe while the exuberant Mexican fans crafted homemade fireworks, as they flung flaming gasoline-soaked rags into the dusty Coliseum air in celebration of Ozzy's appearance.

The February 24th show at the Memorial Coliseum in Lubbock, Texas and the February 25th show at the Lloyd Noble Center in Norman, Oklahoma went on without any major incidents. After eight manic weeks on the road the crew and all the bands on the bill tried to keep the insanity to a chaotic minimum as we looked forward to the upcoming conclusion of the first leg of the tour.

On February 26th we arrived in Wichita, Kansas, to spend another scheduled day off. That evening, Andy Aycock, our bus driver who up until now had kept pretty much to himself, joined us at the hotel bar. I was quite surprised to see him there since it was customary that after a long drive the bus driver stayed in his room resting.

"Hey guys," he said. "I've heard that we'll be in Florida during the next leg of the tour." Kenny Rogers blasted from the nearby jukebox.

"I hope we do," I said. "I'm from Miami and I always look forward to playing down there."

"Well, if we go anywhere near Orlando I would love to take ya'll up for a spin around the countryside," Andy said while sipping his beer.

"You're a pilot?" I asked.

"Yep, I'm also licensed to fly choppers," he boasted.

"You don't say."

The following evening, February 27th, we performed at Wichita's Britt Brown Arena in front of a near sell-out crowd.

Though their onstage chemistry remained intact, the lingering offstage tension between Randy and Ozzy intensified with each passing day. However, it was clear that Sharon's position on Randy's notice was that eventually he would change his mind and stay, just as he had when he finally agreed to play on the live record. On the other hand, Randy's notice became Ozzy's new springboard for plunging deeper into the bottle.

On February 28th, we went back to Texas to perform that evening in Amarillo. This being our last Texas show, Sharon decided that we should skip sound check in the midst of all the previous death threats and the negative publicity surrounding Ozzy and get to the venue right before show time. While we were in our dressing room changing into our stage clothes I overheard the commotion outside our door.

"Boys, the promoter has received a phone call from some lunatic vigilante group threatening to shoot Ozzy onstage," Sharon announced as she entered the dressing room. "He thinks that it's just a prank but we're increasing security just in case." Sharon said.

"Fuck 'em! You can't hurt bloody steel," Ozzy bragged.

"Yeah, but if you piss on it, it will rust!" Tommy joked as he banged his drumsticks on a table.

That night during the show Randy and I avoided

Ozzy. Every time he came near us we ran in the opposite direction just in case the bullet happened to miss him. Fortunately, not a single shot was fired that night. Not that you would've heard it over the band's thunderous volume.

The following show, March 2nd, was at the Hirsch Coliseum in Shreveport, Louisiana. The band and crew were glad to leave all the tension of playing in Texas behind as we drew closer to our much needed tour break.

A local journalist wrote about the show:

> **"Ozzy Osbourne didn't bite the heads off any animals during his concert at Hirsch Coliseum Tuesday night, but there were probably a few two-legged animals out of the 6,585 people present who, expecting gore and grisly goings on, would have liked to bite off his head. Osbourne and his band arrived after a week or so of dire publicity—news which, to date, has had him targeted by animal lovers, doing vile things to the Alamo, conspiring to harm goats, doves and bats and being warned off by district attorneys. After all that, the man got onstage and provided a rather homogenous mix of loud, rather insipid and uninspired sound which sober souls would never confuse with music."**

The March 3rd show at the Centroplex in Baton Rouge, Louisiana was cancelled so I took advantage of the proximity and flew down to Miami for a couple of days and applied for my U.S. citizenship. It wasn't easy to accept the loss of my Cuban citizenship. After all, it was the only connection I had to my native country. But after the incident at the Frankfurt Airport I was left with no other choice but to become a U.S. citizen and receive a valid passport.

So on December 7th, 1982, I was proudly sworn in as an American citizen at the Miami Dade County Auditorium along with a couple hundred fellow Cubans. Through the years I've come to realize that a piece of paper can never change who I am. Now when someone detects my accent and asks where I'm from, I smile and tell them I'm an American from Cuba.

On March 5th I took an early morning flight from Miami to Pine Bluff, Arkansas to meet the band for that evening's performance at the Convention Center. During sound check the backstage area was quieter than usual as everyone was touched by the drug-related death of John Belushi, whose talent and gonzo lifestyle had garnered the admiration of rock musicians everywhere.

That evening during the after-show drive I joined Ozzy in the front lounge before retiring to my bunk.

"Hey Ozz, too bad about Belushi, huh?"

"We all gotta go sometime," Ozzy muttered as he hugged a whiskey bottle and stared at the TV.

"Yeah, but he was so young and so talented. What a fuckin' waste!"

"That's the fucked up thing about death, said Ozzy. "You just never know when your bloody time is up." He offered me a swig from his bottle.

"No thanks, Ozz, I'm gonna hit the bunk soon." I paused for a moment. "Do you believe in God?" I bluntly asked. Though I had a preconceived notion, I wanted to hear it from him.

"You want to know what I believe?" He asked, peering into my eyes. "I believe in me." He paused and took another swig. "I believe in fate. I believe that I'm here for a bloody reason." He was uncharacteristically frank. "You wanna know what I also believe in?" he asked while I listened. "Luck. Most of my life I've been a bloody lucky guy." He stared at the open road. "But lately, I don't know. I just can't explain it." He paused and took a deep breath followed by another swig. "I don't feel so lucky anymore. I feel like something's going to happen to me soon." He said as his blood shot eyes peered into mine.

"What, like you're going to die?" I replied, trying to lighten up the conversation.

"Well, fuck me if I know when I'm gonna buy the bloody farm," he joked. "All I can do is just fucking go for it and hope to die young enough to leave a bloody good-looking corpse. Can you imagine me up there, an old geezer singing?" We both laughed at the sad mental picture. "For some fucking reason everybody thinks that we rock stars are immortal. But you know what? In the end we either burn out with a flash or we get old and die!"

The next evening, March 6th, we performed the final show of the first leg of the tour at the Botwell Auditorium in Birmingham, Alabama. As usual, Little John was hoisted up in the air during the mock hanging execution while we played "Goodbye to Romance." But somehow that night his safety harness slipped and the noose started choking him for real. The crew member whose duty was to hoist him up saw his diminutive body desperately writhing and figured he was just hamming it up. Encouraged by the realistic performance, the crew member began to swing the rope furiously flinging Little John like a kite in a tornado as he gagged and clutched the noose for dear life.

Taken by the spectacle, Ozzy directed all the spotlights on Little John as the crowd cheered his precarious predicament. Finally, the song was over and Little John was hoisted down. The crew immediately realized that there was something wrong and carried him over to the catering room and laid him on a table. While they gathered around him, arguing who would administer CPR, Little John got up, jumped off the table, shot them a bird and got back on stage to continue with the show.

On the morning of March 7th the band and most of the crew flew from Birmingham to Los Angles for our big, 10-day break. On this flight we traveled coach with Ozzy sitting across the aisle from Little John.

"Hey, that looks like Harrison sitting in first class," Little John said as he tapped Ozzy on the shoulder. "You know we did a movie together."

"Yeah, yeah, you've already told me the same bloody story a thousand times," Ozzy replied, annoyed.

"Hell, I'm going over and say hi to him." He made his way down the aisle into first class.

"This is going to be bloody great. Bet ya anything he's going to tell 'im to fuck off and go back to his seat." Ozzy rubbed his hands together, brimming with anticipation.

A few moments passed with no sign of Little John.

"Bloody hell!" Ozzy blurted as Little John poked his head through the curtain holding up a bubbling glass of champagne. He then flashed a contemptuous smile at Ozzy and disappeared behind the curtain.

"Fuck me, Rache. The little bastard's sitting in first class sipping champagne with bloody Hans Solo," Ozzy mumbled.

When we landed in Los Angeles my girlfriend Rebecca, looking as breathtaking as a Malibu sunset, was waiting for me at the gate holding a colorful helium balloon bunch. Mr. Ford, assuming that she had been sent by the movie studio to greet him, approached her with open arms as she ran to my side and kissed me. Meanwhile Little John, who by then was drunk as a skunk, tried to look up Rebecca's mini skirt before Mr. Ford grabbed him by the arm and carried him off.

Since I wanted to spend the whole break with Rebecca, I opted to stay in a hotel rather than at the Arden's.

"This is your lucky day, laddie," Jake told me as we waited at baggage claim. "I just got off the phone with the travel agent and she told me that she can get you a real good rate at the Chateau Marmont. It seems that after the Belushi incident the place is crawling with paparazzi, forcing most celebrities to cancel their reservation."

"Fantastic," I said. "I'll just have Rebecca drive me over."

"Hi. Reservation for Mr. Sarzo," I said as Rebecca and I approached the front desk.

"Oh, yes, your travel agent just called." the clerk said, handing me the registration card. "Who did you say you played with?" He asked before handing me the key.

"The Ozzy Osbourne Band."

"Isn't he the one who bit the head off the bat?"

"Ah, yes, he's the one."

"Really?" He seemed impressed.

"Well, Bianca Jagger just cancelled her reservation. I can give you her usual penthouse suite if you wish."

"That would be nice," I smiled and grabbed the key. Our stay was blissful as Rebecca and I set up our love nest perched high above the Sunset Strip, giving us a taste of what it might be like if we ever took our relationship to the next level.

Early one evening halfway through the break I got a call from Sharon.

"Rudy, can you do me a favor? Ozzy hasn't left our bungalow since we got back. He's really depressed about Randy leaving. All he does is drink and get high." Sharon sounded unusually worn out. "It might cheer him up if you came over to visit for a while." I could tell from her tone of voice that I was probably her last resort.

"Sure," I said. "Oh, by the way, Rebecca's staying with me. I hope you don't mind if she comes along," I asked.

"Whatever. Just try to get here as soon as you can."

"Oh boy," I thought. "This is going to be interesting."

After we drove past the security guard, we were greeted by Sharon in the courtyard outside.

"Thanks for coming," she said, surrounded by a pack of frisky family dogs. "Ozzy's totally out of control. I just don't know what to do anymore. Last night I just couldn't take it so I grabbed his bag of waffle dust and ran out into the courtyard and smashed it on the ground. Next thing I know, Ozzy's lying on the ground snorting it up along with the dogs. These poor babies haven't stopped chasing their tails around the courtyard ever since! We even had to hose down Jet when he wouldn't stop humping our Shetland pony."

As we followed her into the bedroom I found a disheveled Ozzy lying under the covers with bottles of booze covering every inch of the nightstand. He was oblivious to our presence as he stared at the TV. "Ozzy look who's come by to see you. It's Rudy and Rebecca!"

A few uncomfortable moments passed as Rebecca and I remained unnoticed. Suddenly, Ozzy looked in my direction and slowly motion with his fingers for me to come closer until I was just a few inches from his face.

"You go tell your friend that he'd better reconsider leaving the band. You tell him he's fucking up the best thing he's ever had. He's skating on thin ice."

His words were barely discernible as he pointed his trembling index finger at me. I looked into his eyes and could tell he was really hurting. I knew exactly how he felt; I was hurting, too.

Unfortunately Ozzy didn't crawl out of the bottle soon enough to tell Randy how he really felt.

On the morning of March 16th we flew from Los Angeles to Atlanta to begin the second leg of the Diary of a Madman tour.

"Here you go, laddies. Hot off the presses!" Jake said as he handed Randy and me our tour itineraries while we sat at the departing gate.

"Wow, I can't wait to play at the Miami Orange Bowl

this weekend. My parent's house is just a few blocks from there. They're gonna be so excited," I said as I leafed through the pages.

"Rude's, check this out! We're playing the Garden!" Randy said, showing me the date on the page. "I've been looking forward to playing there since I was a kid. It's going to be great. I just know it." He lit up a cigarette. "Come to think of it, maybe I should call up John Stix and arrange to meet some studio musicians while we're in the city."

"So, how was time off?" I asked.

"Oh, except for a couple of nights out in Hollywood I pretty much stayed home practicing my classical guitar and hanging with Jody. How about you?"

"Well, Rebecca and I stayed at a penthouse suite at the Chateau Marmont and got to play house. We had a great time. As a matter fact, we always have a great time no matter what we do."

"Rudes, sounds like you two are getting serious," Randy said. "You'd be crazy to let that one get away."

"Yeah, I know."

"Oh, by the way. I spoke with Kevin while I was home. He wants to know if we don't mind him calling his new band Quiet Riot."

"I don't have any problem with that," I said. "How about you?" "Not really," he replied.

"Oh no, is that Rachel coming over with Ozzy and Sharon?" I pointed out. "I can't believe it. Sharon told me Rachel was having heart problems and was going to stay home during this leg of the tour. I just hope something bad doesn't happen to her while we're out on the road."

The following evening, March 17th, we performed at the Omni Arena in Atlanta, Georgia. When I boarded the bus for sound check I was introduced by Andy, our bus driver, to a pleasant looking lady sitting in the front lounge.

"Hey, Rudy, I want you to meet my wife Wanda," he said. "She's gonna be riding with us for the next few days." We shook hands and exchanged greetings.

Later on, Jake approached me in the dressing room.

"I hope you don't mind Wanda traveling with us. It's just that they've been separated and Andy's trying everything possible to get her back."

After our 10-day break, it was great to get back on stage and perform in front of a sold-out crowd. There's always an extra amount of energy during the first few shows after a break and this one was no exception with Ozzy and Randy reaching new performance heights, hinting to their possible reconciliation.

The next evening, March 18th, we performed at the Civic Coliseum in Knoxville, Tennessee. That night Randy gave an unforgettable performance as he and Ozzy sustained their electrifying onstage chemistry from the previous night. We were without a doubt on our biggest roll.

After the show, I was approached by Jake as we began the 665- mile drive to Orlando.

"Listen, Andy wants to stop at the bus company's depot outside of Orlando and get rid of some of the extra bunks we have since Ozzy and Sharon have taken the back lounge. He says he's got all the special tools there and it shouldn't take more than half an hour."

"No problem," I replied and headed for the front lounge where Ozzy, Randy, Tommy and Don were watching a video of the World War II epic, Midway.

The mood was upbeat with Randy and Ozzy sitting together engaging in small talk and watching the movie. It was in contrast to the somber mood that permeated throughout the tour bus before the break. After one too many kamikaze suicide crashes on the TV screen it was time for me to call it a night and hit my bunk.

19
March 19th, 1982

After a 655-mile drive from Knoxville, Tennessee, we arrived early in the morning at the Flying Baron Estates, home and headquarters of the Calhoun Brothers' tour bus company, located outside of Leesburg, Florida.

"Rudes, Rudes, come on, get up!" I slid the curtains open and saw Randy standing in the doorway of the tour bus.

"What's going on?" I said with a yawn as I wiped the sleep from my eyes.

"We've stopped at the tour bus depot. There's a landing strip here and Andy's going to take Rachel and me up on a plane to see the countryside. Why don't you get dressed and come with us? It'll be fun!"

"What time is it?"

"Oh, I don't know, about 8 a.m.," Randy said with a shrug.

"Oh, that's all right, you go ahead. I'm just going to wait until we get to Orlando to get out of my bunk."

"OK, but you'll be sorry you've missed it!" Randy kidded as I watched him step out into the quiet Florida morning. I immediately pulled back the curtains and went back to sleep.

"BOOM!"

I was nearly thrown out of my bunk by the violent impact that still had the bus rocking. I quickly opened my curtains as Sharon flung the door to the back lounge wide opened.

"What the fuck is going on? Where are we?" Ozzy, Tommy and I followed her into the front lounge.

"Careful there's broken glass everywhere!" Sharon warned as she opened the door leading from the bunk area to the front lounge.

As I side-stepped the broken glass with my bare feet I

realized that the window had been blown to pieces. Through the gaping hole where the window used to be I watched Jake on his knees crying, rocking back and forth pulling his hair.

"They're gone! They're gone!" he cried.

"Get the fuck out of my way!" Sharon shoved Wanda to one side as she stood frozen in the doorway.

"Jake, what the fuck's happening?" Sharon ran up to Jake and shook him by the shoulders.

"Randy and Rachel were on the plane and they crashed." Jake barely pulled himself together as he pointed toward the enflamed car garage.

"You bastard! How could you let them go up on a plane after he'd been driving all night? And without my permission! Don't you know that man had already killed one of the Calhoun's kids in a helicopter crash!" Sharon frantically yelled at Jake as he fell to his knees coiled in agony.

The shocking news had me stunned, numb. All at once, my senses shut down, as a low frequency hum drowned out every sound around me. I became completely disoriented. Every move I made felt like it was in slow motion. I aimlessly wandered around the debris.

As I started coming to my senses I watched Tommy run past me with a small fire extinguisher he had grabbed from the bus. After he emptied the small canister into the rising inferno, Tommy and Don ran in the house looking for a phone. While they frantically ran from room to room they found a man sitting at the breakfast table reading a newspaper unaware that the house was on fire.

"Hey Mister! Your house is on fire! You've got to get out!" Tommy and Don waved their arms trying to get his attention.

Startled by their presence, the hearing-impaired man jumped off the table and realized the predicament as the smoke filled the room. As the fire grew out of control and spread from the garage to the rest of the house Tommy climbed on our bus and drove it away from the flaming structure.

After an exasperating couple of hours the Leesburg Fire and Rescue Unit and Sheriff Departments finally arrived at the scene of the crash.

"It all seemed so innocent," Jake contemplated as we stood among the smoldering wreckage. "When we arrived this morning Andy offered Don and me to take us up. I must admit that it got a bit scary when he started buzzing the bus trying to wake Tommy up. But after a few attempts we just landed. That was it." He sadly explained.

"Why in the world did Rachel and Randy go up on that plane? Randy's afraid of flying and she's got a bad heart."

"Well," Jake said, "right after we landed Andy came up to me and told me that he was going to take Rachel up for a ride. And that being aware of her heart condition he assured me he was just going to take it easy, circle the property a couple of times and not pull any crazy stunts. So when Randy heard that, he decided to join them so he could take some aerial shots with his camera. Poor Rachel ... She was so excited to ride for the first time on a private plane she even changed into her best outfit." After Don answered a few questions from the local authorities I approached him to get his point of view.

"I had my camera and was taking photos of the plane to give Randy afterwards. I had my telephoto lens on and could tell that there was some sort of struggle going on board the plane. The wings were rapidly tipping from side to side. At one point, the plane almost became perpendicular, no more that six feet off the ground. That's when I put down my camera and saw the plane right in front of me. I quickly crouched to avoid getting hit and looked over my shoulder and watched it clip the bus, crash into the tree and explode on impact into the garage."

As he spoke, the tears ran down his face.

In search of more answers I wandered over to our battered bus and examined the two circular punctures formed by the impact of the wing tips. I approximated that the point of impact was not higher than five feet from the ground. I then realized that if the plane had come down just a couple of inches lower it would had crashed into the bus and taken all of our lives.

After the local authorities concluded their initial rounds of questioning they asked us to remove our personal belongings from the bus before they escorted us to a nearby motel. The personal belongings of Randy, Rachel and Andy remained on the bus until further investigation.

The first thing I did when we checked into the motel was to call my parents and give them the tragic news. Fortunately, the Cuban radio stations in Miami had not yet broadcasted any news regarding the crash and I was able to intercept any misinformation. On the other hand, by the time I was able to reach a phone, the Los Angeles radio airwaves were filled with tributes to Randy and misinformation about the crash. My second phone call was to Rebecca.

"Oh, my God, I'm so glad you're alive!" Rebecca sobbed. I could hear that she'd been crying. "All the radio's been announcing is that Randy and members of the Ozzy Osbourne band were killed in a plane crash."

"It was Randy, Rachel and the bus driver," I sadly whispered. "The rest of us are fine."

I spent the rest of the afternoon reliving the crash over the phone with my friends and loved ones and I just couldn't help feeling guiltier with each call at the thought of still being alive. After I had gone through my whole phone book I just had to be alone. So I went for a walk and came upon a church down the street from the hotel. I walked in and noticed that the place was empty except for one lonely soul on his knees praying near the altar. I too wanted to be alone so I kept my distance as I knelt down at a pew near the entrance and prayed. As I closed my eyes and wept, I could hear him sobbing uncontrollably. Even in my darkest hour I couldn't help but feel compassion towards someone who seemed to be in more agony than myself. Suddenly, he let out a bone-chilling moan that reverberated throughout the church.

"Why! Why!?" He cried.

I raised my head and looked over at him. It was Ozzy.

Back in my room, the events of the day kept flashing through my head as I lay in bed trying to make some sense of it all. It was common knowledge within our circle that Andy and Wanda's marriage was on the rocks and he was desperately trying to win her back. There were references by those who witnessed the crash that Wanda was standing in the doorway of the bus as the plane plummeted towards it.

"Why would Andy invite our band members to go for a couple of airplane rides after an exhausting 10-hour bus drive?" I asked myself over and over. Images of Randy struggling with Andy to keep the plane from crashing into the bus kept flashing through my head.

Finally in a slightly more comforting, lucid moment I came to realize that Randy had saved our lives. Later that night, after I had run out of tears, I fell asleep.

The day following the crash, March 20th, Ozzy, Sharon and I took part in depositions officiated by a Florida Lake County notary public. We were all still in a state of shock and it was extremely painful to piece together the events of the day before. Ozzy was so incoherent and distraught that our publicist, Michael Jensen, had to transcribe his affidavit.

In his deposition, Ozzy stated:

"At approximately 9 a.m. on Friday, March 19, 1982 I was awoken from my

sleep by a loud explosion. I then immediately thought that we hit a vehicle on the road.
I then got out of bed rather rapidly screaming to my fiance 'Get off the bus!' Meanwhile my Sharon was screaming to everyone else to get off the bus. After getting out of the bus, I saw that a plane had crashed.
I didn't know who was on the plane at the time. When we realized that our people were on the plane, I found it very difficult to get assistance from anyone to help.
In fact, it took almost a half-hour before anyone arrived. One small fire engine which appeared to squirt three gallons of water over the inferno. We asked for further assistance, such as telephones, and didn't receive any further help. In the end, we finally found a telephone and Sharon phoned her father."

In her deposition, Sharon declared:

"I left Knoxville the night of March 18th on route to Orlando. I went to bed around 11:30 p.m. the night of the 18th. The next thing I knew, I woke with a huge bang and the bus was rocking. My bed was at the back of the bus, I ran to the front of the bus to look out of the windows, I had no idea where I was or what had happened. There was glass everywhere in the bus and everything was upside down. The bus driver's ex-wife said: 'Don't look, don't come out!' I left the bus and saw flames coming from a house, and a big hole in our bus. I ran screaming trying to find out what had happened, but no one would say, then I found out. I asked for a phone, I was told by a man who I did not know that there was no phone and to keep my mouth shut and I did not see anything. I told him to go to hell and then I found a phone. I did not see the crash. All I saw was fire."

In my deposition I simply stated:

"On March 19, 1982, I was asleep in one of the bus's bunks when it was hit by the plane. I awoke after I felt the impact of the plane hitting the bus and ran out to see what had happened and found the plane had crashed into the house and was engulfed in flames."

Wanda Aycock's deposition was taken a couple of weeks later.
In her affidavit Wanda stated:

"On Tuesday March 16, we flew to West Palm Beach to visit with Andy's brother and then back,
Wednesday morning. We got on the bus and left for Atlanta to pick up Ozzy and the band, then on to Knoxville, and then we left immediately after the show for Leesburg. We arrived in Leesburg somewhere around 8:00 or 8:30. Andy pulled into his house, and we got out and stretched, and then we went on to Jerry Calhoun's place, and then we made coffee. Andy asked Donny and Road Manager if they would like to go for a flight, they said yes then they went up for a few minutes and then Andy landed. And then he asked Randy and Rachel if they wanted to go, they both said yes. I was in the bus, and then I heard the noise of the glass breaking on the bus, and then the

explosion when he crashed."

I find it quite interesting in her affidavit that if she was in the
bus, obviously sitting in the front lounge since she didn't
have a bunk of her own to lay on, how did she escape
without a single cut or bruise from the flying pieces of
broken glass that burst throughout the front lounge on
impact. My conclusion is that Wanda was standing in the
doorway of the bus, like a human bull's eye, when Andy
deliberately crashed the plane.

There were extensive investigations within hours of
the crash by the Lake County Sheriff's Department, the
National Transportation Safety Board (NTSB) and the
Federal Aviation Administration (FAA).

A few weeks after the crash, the NTSB concluded its
investigation with this report:

> **"The Beech model F35 collided with a
> vehicle, a tree and residence while Andy
> was executing low passes over a residence
> on the south side of the eastern end of
> runway 11 at the Flying Baron Estates
> airport, near Leesburg, FL. Randy,
> Rachel and Andy were killed and the
> aircraft was destroyed by impact forces
> and fire. There were no injuries to
> persons on the ground but the bus with
> which the aircraft collided was damaged,
> the tree was severed, two automobiles in
> the garage of the Georgian type residence
> were destroyed and the residence was
> extensively damaged when the post-crash
> fire spread to the main part of the
> structure.**
> **The accident involved personnel
> associated with Ozzy Osbourne's rock
> band, who had traveled to Leesburg in
> their private Greyhound type bus after**

262

completing a concert in Knoxville, TN on the evening of March 18th. Andy was employed as the driver of the bus and the group had arrived at the Flying Baron Estates private airport at about 09:00 on the accident date. Prior to the fatal flight, Andy made a short local flight with Don and Jake aboard during which he made several low passes over the area.

After taking off on the second flight with Randy and Rachel on board, Andy made more low passes over the area. The group's bus was parked about 60 feet in front of the north facing residence and on the final low pass the left wing collided with the bus. The aircraft was in a left bank at the time of the collision and the bulk of the aircraft structure crossed over the bus and severed a large pine tree before crashing through the roof of the garage on the west end of the residence where post-crash fire erupted.

Andy possessed a private pilot certificate with ratings in airplanes single and multi-engine land, instruments airplanes and helicopters. The latest medical certificate on file for Andy was dated November 16, 1979. That medical certificate had expired and no record was found that Andy possessed a current medical certificate. Andy's flight logbooks were not received and his recent flight experience was not determined. His application for a medical certificate dated 11-16-79 showed 1,500 flying hours.

The aircraft records were reported to have been on board at the time of the crash and the aircraft history was not determined. The owner of the aircraft, Mr. Michael Partin, remarked that he did not remember whether an annual inspection had been performed within the preceding 12 months. In a cover letter received with his partially completed accident report he stated the following: " ... The plane was stored in a hangar at the Flying Baron Ranch. No one was given permission to fly the plane ... "

The weather was not a factor in the accident. The 09:50 surface weather observation at the nearest reporting station in Orlando, FL showed 1,500 feet scattered, visibility 7 miles with surface winds from 170 degrees at 7 knots.

There was a 5 to 6 foot diagonal slash on the upper left side of the bus about 1/3rd of the way from the front. The bus was parked on an easterly heading in front of the north facing residence and a pine tree standing between the bus and the residence was severed about 10 feet above the ground. The separated outer portion of the left wing that collided with the bus was adjacent to the rear of the bus and outside the post-crash fire pattern. The inboard portion of the left wing including the landing gear and portions of the empennage and "V" tail were outside the garage adjacent to the north wall. The remainder of the aircraft slammed through the garage roof and came to rest inside.

The wreckage was almost totally consumed in the post-crash fire and the readings or settings of the various cockpit instruments, switches, levers etc. were not obtained. The engine sustained extensive fire and impact damage and all of the accessories were destroyed. The propeller was attached to the crankshaft and the outer portions of the blades were consumed in the fire."

The autopsies were performed by the State of Florida's district medical examiner in Leesburg and toxicological studies were conducted at the Federal Aviation Administration's Civil Aeromedical Institute in Oklahoma City, OK.

According to both reports by the NTSB and the FAA, there were no drugs found in Randy's system. Nicotine was the only substance they could find. On the other hand, according to both reports, there was cocaine found in Andy's system. This substantiates my theory on Andy's state of mind at the time of the crash. Toxicology studies on Rachel were not performed.

Among Randy's personal effects that the Leesburg Sheriff's Department itemized were his music case with classical sheet music, a micro cassette tape recorder with an extra tape and his portable music stand. Since we had just started the second leg of the tour Randy was looking forward to learning the new batch of classical lessons he had purchased while at home and to monitor his progress with the tape recorder.

Later that evening, after we concluded our depositions, we flew from Orlando back to Los Angeles. It was a rather uncomfortable flight as we solemnly sat among the happy children returning home from their Disney World vacations. I looked into their faces and prayed that none of them would ever feel the pain I felt that night.

"Rudy, look at him. My poor Ozzy," Sharon whispered and

shook her head while the three of us sat together in the back of the plane. "He hasn't stopped crying since yesterday. I don't know what I'm going to do. I'm afraid that if we get off the road he might hurt himself." Sharon put a blanket over Ozzy's shoulder as he sobbed in the window seat. "Do me a favor.

From now on when you're all onstage he's going to need somebody to play off. I think he'll be comfortable with you. So please be there to support him." I watched him sob with his head buried in his blanket.

I pondered one thing:

"How am I going to support him when I need all the support I can get?"

20
Why Him and Not Me?

There are some things in life that you just can't replace, like the love and affection from dear friends such as Rachel and Randy, and the impassioned sound of his guitar. We never tried to. We just tried to pick up the pieces and carry on the best we could.

Upon our arrival in Los Angeles on March 21st, one of Sharon's first tasks was to deal with the next couple of weeks' worth of tour dates. The March 20th concert at the Tangerine Bowl in Orlando, Florida and March 21st performance at the Orange Bowl in Miami were cancelled immediately after the crash. The following shows, March 24th at the Capitol Center in Largo, March 25th, at the Broome County Arena in Binghamton, New York, March 26th at the Spectrum in Philadelphia, Pennsylvania, March 28th, at the Nassau Coliseum in Hempstead, New York, March 29th, at the Brendan Byrne Arena in East Rutherford, New Jersey and March 30th, at the Civic Center in Hartford, Connecticut we're postponed. Also, Ozzy's March 27th in-store" appearance at the Discomat in New York City's Time Square was cancelled.

The tour was then scheduled to resume on April 1st. We had less than two weeks to find and break in a guitarist. Randy's death deeply touched musicians around the world. As soon as reports of the crash hit the news media phone calls from guitar players in Europe, England and the United States started coming in offering their sympathy and assistance to help us continue with the tour. There's no doubt in my mind that Sharon's main objective was to keep Ozzy occupied with the guitar player auditions and to get us back on the road as soon as possible in order to prevent him from slipping into an irreversible depression and committing the unthinkable.

Randy's rapid fire rhythm guitar and classically

influenced soaring solos had defined the Ozzy sound. So our biggest task was to find a suitable guitarist who could pay homage to his talent and memory by executing the songs as closely as possible to the way in which he performed them. Even though his musical style would influence a generation of musicians to come, at that moment in time it seemed impossible to come across a guitarist capable of emulating Randy's innovative style.

As soon as we started the auditions we were confronted with a new set of depressing circumstances. Just a few days earlier, we were performing with the most gifted musician I had ever known, someone who could interpret blazing renditions of his musical compositions as effortlessly as taking a breath. And now we were in a rehearsal room filled with sadness and grief while the endless parade of guitar hopefuls struggled to muster a mere speck of Randy's prowess.

After the first day of emotionally draining and futile auditions it
occurred to me that maybe my brother, Robert, should came to Los
Angeles and tryout. I had always regarded Robert as a great musician
and felt that he was more talented than any of the guitarist who had
already auditioned.

"So what do you think? You want to give it a shot?" I asked Robert over the phone.

"Well, you know how much I respect Randy. He's got a unique style and I wouldn't want to change a note," Robert said.

"Good, that's exactly what Ozzy wants. Here, he wants to talk to you.

Ozzy grabbed the phone. "Robert, can you send me a demo tape?" Ozzy asked.

"Well, the only thing I have is a tape of my old band, D.L.
Byron, but it's not in the same style as what you guys

are doing." "Well, can you fly here and try out then? Your brother tells me that you're exactly what we're looking for."

"Yeah, I guess I can," Robert replied.

"Good, I'll have Sharon call you with the details."

Though it was hard to spend hours auditioning guitarists, it soon became clear that being alone in my room was even more difficult since the various stages of grief had begun to set in.

I had already experienced denial at the crash site as I aimlessly wandered through the debris littered field hoping to find Randy and Rachel alive and safe, away from the burning wreckage. In such an unexpected tragedy there was no chance for bargaining.

Acceptance was inevitable as a fireman advised while I peered into the smoldering car garage, "Son, you don't want to go in there. Just remember them the way they looked the last time you saw them alive. Any anger that surfaced was overcome by guilt as we all shared the sentiment of. "Why them and not me?" And in my case, the guilt was compounded with the belief that Randy had struggled with Andy and managed to save all of us asleep in the bus.

But now I was going through the most intense stage of depression I had ever experienced. If it weren't for my religious beliefs and Rebecca's consolation I would have been left with even more emotional scars. But slowly the simple things in life began to take on a deeper meaning. I began to understand how fragile life really is and to be grateful for the everyday gifts that it brings. It was time for me to take a good look at myself and re-evaluate my life. And so I began.

As soon as Robert arrived he spent most of his time in his hotel room learning the songs and concentrating on capturing all of Randy's musical nuances. His brotherly solace and musical talent made the audition process less painful. It quickly became clear to everyone, including

269

Ozzy, that Robert was by far the best candidate for the job.

While Ozzy flew to New York City to fulfill a previously scheduled "David Letterman Show" appearance, the rest of the band carried on with the auditions. That evening while I watched the TV interview I couldn't help but feel compassion for Ozzy as the subject Mr. Letterman was most interested in was the biting the head off the bat incident.

The following day, upon Ozzy's return from the East Coast, another guitar hopeful showed up to audition. His name was Bernie Torme. The tall blonde Irishman was a veteran of Ian Gillan's band, the former Deep Purple vocalist. While in the midst of recording his own solo album, Bernie had flown out at the behest of the Jet Records in London. Just as Don Airey had done with every other auditioning guitarist, he and Bernie went over the songs the evening before Tommy and I joined them for the audition. Unbeknownst to all of us, Bernie had been assured by Jet that he had the job and was totally perplexed upon arriving at the auditions and finding Robert and the other hopefuls present.

During this time we all took a break from the daily audition schedule to attend Rachel's memorial service. Sharon, who considered Rachel more of a friend than an employee, was deeply grieved during the service. I had never been to a funeral home before and didn't know what to expect from the gospel music-filled service. But by the time the sermon was over, the preacher's uplifting words had us all convinced that Rachel was now in a better place.

Right after the service we returned to the rehearsal hall and continued with the auditions. Even though Bernie worked extra hard to get a grip on Randy's guitar style, the seasoned musician struggled during his tryout. This was due mostly to his unfamiliarity with the material off the Blizzard of Ozz and Diary of a Madman records.

On the morning of March 24th, we all gathered to attend Randy's 12:30 p.m. memorial.

"You know, I just don't understand it," Ozzy slurred as Sharon caressed his shaking hands in the limo. "I drink myself into bloody oblivion every night, I get stoned out of my mind and abuse myself all these years and the guy who kept his nose clean is the one who buys the bloody farm. I just don't get it. Why him and not me?" He paused while he stared out the window. "The hardest thing of all is facing Delores. I just feel so guilty and responsible. Here I go and take her son away from her after she puts her trust in me. And then what happens? I bring him back home in a box." Ozzy wept as Sharon consoled him.

When we arrived at the church, the first person I approached was Jody. Sometimes you associate couples with their mates and the impression made by her solitary presence was yet another reminder of the emptiness we all shared.

"Jody, it's so good to see you," I barely uttered.

"You know," Jody sobbed as she held her crumpled handkerchief, "I was driving and 'Crazy Train' came on the radio and then a couple of more Ozzy songs. I was so happy, just singing along and then the DJ came on with the news of the crash. I started crying so hard that I couldn't see the road. I just had to pull over and…" We hugged while she broke down and cried. As Jody composed herself I watched Ozzy weeping on Delores' shoulder.

Unlike Rachel's uplifting memorial, Randy's overcrowded service was filled with grief and sorrow. Even though I was comforted by Rebecca's presence, the swirling pool of mixed emotions filled with guilt, grief, and "what ifs," was tearing up my soul as I stared at Randy's portrait next to his closed casket during the service. After the service Ozzy, Tommy, Kevin DuBrow and I were among the pallbearers who carried Randy's casket into the hearse for his final journey.

As the long motorcade made its way from Burbank to San Bernardino I couldn't help but reflect on the countless times that Randy and I had ridden the same roads on our way to rehearsals and performances. A couple of solemn hours later we arrived at the Mountain View Cemetery in San Bernardino where family, friends and fans gathered to pay their last respects. After a brief graveside service, Randy was laid to rest, just a few miles from the Orange Pavilion, the place where it all began just 12 months before.

After the burial I opted to drive back to Los Angeles with Rebecca instead of riding in the limo with Ozzy and Sharon.

"You're not going to believe this!" Rebecca was incensed while I started her car. "As I was leaving the church Little John asks me to give him a ride to the cemetery. So on the way here he starts hitting on me. He suggests getting on my lap and taking over the steering wheel while I work the pedals. The little pervert, I almost smacked him and left him on the side of the road!"

It was the first amusing moment in almost two weeks and I couldn't help but crack a smile.

As April 1st drew closer there had to be a decision made regarding the new guitar player. By now it had come down between Bernie and Robert. There was never a question about Bernie's proven musical abilities but his bluesy style didn't quite compliment Randy's classical thumbprint, the heart and soul of the band's sound. So since Robert was able to emulate Randy's nuances, he got the job. In the middle of all the grief, I was pleased to give my brother the good news.

These were trying and confusing times for everyone and there was plenty of miscommunication between the Los Angeles and London Jet offices. So the following day when Bernie was told about the decision to go with

Robert he then informed Sharon and Ozzy that he had already been promised the job by the people in the London office and that he had already received an advance before leaving home. This left Ozzy and Sharon with no other choice but to take Bernie out on tour.

At this point I was just too emotionally beat up to face Robert and tell him the news. Nevertheless, I told him about the circumstances and since all he wanted to do was to pay tribute to Randy and help us finish the remaining tour dates he took the news in stride and graciously accepted the situation.

On March 29th we flew to Bethlehem, Pennsylvania, to continue with rehearsals and prepare for our first show with Bernie. At this time Pete Mertons, Randy's tech from the very beginning, became my bass tech. Even though Bernie had brought his own guitar tech, Pete was too aggrieved to look after another guitarist.

Besides rehearsing the set list on his own, Bernie spent many hours going over the intricate guitar parts with Don, who made sure that Bernie adhered to Randy's original guitar lines and not reinterpret them the way he would've like to.

Sharon was concerned about Bernie's image, which was a cross between Sid Vicious and Jimi Hendrix, not fitting in with our medieval stage production.

"Boys, we've got to do something about Bernie's looks," she remarked as she pulled Tommy and me aside during a rehearsal break.

"You've got that right," said Tommy. "If you dropped the guy looking like that anywhere in Texas they'd shoot him on the spot and then ask him what freaking planet he's from."

"Rudy, do you have any spare stage clothes that he can borrow?"

"Yeah, I've got a couple of leather vests."

"And by the way," she added, "we need to do something with his hair. Perhaps you could style it for him."

"Well, I can give him a trim but I'm not sure
about a makeover," I explained.

"Unfortunately we're in the middle of bum-fuck," she
said, "and I wouldn't even know where to start
looking for a hairdresser.

I'm sure you'll do as good a job as anyone else
around these parts."

Bernie had never been in a situation where he had to
alter his image in order to suit the stage production, so
when confronted by Sharon he was a bit resistant,
especially about his hair. But he ultimately complied.

On the afternoon of April 1st we rode in our new tour
bus to Bethlehem's Stabler Arena for our first sound
check without Randy.

It was an extremely uncomfortable feeling for everyone
to be on that stage. For Bernie, this was his first chance to
perform the whole set in front of the castle. Needless to
say, he was wound pretty tight. Besides not feeling
completely sure about the songs and dealing for the first
time with our mammoth stage, the rest of his equipment
had yet to arrive from England. Since Bernie was rushed
over to Los Angeles, he had left home with only one
Fender Stratocaster while the rest of his gear was shipped.

So with just a few hours before show time, the crew
searched all over town and replaced most of the missing
equipment with rental gear. In an ironic twist, when the
crew couldn't manage to come up with the suitable effects
pedals, Bernie reluctantly used some of Randy's spares.

Before the show the mood in our dressing room was
eerily quiet as feelings of uncertainty kept rushing through
my mind. How was it going to feel to be performing
without Randy? Was Bernie going to be able to pull it off
after so few rehearsals? If the show didn't go well would
Ozzy call it quits and drink himself into oblivion again?
Certainly, this was not the best frame of mind to be in
before going on stage in front of a sell-out crowd.

As I was getting ready, I watched Bernie standing in front of a mirror skeptically checking out his new blonde shaggy haircut and hand-me-down purple leather vest.

"Now that's more like it!" Sharon remarked. By the look on his face I could tell he was uneasy with his new image; he now resembled Randy a bit too much.

They say that time heals all wounds. But I can assure you that some take longer while others never heal, especially when the lights went down and the roar of the crowd swelled to a deafening thunder while Randy's guitar intro from "Diary of a Madman" blared through the PA. The portcullis raised, I stepped on stage, looked to my left and Randy wasn't there. I then gazed at the audience through misty eyes and read the numerous banners hanging from the balconies:
"We Miss you Randy," "You Can't Kill Rock n Roll," "God Bless Randy." As Tommy's drum fill kick started the set, I hung my head low, went into autopilot and tried to survive the show.

I don't know many guitar players who could stand the kind of pressure Bernie had to endure that first show. Besides not having all of his own gear, he was unaccustomed to playing under such odd theatrical conditions. Fortunately, the fans and their overwhelming appreciation, especially Bernie's, helped us make it through the show.

Backstage after the show, Ozzy was kindly supportive of Bernie, who had struggled through most of the set.

"Don't know how you did it, mate, I would've shit my pants out there if I was in your shoes."
"You know, I think it was all going pretty well," Bernie said, "until Randy's foot pedal started coming on and off all by itself in the middle of the show. I've never seen anything like it. It was as if the pedal had a mind of its own."
Personally, that first show was the toughest 75

minutes I had ever spent onstage. So immediately after I got out of my sweaty stage clothes I slipped into the bus in search of sanctuary, climbed into my usual driver's side, upper rear bunk, pulled the curtains and went to sleep. But as I laid in the dark the boom of the crash kept echoing in my head. Exasperated and tormented, I jumped out of that berth and moved to the furthest one available. I didn't care that it was the one on the floor next to the toilet.

As I tried to sleep, I painfully reflected on the events of the past two weeks and realized that not only had we lost Randy, the heart and soul of the band, but the band as we knew it had also perished with him.

The following evening, April 2nd, we performed at the Boston Gardens in Boston, Massachusetts. Besides trying to fit in with the image and sound of the band, one of the toughest challenges that Bernie had to face was Sharon's new policy of "no alcohol allowed backstage and in the bus." Though the mood backstage prior to the crash had always been rather sedate and the drinking kept to a bare minimum, Sharon was now struggling to keep Ozzy from completely immersing himself in the bottle. The rebellious Irishman quickly found, however, a few kindred spirits in the members of UFO as he spent most of the time backstage hanging out in their dressing room.

By the second night, Bernie started to perform a bit more relaxed on stage and even began injecting a bit of his own style into the show as he played with his teeth and flung his guitar up in the air during a bluesy solo spot.

As Sharon had suggested after the crash, Ozzy started coming over to my side of the stage during the show to pull my hair and grab me in a half nelson choke hold as he used to do with Randy. As I began playing the intro to "Believer," Ozzy came over to my side with his head bopping and handclapping when he suddenly stopped and grabbed my arm and yelled,

"Your bass doesn't have any bloody frets!"

"Good one, Oz!" I thought since I'd been playing the same bass for a year and now he finally realizes that it's a fretless!

A local rock journalist wrote these words about the evening's performance:

> **"The only animal you'll ever see on stage is Ozzy Osbourne as quoted Wednesday by his fiancee Sharon Arden regarding the rumors of animal killing during his concerts. Osbourne, who bit into a dead bat in Des Moines, Iowa, last January, did not bite into anything tossed on stage last night. The set summary:**
>
> **New guitarist Bernie Torme (replacing Randy Rhoads, who died in a plane crash two weeks ago) began his screech-and-feedback guitar solo at 9:46 during "Suicide Solution" and finished at 9:50. Drummer Tommy Aldridge began his bang-bang and crash solo at 9:51 and finished at 9:54. As the show neared its end, the band played "Believer," a cement mixer of plodding rhythm and no-end guitar, and moved into "Flying High Again," where Osbourne yowled about mama worrying because he's a bad boy. It was then time for the Black Sabbath medley, "Iron Man"/"Children of the Grave," where Osbourne sang The Pertinent Question for the Evening: "Is he alive or dead?/ Has he a thought within his head?"**
>
> **Osbourne and company encored with Sabbath's biggest hit, "Paranoid," where the singer yowled,**
>
> **"People think I'm insane" as his four henchmen churned out the thick slabs of metal chords. But Osbourne's no trouble to anyone, just another heavy metal**

geezer plying his trade."

Though it was common knowledge within our circle that the main reason we went back on the road so soon was for Ozzy's sake, to most of the public, such as the above rock journalist, our sudden return to the road had been misunderstood to mean "replacing Randy Rhoads."

The following evening, April 3rd we performed at the Coliseum in New Haven, Connecticut. During sound check Sharon informed the band about the newly added string of dates.

"We should be finished with the U.S. and Canada by the end of June. Right after that we'll be in Japan for a couple of weeks." "I'm sorry, Sharon," said Bernie, "but when Dave Arden hired me I was adamant about my availability for just a couple months. You see, I'm in the midst of recording my solo album. I even had to reschedule tour dates in order to be here."

"You mean you rather be playing in shitholes on your own than to be playing arenas with Ozzy?" Sharon was miffed.

"Sorry Sharon, but that was my deal with David."

"Well, if that's what you want, then so be it." Sharon abruptly left the room in search of Ozzy.

On April 4th we arrived in New York City to spend our day off prior to the much-anticipated Madison Square Garden show. Ozzy, Sharon, Tommy and I stayed at Don Arden's penthouse suite at the posh Helmsley Palace Hotel. With Bernie's imminent departure we were once again in a frantic search for a guitarist. Desperately looking for suggestions, Sharon placed a phone call to the Epic Records office where one of the executives recommended Ray Gomez, a young Moroccan CBS Records solo artist. Ray was a musician's musician with a string of recording and touring credits with such jazz/rock fusion musical icons as Stanley Clarke and Herbie Hancock. He was the kind of solo artist that Randy aspired to be. So after a dinner meeting between Ray, Ozzy and Sharon, she arranged for Ray and Don to go over the songs backstage during sound check. That evening Robert came to visit me at the hotel.

"Rudy, I heard Ozzy's still looking for a guitarist. Do you think I should let him know that I'm still available?"

"You know, every night it kills me when I go on stage and everything seems the same except that when I look to my left Randy's not there. I don't think I can keep going much longer."

I said as I gazed down at the city lights. "You're my brother and I can't ask you to join something that I can't bear to be a part of. I don't know what I'll be doing next. I just know I can't continue playing in the band after this tour."

Robert understood and opted not to pursue the matter any further.

A few years later Robert attained success as a founding member of the highly acclaimed rock band Hurricane.

The following day, April 5th, I went to sound check early in case Don needed me to go over the songs with Ray.

"Hi, I'm Rudy. I love your playing on Stanley Clarke's School Days."

"Well, thanks," he said with a confident smile. Don offered:

"We're just going over some of Randy's signature guitar riffs.

Ray feels he can join us on stage tonight."

"We can't go up there without a rehearsal," I said. "This is the Garden, the biggest night of the tour!"

"Ah, no problem! How hard can this gig be?" Ray replied. "It's only rock and roll."

Don rolled his eyes. Though more than qualified, Ray's overconfidence didn't go over well as we continued our pursuit for a suitable guitarist.

After a handful of shows without Randy, I was slowly building an emotional wall on stage that I could hide behind. But that evening the wall came tumbling down as I gazed out into the audience with teary eyes and saw the sea of banners draping from the balconies. This was not just another show, this was Randy's New York City wake. So I hung my head low and struggled to play as a puddle of tears formed around my feet.

21
That's the Bloodiest Daft Idea I've Ever Heard

From the first moment I picked up a bass guitar I dreamed of how thrilling it would be to headline Madison Square Garden. But that, night as we performed without Randy, the dream turned into my saddest moment on stage. As soon as we took our last bow and returned to the dressing room, I quietly peeled off my clothes and sat in a corner, trying to leave the show behind.

Much to my surprise, when we arrived back at the penthouse suite there was a record company party in full swing, a celebration of the Diary of a Madman record going double platinum.

"Congratulations Rudy, great show!" Tony Martel said as he shook my hand. "This is for you. Thanks for working so hard to promote the record."

I stood among the reveling partygoers holding back my tears and wishing that Randy were around to hold the framed platinum discs with me. After all, it was his unique contribution to the records that propelled the band to multi-platinum heights.

By then, I was too emotionally beat up to hang out at the party so I slipped away into my room. While I lay in bed watching TV I couldn't help but glance at the platinum albums leaning against the wall. Suddenly, pools of emotions swirled through my mind, recalling moments of joy, sadness and anger. It was all too much for me to handle so I got up and stashed the award in the closet.

In a futile attempt at slumber, I tossed and turned as the hum of the party filtered through the door. A few minutes later I heard a knock.

"Come in!" I shouted.

"Rudy, there's a young man up in the penthouse that has flown in from California to audition," Sharon said as she poked her head in the room. "Would you mind going over the songs with him?"

"Yeah, no problem. I can't go to sleep anyways. What happened to your neck?" I asked, noticed her bandage.

"Oh, just some bloody idiot threw a firecracker on stage and it exploded on my neck while you boys were on. They dragged me off to the medic backstage and he gave me couple of stitches. But don't worry, I'll be fine. You know what they say: You can't hurt steel." She smiled and bolted out of the room.

Sharon was the strongest individual I had ever met. I guess she had to be that way in order to keep Ozzy's career on track while preventing him from completely going off the deep end.

"Hi I'm Rudy." I introduced myself as I walked out of the private elevator into the spacious penthouse.

"Nice to meet you, I'm Brad." The sandy-haired young man introduced himself as we shook hands. After a bit of conversation I learned that we had a few things in common: a shy disposition and the willingness to work.

"So, are you familiar with the songs?" I asked.

"Well, not really." He strummed his unplugged red Fender Stratocaster. "Actually, I got the call from Sharon just a couple of days ago to come out and audition. When she put Ozzy on the phone he just rattled off the set list. So after we hung up I called up my friends and asked them to borrow their old Black Sabbath albums and any of the Ozzy solo stuff they had. And here I am."

"Well, I don't know if Ozzy and Sharon told you this, but what we really need is someone who can sound and play the parts just like the record."

"Yeah, that was the first thing Ozzy mentioned. It seems that you guys are not happy with whoever is playing guitar now." "He's actually a real good player," I said, "but it's just that he has a whole different style from Randy, more bluesy and loose, and we need someone who can play the rhythm parts chunky and tight, just like the record. Are you familiar with Randy's playing?"

"Oh, yeah, I saw him when you guys played at the Day on the Green in Oakland last July. I was blown away by his technique." "Yeah, that was a crazy show. We went on so early in the morning that it felt like I just rolled out of bed onto the stadium stage."

"Yeah, I love playing the big shows, too," Brad agreed.

"Oh, who did you play with before?" I asked.

"I was in a band called Rubicon a few years back."

"Oh yeah, I remember! I saw you guys on TV when you played the Cal Jam 2. You guys were smoking!"

That night, as I watched the snow fall over Manhattan, I had a hunch that Brad was going to do just fine.

The following morning, April 6th, I woke up in the middle of a record-breaking spring blizzard that blanketed Manhattan with nearly a foot of snow overnight. We were snowed in, which meant I had no other choice but to eat at one of the hotel's overpriced restaurants.

So I decided to dial up Jake and get some cash.

"Mr. Duncan's room please," I asked the operator.

"Sorry, but Mr. Duncan has checked out. I've been asked to direct all his calls to Mr. McNeny's room."

"Hi, this is Larry." I heard an unfamiliar southern drawl at the other end.

"Hey, Larry, this is Rudy, Ozzy's bass player. I'm looking for Jake."

"Well, hello Rudy, I was wondering when I was going to hear from you. Jake's no longer with the tour. I'm the tour manager now. Why don't you come down to my room so I can give you your per diem."

Even though Jake was a hardworking, likeable guy, I wasn't a bit surprised about his hasty departure. After the crash, Sharon placed a large portion of the blame on Jake's shoulders. She felt that Jake should have gotten her up and told her about Rachel's and Randy's intention to get on the plane with Andy. And since she had knowledge of Andy's previous fatal crash she would have prohibited them from flying with him, thus preventing the tragedy.

"Nice to meet you, Rudy. Come on in." Larry shook my hand as he welcomed me into his room.

"Wow, bet you get mistaken for Eric Clapton all the time," I said. I couldn't help notice Larry's uncanny resemblance to "Slow Hand."

"Well, as a matter of fact, I happen to be his tour manager. You won't believe how many people ask me for his autograph even when we're both standing together," he laughed.

Larry and I hit it off right away. Within a couple of days, his laid back Southern disposition brought our tour a much-needed sense of serenity. Later that afternoon, Don, Brad and I gathered in the penthouse suite to go over the songs.

"Hey, guys. I just wrote this song for Randy," said Ozzy, still high from the night before.

He stumbled into the room as we gathered around the living room grand piano.

"It goes like this." Ozzy then started to rock slowly back and forth, clapping his hands. "Isn't life strange..." He sang as Don, Brad and I just looked at each other.

"Ozzy, ah, don't you think it sounds a bit too much like the Moody Blues song?" I hinted, choosing my words carefully.

He mulled it over for a moment, turned around and wobbled back to his room. A couple of minutes later he returned.

"Guys, guys. I got an idea for a song," he proudly announced, interrupting our rehearsal. "It goes like this." Once again Ozzy rocked slowly back and forth, clapping his hands. "Isn't life strange ..." he sang.

"Ozzy, I still think it sounds a bit too much like that Moody Blues song," said Don said ever so politely. And once again Ozzy wobbled back to his room.

His relentless pursuit to write this song continued for the next few weeks as we continued reminding him of its similarity to the Moody Blues' classic.

On the morning of April 7 th we rode our tour bus through the snowy streets of Manhattan bound for Providence, Rhode Island for that evening's performance at the Civic Center. The plan was to have Brad travel with us in the bus while he practiced on his own and became familiar with the set. Even though Bernie's departure was amicable for both sides, traveling with his replacement put him in an uncomfortable position. Still, being a consummate professional, Bernie handled it well and stayed with the tour until Brad was ready.

Meanwhile, Brad sat in his hotel room for the next few days playing along to a tape from one of our shows with Randy.

The following shows, April 9th at the Memorial Auditorium in Buffalo, New York and April 10th at the War Memorial in Rochester, New York went rather well as Bernie started getting a grip on the songs. Impressed by his performance, Don tried to change Bernie's mind about leaving, but the Irishman man was set on pursuing his solo career.

On April 12th, before that evening's performance in Binghamton, New York, Brad heard a knock on his hotel room door.

"Bradley, are you ready to play tonight?" Ozzy asked as

Brad answered the door. "Bernie's anxious to go home.

What do you think?"

"Sure, I'll give it a shot," Brad answered.

That afternoon during sound check we managed to plow through half the set with Brad before the doors opened, as this was his only opportunity to rehearse the songs with us onstage. To his advantage, the venue couldn't hold the castle production, so Brad did his first performance without the usual production obstacles. That evening Brad pulled off a nearly perfect performance in front of 7,0 people. His only blunder happened during "Revelation Mother Earth" when he got lost in the middle of the song. Besides getting a dirty look from Ozzy, he came out of it pretty much unscathed. Meanwhile, per Ozzy and Sharon's request, Bernie had been on stand-by and ready to come on stage in the event Brad didn't work out.

After the show it was evident that we could carry on with Brad. So after a small backstage send-off, Bernie returned to England to continue his solo pursuits.

As we carried on with Brad we performed on April 15th at the Coliseum in Fort Wayne, Indiana, followed by the April 16th show at Roberts Municipal Stadium in Evansville, Indiana and the April 17th performance at the Freedom Hall in Louisville, Kentucky.

Just like Bernie, Brad favored playing single coiled Stratocasters. But unlike Bernie, he somehow managed to get a fat, crunchy tone similar to Randy's Les Pauls and Jacksons. It wasn't until the latter portion of the show when Brad would then strap on his Les Paul for the Black Sabbath numbers. As far as his image was concerned, Sharon didn't feel that Brad needed a makeover to fit in with the production. All he required was one of my hand-me-down stage outfits.

As we carried on with the April 19th performance at the Civic Center in Roanoke, Virginia, the April 20th show at the Hampton Coliseum in Norfolk, Virginia, and the April 21st performance at the Richmond Coliseum in Richmond, Virginia our sound started to gel with Brad's to the point where we felt that we could finish the tour with dignity. Whereas Bernie had struggled to get a grip on Randy's style, Brad's funk rhythm guitar chops helped him emulate Randy's fiery rhythm style.

In the aftermath of the crash, Sharon had masterfully dealt with the tour's logistical nightmares while keeping Ozzy in check. But just as with the best jugglers, sooner or later those plates will stop spinning and crash to the ground. In his typical, dysfunctional way, Ozzy had gone through the stages of grief out of sequence. It wasn't until a month after the crash that he began to enter his anger stage.

At this point, Ozzy began drinking heavily again and started acting resentful towards Brad and urged Sharon to continue looking for another guitar player. It was rather disturbing to watch Brad, who was doing a great job, being verbally abuse by an inebriated Ozzy.

On the evening of April 23rd we performed at the Freedom Hall in Johnson City, Tennessee. The following date, April 24th at the Memorial Auditorium in Greenville, South Carolina was replaced with a show in Largo, Maryland. Also, the April 25th show at the Coliseum in Charlotte, North Carolina was cancelled and replaced with a gig in Richmond, Virginia.

On the evening of April 28th, a couple of weeks after our first show with Brad, we performed a live radio broadcast from the Mid-South Coliseum in Memphis, Tennessee. Needless to say, the band never sounded the same without Randy. But nevertheless, Brad did a superb job that night as he poured his heart and soul into his playing, more than likely to retaliate for Ozzy's harassment.

The following dates, April 29th at the Municipal Auditorium in Nashville, Tennessee, April 30th at the Coliseum in Greensboro, North Carolina, and May 1st at the Cumberland County Auditorium in Fayetteville, North Carolina were filled with tension as Ozzy's drinking and hostility towards Brad worsened.

On May 2nd Sharon suddenly put the tour on hold and whisked the band back to Los Angeles in a move to prevent Ozzy from having a complete meltdown. In order to accommodate the tour break, the following dates were cancelled: May 2nd in Hampstead, North Carolina, May 4th in Wheelington, West Virginia, May 5th at the Fairgrounds Coliseum in Columbus, Ohio, and May 6th at Hara Arena in Dayton, Ohio. Also, the following Canadian dates were postponed: May 16th in Ottawa, May 17th in Montreal and May 18th at the Maple Leaf Gardens in Toronto. The May 19th show in Cape Cod, Massachusetts was cancelled as well.

For me, this unexpected three-week break was a welcome opportunity to get away from the frenzied pace of our tour and peacefully reflect on how my life had changed since the crash. Mourning Randy was a new experience for me since I had never lost a loved one before. As the days went by it became clear that some of the ways in which I could honor my friends was by striving to strengthen my spirituality, by acknowledging all the wonderful gifts that life brings and by living each day to the fullest, as if there is no tomorrow, for some day tomorrow will never come.

On previous tour breaks I struggled to relax and leave the hectic pace of the road behind. I would be at a movie or a restaurant and suddenly experience panic attacks as I constantly checked my watch, imagining what I would be doing at that very moment if I were back on the road. But as I slowed down my pace, I began to enjoy the peaceful tranquility of my time off the road with Rebecca.

Meanwhile, Sharon had completely lost control of Ozzy upon returning to Los Angeles, as he plunged into his longest binge. If the idle mind's the devil's playground then the devil must have found a hell of an amusement park inside Ozzy's head as he embarked on a quest to find the "next guitar hero."

One evening, a friend picked Ozzy up and drove him to a rehearsal studio where he was introduced to a young local guitar player named Marq Torien. Before the young man played a single note, the friend made sure that Ozzy was in the right mood by pumping him with enough blow to stun a rhinoceros.

"I can't bloody believe it! He's great! He's the next big thing!" Ozzy yelled as he jumped around the room while Marq churned a flurry of guitar riffs and hammer-ons. "That's it! I want you to start rehearsing tomorrow with Rudy and Tommy." Ozzy told Marq as the friend shoved more blow up Ozzy's nostrils.

The next afternoon Tommy and I went down to S.I.R. Studios in Hollywood to rehearse with Ozzy's latest discovery. Halfway into "Crazy Train" Tommy and I looked at each other in total disbelief. "Damn, that's some new kind of information coming out your guitar, boy," Tommy said in total frustration as he threw his drumsticks on the ground.

"What do you mean?" Marq asked confused.

"For starters, it sounds like a freakin' train wreck, you haven't played a right chord pattern or solo yet. Have you heard the record?"

"Well, yeah," Marq replied.

"And you can't tell that what you're playing is in the wrong key?" Tommy asked with disbelief.

"Well, it sounds fine to me," Marq replied.

Tommy and I just looked at each other and shook our heads. "We got to call Sharon right now and nip this in the bud." Tommy whispered as I leaned over his drum kit.

The next morning Ozzy resisted our advice.

"Well, how about if we bring him on the road like we did with Brad and break him in during the sound check?"

"Ozzy, you don't understand," Tommy insisted. "The kid can't tell whether he's playing in the right key or not. He just doesn't get it and he might never get it."

"Oh, bloody hell," Ozzy pondered. "Well all right. I'll call him and tell him he's not going to work out."

A few years later Marq, sans his guitar, tasted success as the lead singer for the multi-platinum '80's heavy metal band the Bullet Boys.

After exhausting all the possibilities in Los Angeles, Sharon and Ozzy flew to England to continue their search for the "next big thing." Knowing how much Ozzy and Sharon loved and respected Randy, I don't think they were trying to replace him. More than likely, this was just another one of Ozzy's dysfunctional ways to deal with acceptance. I don't think he was looking to replace Randy; he was looking for Randy himself.

At the suggestion from the members of our opening act, Magnum, Sharon and Ozzy auditioned a young guitar player by the name of John Sykes from the British rock group Tygers of Pang Tang. His rock-star image and guitar chops greatly impressed them during the auditions. But then once Ozzy and Sharon expressed their interest in John, his personal manager stepped in and made certain unrealistic demands. The terms did not sit well with Ozzy and Sharon and they decided to continue with their search. A couple of years later John Sykes attained success as the lead guitarist for the legendary British blues rock band Whitesnake and later with his own group Blue Murder.

Upon Sharon and Ozzy's return from England, we kicked off the next leg of our tour on May 20th with a performance in Hartford, Connecticut. The first thing I noticed was the change in Ozzy's attitude; he looked calm and focused. Also, it appeared that he had accepted carrying on with Brad, at least until the end of the tour.

Furthermore, it seemed I wasn't the only one who was taking stock of their lives as Sharon and Ozzy made the surprise announcement of their plans to get married. With only a few weeks to go before the nuptials, arrangements were quickly put in motion for the wedding to take place in Maui on the Fourth of July, just a couple of days after our scheduled show in Oahu. From Hawaii we would then continue our tour with our first string of Japanese dates.

So with this new positive attitude following our three-week tour break we continued the last few weeks of our North American tour. The following previously scheduled Canadian dates had to be rescheduled or replaced in order to accommodate the break: May 21st in Winnipeg was replaced with Harford, Connecticut. May 22nd in Regina was replaced with Portland, Maine. May 23rd in Calgary was replaced with the Meadowlands in New Jersey. May 25th in Edmonton was replaced with Columbus, Ohio. May 27th in Vancouver, British Columbia was replaced with Springfield, Illinois.

During the Meadowlands show we were visited by the friendly folks from a new cable channel called MTV.

"Guess what?" Sharon excitedly announced,

"These gentlemen want to broadcast our show live on MTV."

"What the fuck's MTV?" Ozzy asked.

"Oh, it's a cable channel that plays music videos 24 hours a day," the executive proudly explained.

"Well, that sounds like the bloodiest daft idea I've ever heard. Who the bloody hell will want to sit in front of the telly and watch a bunch of geezers prancing around all day long?" Ozzy said, as he wobbled out of the dressing room.

As we continued, the May 28th performance in Seattle, Washington was rescheduled for a later date and replaced with a show at Poplar Creek outside of Chicago, Illinois. The May 29th show in Spokane, Washington was rescheduled. Then May 30th was added with a show at Castle Farm in Charlevoix, Michigan. The May 31st concert in Portland, Oregon was rescheduled and replaced with a show at Pine Knob outside of Detroit, Michigan.

We then began the month of June making our way west through Canada with the following rescheduled dates: June 2nd in Ottowa, June 3rd in Montreal, June 4th in Toronto, June 6th in Winnipeg, June 8th in Edmonton, and June 10th in Vancouver.

When we arrived in Seattle, Washington, on June 11th Larry suggested that we use the city as our hub for the next five days. That evening, in a futile attempt to expose Ozzy to something else besides heavy metal, Sharon dragged us to see the touring production of Annie at a nearby theater. Needless to say, Ozzy fell sleep before the second act.

"Ozzy, I can't believe you snored throughout the whole performance!" Sharon complained as we left the theater.

"Are you kidding?" Ozzy yawned. "That was best bloody sleep I've had all tour."

The next day, June 12th, we performed in Seattle in front of a sold-out crowd. Then, the very next morning we boarded a flight to Anchorage, Alaska to perform at the most suitable rock venue in town, the high school auditorium. Since the show was sold-out in a matter of minutes, Sharon added a second show performance for that same evening. While most of our crew stayed behind to enjoy all the natural wonders the last frontier had to offer, the rest of us were glad to spend a couple of days off in the cosmopolitan surroundings of Seattle.

As we continued with the last two weeks of our tour, on June 16th we performed in Spokane, Washington followed by Portland, Oregon on June 17th. On June 18th we arrived in San Francisco to prepare for the following day's pre-production rehearsals of our upcoming MTV live broadcast. Basically, the show was going to be exactly what we had been performing all along except for the inclusion of a laser show. Since time was of the essence, Sharon decided to test the lasers during the following show at the Oakland Coliseum.

Ever since the July 4th "Day on the Green" shows the previous year, San Francisco had become one of my favorite cities. So I arranged for Rebecca to fly up and join me on a romantic day off in the city by the bay.

That evening Sharon and Ozzy invited us to go see

Elton John perform at Berkeley's Greek Theater.

"Oh, you'll like Elton. We've been neighbors for years," Sharon said as we rode in the back of the limo. "When he's out of town I sneak in his house, go through his closet and put on his stage clothes. It's so much fun!" Sharon flashed a wicked grin. "I bet my boobie would look awfully cute wearing the Donald Duck suit." Sharon teased Ozzy with baby talk as he gazed out the window.

On June 19th we performed at the Oakland Coliseum where the sold out crowd got a surprise treat as they witnessed a spectacular laser show. Apparently, the laser company was trying their best to impress Sharon with their technology as they projected an array of gothic themes such as bats, crosses, the Ozzy logo all throughout the show. Also, I was pleasantly surprised by the sold-out crowd, since our previous show in the area, December 30th 1981 at the Cow Palace, was such a disaster.

The following day, June 20th, we performed in Bakersfield, California followed by the June 21st performance in Reno, Nevada. The next morning we arrived in Los Angeles for a couple of days rest before the taping of our MTV broadcast.

On June 23rd we traveled about 60 miles from Los Angeles to Irvine Meadows for our final performance of the tour. It had been an amazing, bittersweet journey since we started the Diary of a Madman tour. And even with all the distractions that the taping of a live performance added to the occasion, I couldn't stop thinking about how much I missed Randy, and how I wished he could still be with us to enjoy all the success that came as the result of his unique talent and hard work.

22
The Most Awesome Bachelor Party Ever

Through the decades the islands of Hawaii have become a favorite lay-over spot for rock bands making their way to or from Japan and other Pacific Rim destinations. The sultry island breezes and the laid back atmosphere make this a perfect place for any band, crew and their families to unwind after a long tour.

On the morning of June 27th, our large entourage checked into the Kahala Hilton resort situated on a private beach near Waikiki. Since Rebecca's birthday was just a few days away, I asked her to join me in what promised to be 10 days filled with fun and relaxation.

The following evening, June 28th, we performed at Honolulu's NBC Coliseum in front of a sold-out crowd. I was impressed to see all the local headbangers going crazy during the show in complete contrast to their usual mellow and relaxed "hang loose" surfer attitude.

After the show, we stayed in Honolulu for one more day before moving over to Maui on June 30th for Ozzy and Sharon's wedding festivities. During our week in the then low-key and sparsely populated island we stayed at the Maui Princess resort. The hotel's lush, romantic gardens and private beaches were the perfect setting for the couple's sunset nuptials.

On the evening of July 1st, Rebecca celebrated her 21st birthday at a quaint dinner party along with Tommy's fiancee, Alison, who also happened to share the same birthday. Though we had known each other for less than a year, Rebecca had grown from a wide-eyed girl into a worldly young woman before my eyes.

The next afternoon when Rebecca and I returned from the beach there was a phone message from Larry asking me to meet him in his room. When I arrived, Tommy and Brad were already there.

"OK, guys. You've got to promise to keep this mum.

Especially you, Rudy and Tommy; you've got to promise not to say anything about this to your girlfriends." Larry was adamant. "I've put together for Ozzy the most awesome bachelor party ever. I just got back from a meeting with the hotel's concierge and he's taking care of all the arrangements. He's promised plenty of booze and food. And for those of you who want to partake," Larry proudly announced with a Cheshire cat grin, "we've got Korean hookers."

"All right! Korean hookers!" Tommy shouted. "Me love you long time!"

The following evening, July 2nd, the rowdy bunch—our crew, band and friends—met at the hotel lobby for a round of drinks before piling into a passenger van and a limo, headed for what promised to be an unforgettable evening filled with debauchery. Meanwhile, Sharon made her own plans to celebrate her bachelorette party with all our girlfriends and wives.

"Where the fuck are we going?" One of the crew angrily slurred. "We've been riding for over an hour. We've got to be going in circles 'cause this fuckin' island ain't that big!"

"It looks like we're here," said our driver as the limo ahead of us pulled into the driveway of a desolate industrial park.

"Larry, are you bloody sure we're in the right place?" Ozzy wondered.

"Yeah, this is the address I've got written down," Larry replied as he double-checked the directions.

"Well, this doesn't look like the right spot for a Chuck E. Cheese, much less a whorehouse," Tommy said, as our motley bunch banged on every security door in the lifeless compound.

"Hey, I've found it!" a crew member yelled from the end of the driveway.

Like a bunch of ravaging pirates we stomped our way up the narrow staircase to the upper floor of the concrete building.

"Welcome. Please come in and have a seat." One of four elderly Asian women welcomed us into the sparsely decorated room furnished with folding tables and chairs. As I took my seat I noticed the single can of Budweiser placed at each plate setting. Next, I noticed the trays filled with mounds of sardines, crackers and Vienna sausages set on each table.

"What the bloody hell is this!" Ozzy complained. "This better be a joke. We didn't fuckin' drive for two hours to get to this shithole and eat these bloody wienies and crackers!" He flung a sausage against the wall.

"Man, all I know is that these Korean hookers better be drop dead gorgeous 'cause the food really sucks," Tommy said.

In a desperate attempt to fix the situation, Larry pulled one of the old Asian women aside and complained about the arrangements. "Guys, we're out of here," Larry suddenly announced. "But we haven't seen the Korean hookers yet!" the crew complained. "Oh, yes you have. It's these old hags. They are the hookers!" Larry sprang as we cleared the room faster than roaches at the flip of a light switch.

"Where the hell are we gonna go now?" Tommy asked as we gathered outside in the parking lot.

"I've got an idea," Larry suggested. "Why don't we go into Old Lahaina? It's got the only club in town." "I've been drinking all day," Ozzy said. "I'm tired. Does anyone know where we can get some blow on this bloody island?"

"Hey Ozz, I got the phone number of this guy I met by the pool," said one of the two photographers covering the wedding for the rock press. "He told me to give him a call if we needed anything."

"Fuckin' great! Call him right now," Ozzy replied. "I will but I'm going to need a car to go and pick it up."

Larry intervened.

"OK, this is what we'll do then. You both go in the limo and get the stuff. Meanwhile we'll take the van into Lahaina and meet you guys at the club."

An hour later we arrived at the club situated on the then sleepy little commercial strip in Old Lahaina.

"Hi, we're with the Ozzy Osbourne band," Larry said to the burly Samoan bouncer.

"I don't give a fuck who you guys are. It's a $10.00 cover charge with a two-drink minimum. And what's with him?" The bouncer pointed at Ozzy, who was being held up by a couple of our crew. "Oh, he's all right. He's just a little tired," said Larry. "This is his bachelor party and he's just having a bit of fun."

"I don't want any trouble from you guys," he warned. "One complaint and I'll kick your asses out!"

As soon as we entered the bar we realized that the place was completely dead. By now the most awesome bachelor party ever had turned into a completely disaster.

"I hope the guys get here with the blow soon," said one of the crew. Suddenly, the bouncer and a bartender grabbed Ozzy's limp body and dragged him out in the street.

"Hey, what do you think you're doing?" Larry yelled as he chased after them.

"This is a bar, not a hotel," said, the bouncer. Just then the limo carrying the photographers arrived.

"So, did you get the stuff?" one of the crew excitedly slurred. "Well, yeah, but the trip back was so long and we we're really tired. So we did a few bumps and before we knew it all the blow was gone."

"That's it! Party's over guys," Larry announced. "We're going back to the hotel." He picked Ozzy up and shoved him into the back of the limo.

When I got back to the room Rebecca hadn't returned yet from Sharon's party. A couple hours later she walked in.

"Oh, you're back already?"

"Yeah," I grunted as I peered sleepy-eyed from under the covers.

"Oh, we had so much fun!" Rebecca beamed as she lied down next to me.

"First, Sharon took all the girls out to dinner at the fanciest restaurant in the hotel. Then we went bar hopping in the hotel. After that we went for a walk on the beach. Sharon got so wasted that her zipper broke and her skirt fell down to her ankles. She just didn't care. She kept on walking, dragging her skirt in the sand. It was so funny! So, Alison and I walked behind her holding up the skirt until we found a safety pin." She was laughing.

"Sounds like you guys had a great time," I yawned.

"Yeah, we did. Hey, so how was your big old rock star bachelor party?" "Actually, it sounds like you guys had a better time than we did. Oh, I'm too tired right now. I'll tell you all about it in the morning." I turned over and went to sleep.

On July 4th we all gathered before sunset on the hotel's sprawling beach-side lawn to attend Ozzy and Sharon's wedding.

Don Arden and Ozzy's family, including his mom, flew in for the celebration. Tommy and Alison served as best man and bridesmaid.

The setting could have not been more romantic as Sharon, dressed in a white lace gown, was proudly led down the aisle by her father while the sun dipped into the ocean, gently painting a multitude of hues across the sky. As they approached Ozzy, Don joined his and Sharon's hands before the preacher commenced the ceremony. And just as Randy had predicted the year before, Ozzy and Sharon became husband and wife.

Following the ceremony, the guests were treated to a traditional Hawaiian luau complete with hula girls and band. Later on, after a few too many Polynesian cocktails, Brad, Ozzy and I borrowed the band's acoustic guitar and upright bass and performed an unplugged rendition of "Paranoid" much to the delight of our guests and the uninvited hotel guests who had crashed the party and joined the raucous celebration.

Eventually, all good things had to come to an end. So on July 6th, we left the tranquil beaches of Maui bound for the bustle of Osaka, Japan's second largest metropolis. Our visit to Japan was just another bittersweet reminder of Randy, who had garnered a large legion of Japanese fans from his Quiet Riot and Ozzy recordings.

As we traveled throughout Japan, I met a myriad of fans that would politely approach me and ask the question: "What was Randy Rhoads really like?" I gladly spent countless moments, relaying through an interpreter or doing my best with hand signs, to share stories about Randy. But most of all I wanted the fans to know how much Randy had looked forward to performing in Japan and how the Japanese fans held a special place in his heart.

Since this was Ozzy's first visit to Japan as a solo artist Mr. Udo, the promoter, limited our tour to a minimum amount of shows. On the evening of July 9th we performed in Osaka, July 11th in Nagoya, July 13th in Kyoto and July 15th in Tokyo.

I was extremely impressed by how efficiently Mr. Udo ran his operation. Every detail was handled by a team of experts.

How the band, crew, luggage and equipment traveled was expeditiously handled by Mr. Udo's staff. Even our backline was setup by the Japanese crew after they took notes during our own crew's first show set-up.

Another thing that impressed me was how polite the Japanese fans were. Before each sold-out 7 p.m. show I watched the unusually polite audience sitting quietly, as a soft-spoken female announcer came over the house PA and warned them about any possible misbehavior including standing during the show. This drove Ozzy nuts since he was used to having the audience respond to his commands like "Go Crazy!" throughout our performance. Also, since traditionally in a Japanese show there's no opening act we had to add "No Bone Movies" to our set. These were the only dates where that song was performed live while I was in the band.

On July 16th, after an extremely successful tour we flew back home to Los Angeles for a three-week break. During this time,
Sharon and the band gathered at the Jet office to watch the final edit of the June 24th Irvine MTV performance.

"What in bloody hell is that?!" Ozzy slurred as he pointed at the TV monitor.

"Ah, it's the bats," said one of the laser technicians.

"Shit, they look like bloody squirrels with wings," Ozzy complained.

"What the fuck happened!?" Sharon cut in.

"Well, when we did the pre-production rehearsals at the Oakland Coliseum," the tech explained, "it was indoors and with all the haze from the fog machines you could clearly see the reflection of the lasers. But once we got outdoors at Irvine all the fog dissipated and we had nothing to reflect the lasers onto. We were left with no other alternative but to video the laser bats in our studio and super impose them into the footage."

"I hate it Sharon! It's crap!" Ozzy yelled as he stormed out of the room.

Even though the lasers blunder was never corrected, the live performance was aired on MTV the following Halloween night.

As I watched the video I realized how horribly mechanical my performance had become. Any of the joy and celebration I felt every night onstage while Randy was with us was gone. The emotional wall I had built not only shielded me from the rest of the band and audience but also alienated me as well. I had become a robot. I didn't know how or when, all I knew was that I didn't want to carry on like that any longer.

As I was leaving the Jet office I watched Ozzy stumbling around the parked cars.

"Ozz, what are you doing?" I asked. Ozzy quietly shushed me as he put his finger to his lip.

"It's payback time," he said, deflating the laser technician's tires.

23
You People Think I'm Crazy?

On August 6th, the band and crew gathered in Dallas, Texas to perform outdoors at the Cotton Bowl's Texxas Jam along with Foreigner and other major acts.

That afternoon I was sitting in the hotel's lobby bar with Larry having a drink when he a concierge approached.

"Mr. McNeny, there's an overseas call for you." Half a vodka- tonic later Larry returned.

"Well, you're not going to believe this. That was Sharon. Ozzy's shaved his head!"

"What!" I yelled in disbelief. In the 80s, shaving the mane was career suicide.

"Yep, you heard me right. Sharon just told me that a few days ago they got into an argument at the Arden's home in Wimbledon. Ozzy was complaining to Sharon about her not letting him have any cash so she pulled out a 20 pound note from her purse and threw it at him. And that was it. Ozzy grabbed the money and ran away. After a couple of days she still hadn't heard from him and with these shows coming up, Sharon hired a detective to track him down. After searching for a couple of days, the detective found Ozzy back in Aston, his home town, passed out at the bar of the local pub with his head shaved." Larry shook his head, barely containing his laughter. "Oh my God!" I winced at the thought of Ozzy's shaven head shining brightly in the Texas sun.

"No, wait. It gets better," Larry smirked. "Sharon wants you to get a wig and cut it like Ozzy's hair."

"I've never cut a wig in my life! I wouldn't even know where to begin," I balked.

"Well, that's what she wants and she's counting on you," Larry replied.

"So why the hell did he shave his head?" I asked.

"Sharon said that Ozzy didn't want to come back on

the road to do these shows, so he figured that if he shaved his head Sharon would have to cancel."

The cocktail waitress approached.

"Another round gentlemen?"

"I'm done. I think I'd better be sober for this," I said and walked over to the concierge in search of the nearest beauty supply store.

In my room later that night I laid in bed watching TV occasionally glancing at the long, blonde wig on top of the spooky white Styrofoam head. Finally, I mustered up enough courage to grab my scissors and start hacking away at the wig. But no matter how hard I tried to make it look like Ozzy's signature mane, the layers just fell flat. In the end it looked like Doris Day.

The following afternoon August 7th, we all anxiously waited in our dressing for Ozzy and Sharon to arrive from the airport.

"I just got off the phone with Sharon," said Larry, "and they're on their way. She doesn't want anyone to make remarks to Ozzy about his shaved head." The wall clock signaled 20 minutes till show time.

"Where's the wig?" Sharon bluntly asked as they entered the dressing room. I quickly handed it over to Sharon who placed it on Ozzy's head.

"Sharon, I look like the bloody village idiot!" Ozzy complained as he stood in front of the full-length mirror.

"Quick! Give me the scissors!" Sharon demanded as I pulled them out of my bag. "Now, get me a spray water bottle. We've only got five minutes before show time."

As soon as Sharon wetted Ozzy's wig it suddenly began to take shape as the layers started to appear. She then added a few extra layers before fastening the wig with a rolled bandana onto Ozzy's head.

"There, you looked beautiful now."

"I still look like a bloody cunt." Ozzy mumbled.

"Come on let's go!" Larry shouted. "They've started

the intro tape."

When we took the stage at 5 p.m. it was 110 degrees in the shade as the blinding Texas sun hung on the horizon like a giant ball of fire. I looked over at Ozzy and saw the sweat rolling down from underneath his wig as we kicked into our first song, "I Don't Know." At the end of the tune, Ozzy addressed the sold-out stadium crowd. "You people think I'm crazy?" Ozzy yelled into the mike as the crowd responded affirmatively. "Well, let me show you how fuckin' crazy I am!" Ozzy ripped his wig off and threw it into the crowd.

The audience went insane as we segued into "Crazy Train." Suddenly, there was pandemonium backstage as stage left and right filled up with astonished onlookers. While I gazed at Ozzy's head shining like a disco ball all I could do was wonder where the hell we were going to find another wig for the next show.

The following afternoon, August 8 th, we arrived in New Orleans to perform later that evening at another outdoor festival with nearly the same line up. As soon as we checked into the French Quarter's Royal Orleans Hotel I went on a mad hunt for the nearest beauty supply store. But being Sunday, they were all closed. So I had to settle on a "Merlin the Magician" wig that I found at a Bourbon Street magic shop.

As soon as we arrived backstage at the festival grounds I went into the makeshift trailer that served as our dressing room and began to hack away at the wig. But since it was a cheap novelty item, every time I tried to layer it chunks of hair would fall off the cap.

"Ozz, listen, man, this is the best I can do with this cheap piece of crap."

Ozzy applied fake blood onto his shaved head. He grabbed the wig, secured it with a rolled bandana and checked himself out in front of the full-length mirror.

"Fuck, I look like a bigger cunt than I did yesterday." He tossed his waist-long mangy wig back and forth,

304

looking like a deranged flower child.

After a couple of hours' rain delay we finally hit the stage. Though we weren't being punished by the blazing sun, still the 95 degree with 100 percent humidity Louisiana weather was unbearable. As our intro tape rolled I could see Ozzy pacing like a caged tiger on the side of the stage. As he entered from stage left, he yanked his wig off and flung it as far back as he could into the roaring audience. And that was the end of the wigs.

The following morning, August 9th, we flew back to Los Angeles for a 10-day break. During this time I got a call from Kevin DuBrow asking if I would like to play on "Thunderbird," a tune for the new Quiet Riot record. Kevin had written the song for Randy right after he left home to join Ozzy and I was very familiar with it since I had already played it during a few gigs with DuBrow.

As DuBrow, Frankie Banali, Carlos Cavazo, the band's producer Spencer Proffer and I crammed into the small tracking room at Pasha Studios in Hollywood the mood was fresh and upbeat, a complete contrast to the somber mood that lingered over most of the Ozzy band's performances. Sitting in with my old friends, especially Frankie Banali whom I had grown up playing with back in Florida, felt as comfortable as putting on an old pair of sneakers.

"So do you remember any of the old songs?" Kevin asked me after we finished tracking the rhythm tracks to "Thunderbird."

"I don't know, it's been a while since I played any of them." "How about "Slick Black Cadillac"?" he asked about our old Quiet Riot staple.

"Well, if you give me a few minutes to run it down with Frankie and Carlos I'm pretty sure it will come back."

After a couple of run-throughs we were ready to lay it down. By the end of the evening I had recorded almost half the album.

As I was leaving the session I ran into Quiet Riot's bassist Tony Cavazo, Carlos' brother. He had come in to record the Slade classic "Cum on Feel the Noize."

"Listen, this is what I'm going to do," I heard Frankie tell the band as they huddled outside the control room. "We all know how much Spencer's pushing for us to record this song no matter how much we hate it. So, when we start tracking I'm going to play it as straight and boring as possible. I'm sure Spencer will drop the idea after he hears my drum take."

I decided to stay and watch the percussive sabotage. But once Spencer hit the "Record" button Frankie couldn't play bad even if he had a gun held to his head.

"We got it! It's a take!" Spencer smiled and gave the thumbs up from behind the recording console.

In the days that followed I recorded the rest of the Quiet Riot record's bass tracks with the exception of "Metal Health" and "Don't Wanna to Let You Go," which had been previously recorded by Chuck Wright. As I continued to spend more time in and out of the studio with my old friends I realized that I had already found the fresh start and emotional refuge that I was looking for in Quiet Riot.

Leaving a top International act like Ozzy and the company of some of my closest friends for the uncertainty of an unknown band like Quiet Riot was the hardest decision I have ever made in my life. But my happiness and peace of mind outweighed everything else. To be honest, it felt like God had already made the decision for me.

On September 19th, Sharon, the band and crew arrived in New York City to rehearse and record Speak of the Devil, Ozzy's live recordings of some of his old Black Sabbath classics. Throughout the years, titling both the MTV Halloween Live from Irvine Broadcast and this collection of Black Sabbath tunes called Speak of the Devil has created much confusion among Ozzy fans.

306

The day following our arrival, Tommy, Brad and I started rehearsals at a gloomy midtown Manhattan studio. We had only five days to learn "Symptom of the Universe," "Snowblind," "Black Sabbath," "Fairies Wear Boots," "War Pigs," "The Wizard," "N.I.B.," "Sweet Leaf," "Never Say Die" and "Sabbath Bloody Sabbath."

"Now boys, don't expect to see much of Ozzy at rehearsals.

He's not being very cooperative," Sharon apologized. "So you're all pretty much on your own. Just remember that this is a live record and there'll be no overdubs for you boys afterward. So make sure that you're all well rehearsed because if you make a mistake it's going to wind up on the record. And by the way, since we're going to include Randy's live versions of "Iron Man," "Children of the Grave" and "Paranoid" on the record don't bother rehearsing them."

Since I wasn't very familiar with the songs we were learning, I continuously struggled to make some sense out of Black Sabbath's convoluted arrangements with their erratic tempos and rhythm changes, a complete contrast to Randy's flowing writing style. One afternoon, as we continued rehearsing without Ozzy, we were plodding through the monotonous diminished riff of the song "Black Sabbath" when I realized how low the band's morale had sunk. Here we were rehearsing for one of Ozzy's records and he didn't even bother to show up once. If there was ever any doubt about me leaving the band, going through these rehearsals removed them.

On September 26th and 27th we recorded "Speak of the Devil" live at the Ritz in New York City in front of a rowdy, sold-out crowd. On the afternoon of the 26th, as we began our sound check I noticed that the old converted Latin ballroom had the perfect acoustics for our needs—

not too booming or flat, just warm and intimate. For these live recording sessions we had to make a few technical changes in order to maximize instrument separation. One of the most crucial adjustments was the removal of the side-fill monitors. Without the aid of these pumping walls of speakers I was forced to spend the whole show anchored to the front of Tommy's drum riser to hear him over the volume of our backline.

Ozzy finally surfaced for sound check and since he hadn't rehearsed with us he experienced difficulties remembering the lyrics he had sung so many times with Black Sabbath. With no time to go to a music store and purchase a stand, Ozzy grabbed a folding chair and placed it next to him in front of the stage. He then put a desk lamp on top of the chair to light up the pages of the notebook where he had scribbled his lyrics.

As we ran through the set list "The Wizard" came up next. Ozzy pulled a harmonica out of his back pocket and began to play the signature intro. Every single hair in my body stood up as the eeriest sound I've ever heard blared out of the PA.

"Oh my God! Ozzy that sounds great! I didn't know you could play the harp like that!" I told him in awe.

"I didn't know if I could still remember how to blow this thing.

But I guess it's just like riding a bloody bike." He smiled while he glanced at the lyrics to the next song.

Instead of putting on the usual spectacle, the mood of the live recordings was rather casual with the emphasis on capturing the tightest performances possible onto the tape machines housed inside the Record Plant's mobile studio parked in the alley behind the stage. We all dressed down for the occasion, especially Ozzy, whose recently shaved head was starting to grow back in. He stood center stage reading the lyrics from his notebook while we performed.

One of the biggest challenges I faced during the live recordings was to stand in one place. And after tapping my foot to the rhythm of Tommy's drums for two nights in a row I was left with a sore right knee for the next couple of weeks. Not only was it unnatural for me to stand still in one spot during the show but also for the fans that were used to watching my antics on stage. So throughout the show I watched the audience gathered in the front rows beckoning for me to come closer to them.

In order to make the show satisfactorily long enough for the audience, we also included "Iron Man," "Children of the Grave" and "Paranoid." Since Sharon had mentioned that Randy's versions would be the ones included on the record, I ventured beyond my comfort zone and got closer to the fans.

"Wow, I can't hear any of Tommy's playing from here," I thought while I banged my head down stage along to our old Sabbath closers.

A couple of months later while I listened to the final mixes of Speak of the Devil I was appalled to hear my sloppy playing on these three songs since the powers that be decided to save Randy's versions for the "Tribute" album.

On September 28th the band, sans Ozzy and Sharon, flew back to Los Angeles. During the flight Brad and I hung out on the back of the empty plane.

"Hey Rudy, do you want to hear a couple of new mixes of my band?" Brad asked as he pulled a cassette out of his Walkman. "Yeah, sure," I replied and began to listen. "What's the name?" "We've been calling it Ranger," he explained, "but we might have to change it to something else."

I continued to listen to most of the songs that would make up Night Ranger's debut album.

"Do you want to hear my new band?" I asked Brad.

"You have a new band? You dog!" he remarked as I handed him the cassette.

He listened.

"This is cool. What's the name of your band?" He

pulled off one of the headphones.

"It's called Quiet Riot."

Brad smiled and gave me the thumbs up as we both continued listening to each other's bands.

Immediately after I returned to Los Angeles I officially became a member of Quiet Riot. My next order of business was to make the hardest phone call of my life.

"Ahhh, hello, Sharon?"

"Hi Rudy, is everything all right?"

"Well, I don't know how to put this but I've joined Quiet Riot." The uncomfortable silence on the other end felt like an eternity. "The album doesn't come out until March, so if you want me to do the U.K. dates I will be available and ..."

"Forget it! Nobody leaves Ozzy!" she bellowed and hung up. And so my adventures in the land of Ozz ended just as they began, with a phone call with Sharon.

24
Closure

Through all these years, a day hasn't gone by without me thinking about Randy. Quiet Riot's Metal Health, the debut album from the band he founded, reached the top of the Billboard charts in November of 1983. The record was dedicated to his memory and included "Thunderbird," the song that planted the seed for my return.

But it's not my recollections of Randy during our struggling days in Quiet Riot that linger. It's the warm memories of when we toured with Ozzy as I proudly watched him from across the stage dazzle crowds in Europe, Britain and North America that continue to put a smile on my face.

As the Lord continued to shower me with blessings, Rebecca and I were married on June 24, 1984. The trust, faith and love we have for each other have been the cornerstones of our relationship. She has been the voice of reason through all the ups, downs, and sideways of my music career beginning with Ozzy on through Quiet Riot, Whitesnake and now with Dio, the band led by the man who took Ozzy's place in Black Sabbath, heavy metal icon Ronnie James Dio. Isn't life wonderfully strange?

In the summer of 1984, Quiet Riot was booked at an outdoor festival on a bill that included Triumph, Motley Crue and Ozzy among many others. After checking into our hotel I ventured over to where most of the other bands on the bill were lodged. Upon entering the lobby I was glad to recognize a few familiar faces.

"Hey Rudes," Tommy shouted. "Park your carcass over here." "T.A., it's so good to see you," I said as we shook hands.

"You too Rudles. Hey, how come you guys aren't staying at this hotel?" Tommy asked as he ordered me a drink.

"Well, as you probably know, Kevin's made some disparaging comments in the press about Ozzy and most of the L.A. bands. He's pissed off a lot of people and some of them are on the bill tomorrow. So our manager booked us in a hotel across town in order to avoid any confrontations. By the way, where's Ozzy?"

"Oh, man he's on a huge bender tonight. Look at him, he's worse now than when you were in the band."

At that moment, Ozzy, looking like trouble waiting to happen, staggered by our table. Suddenly he did a double take and came charging towards me.

"You scum bag! Get out of my sight!" Ozzy yelled at me as the hotel security rushed over.

"T.A., I think I'd better go," I said as I got up to leave, trying to avoid a scene.

Just then, Ozzy threw a sucker punch and hit me on the left side of my face. As I turned to defend myself I watched him slump over, dragged away by two security guards. It wasn't his drunken off balance punch that hurt. What really hurt was feeling the wrath of someone who I held in such high esteem, someone I owed my career to and had shared the darkest moments of my life.

Eventually, Ozzy and I made our peace after I left Quiet Riot in January of 1985. And even for a brief period Sharon represented Tommy and me while we attempted to put our own band together prior to us becoming Whitesnake's rhythm section in 1987.

Over the last 20 years Delores' wish has been for Randy's name to live on forever in our hearts like an eternal flame. As she carries on with her goal, Delores founded The Randy Rhoads Memorial Scholarship Endowment at both UCLA and California State University in Northridge (CSUN) classical guitar departments in 1993. Every year Delores participates in the auditions and helps decide which of the applicants will be among the 20 recipients.

On January 6, 1999, Rebecca and I were invited by Ozzy and Sharon to attend the Black Sabbath reunion show at the Los Angeles Forum. After the show we went backstage.

"My goodness, how've you both been?" Sharon gave us a kiss and a hug as she welcomed us into Ozzy's dressing room.

"Oh, I've been busy touring with Quiet Riot," I explained as I watched Ozzy sitting on a couch chatting with some music business types.

"I know, I've been following your tour on Pollstar," Sharon smiled. "Ozzy, look who's here. It's Rudy and Becky." He waddled across the room looking drained and disoriented

"Great show, Ozz! You sounded better tonight than you did 20 years ago," I told him, and he hugged me. "When I watched you singing 'Paranoid' I couldn't help reminisce about the time we played it unplugged at your wedding luau in Maui."

Slowly, that familiar boyish expression and mischievous grin appeared on Ozzy's face as I continued to lead him down memory lane.

"You know, the saddest thing is that Ozzy doesn't remember much from those days," Sharon told us as Ozzy was escorted out of the dressing room. "After all this time it's never been the same. Those days we all spent together were the best," Sharon said as we hugged and said our goodbyes.

On our way home I reflected on Sharon's bittersweet confessions and realized I wasn't alone in regarding the days we all shared with Randy as the best of times. Also, that night it became evident to me that if Ozzy didn't have much of a recollection of those days then someone else would have to tell the story.

In January of 2004 I was asked by Randy's family

and Dave Widerman, Guitar Center's Director of Artist Relations, to say a few words about Randy during his long overdue induction ceremony to the Hollywood Walk of Fame. The event was attended by Delores, Randy's siblings Kelly and Kathy, his girlfriend Jody, and Ozzy and Sharon. Also on hand were rock luminaries Lemmy Kilmeister, Zaak Wylde, Yngwie Malmsteen, Nuno Bettencourt, John 5 and Frankie Banali, among others. As I stood at the podium in front of the multitude of Randy's fans and the media I read these words:

"I met Randy in the summer of 1978 when I auditioned for Quiet Riot, the local Los Angeles band he formed in the mid '70s. The first thing I noticed about Randy was how effortlessly he managed to alternate from playing rhythm to soloing without losing the fullness of his sound. Though we were just jamming on a blues-based riff I could tell that he had a rich musical vocabulary reaching well beyond the average rock guitarist.

During the next couple of years, Quiet Riot performed at the Whiskey, Roxy and Starwood, not far from where we are gathered today. As we struggled to get the attention of the music industry during the New Wave and Punk era, we managed to carry on with the support of our local fans' love for Randy and the band.

It was during this period that Randy asked me join the teaching staff at Musonia, his mother Delores' music school. I watched him daily teach his students, some who are present here today, with love and dedication. One afternoon I asked him about his approach to teaching. Randy told me he believed that his students weren't any different than he was at their age. They just couldn't wait to get up on stage and tear things up and that it was his responsibility to prepare them for that moment the best he could.

314

In the winter of 1979, Randy left Los Angeles to join Ozzy Osbourne and form one of the most prolific musical partnerships in heavy metal history. After being creatively stifled by the local L.A. music scene, Ozzy gave Randy the complete freedom and encouragement to fulfill his musical potential as a guitarist and composer.

While in England, Randy took the opportunity to further his musical knowledge by taking classical guitar lessons from some of the most renowned guitar teachers in London. His newly acquired musical skills can be heard on "Revelation Mother Earth," "Diary of a Madman" and Dee, a composition written for Delores, just to name a few.

In March of 1981 Randy recommended me to Ozzy and Sharon and shortly thereafter I became the bass player on the Blizzard of Ozz and Diary of a Madman tours. I'm eternally grateful to Randy for giving me the opportunity to share all the wonderful and crazy, fun-filled moments we all shared together.

While on the road, Randy would go through the Yellow Pages as soon as he checked into his hotel room and phone a local music school to book a classical guitar lesson. Most of the time, Randy wound up giving the star struck local music teacher the guitar lesson but still pay for the lesson himself. You see, in his heart Randy never lost his love for teaching.

As we are all gathered here today to celebrate Randy's contribution to the world of music it breaks my heart that he is no longer with us. But I rejoice knowing that his music lives on every time I hear "Crazy Train" being played by a young guitarist while checking out a new amp at Guitar Center, when it's played over the P.A. at a sporting event or when I turn on MTV to watch "The Osbournes."

Randy, we miss you and we love you.

315

Thank you for coming and sharing this joyful occasion with all of us. God bless every one of you."

At the end of the ceremony his bronze plaque was unveiled. As the attendees gasped in horror I realized that Randy's last name had been spelled "Rhodes" instead of "Rhoads."

In the middle of all the pandemonium, I was sure I could hear Randy giggling.

Randy and me during Quiet Riot days at the Starwood.

Near the end of Quiet Riot at the Whisly a Go Go.

On tour Randy looking through the Yellow Pages for a Classical Guitar teacher.

Randy and Sharon enjoying a bumpy flight.

Ready to set sail off Cape Cod.

Randy enjoying a smoke and a giggle.

A perfect day to go sailing.

Taking a turn at the helm.

Randy and Ozzy cavorting in the sun.

Ozzy backstage with Motorhead at Port Vale.

Randy sightseeing in London.

With Sharon at the Arden's Christmas party.

Randy and Ozzy goofing around with stage props.

With Ozzy during the Diary of a Madman Tour.

Ozzy and Sharon backstage in Anchorage.

A bewigged Ozzy heading to the stage in New Orleans.

Playing Paranoid at the Osbourne's wedding.

Mr and Mrs Osbourne

Ozzy and Sharon sightseeing in Tokyo.

The Sarzos in Miami, 1961.

With my Yorkshire Terrier, Tory, my comfort and muse during the penning of this book

With Rebecca on our weeding day, June 24, 1984

Printed in Poland
by Amazon Fulfillment
Poland Sp. z o.o., Wrocław